Performance Funding for Higher Education

Performance Funding for Higher Education

Kevin J. Dougherty, Sosanya M. Jones,
Hana Lahr, Rebecca S. Natow, Lara Pheatt,
and Vikash Reddy

Johns Hopkins University Press
Baltimore

Johns Hopkins University Press
2715 North Charles Street
Baltimore, Maryland 21218-4363
www.press.jhu.edu

Library of Congress Cataloging-in-Publication Data

Names: Dougherty, Kevin James, author.
Title: Performance funding for higher education / Kevin J. Dougherty, Sosanya
    M. Jones, Hana Lahr, Rebecca S. Natow, Lara Pheatt, and Vikash Reddy.
Description: Baltimore, Maryland : Johns Hopkins University Press, 2016. |
    Includes bibliographical references and index.
Identifiers: LCCN 2016002107 | ISBN 9781421420820 (pbk. : alk. paper) | ISBN
    9781421420837 (electronic) | ISBN 1421420821 (pbk. : alk. paper) | ISBN
    142142083X (electronic)
Subjects: LCSH: Universities and colleges—United States—Finance. |
    Education, Higher—United States—Finance. | Government aid to higher
    education—United States.
Classification: LCC LB2342 .D668 2016 | DDC 378.1/06—dc23
    LC record available at http://lccn.loc.gov/2016002107

A catalog record for this book is available from the British Library.

*Special discounts are available for bulk purchases of this book. For more information, please contact
Special Sales at 410-516-6936 or specialsales@press.jhu.edu.*

Johns Hopkins University Press uses environmentally friendly book materials, including
recycled text paper that is composed of at least 30 percent post-consumer waste, whenever
possible.

Contents

APPENDIXES

Acknowledgments

We wish to thank Lumina Foundation for its support for this research. The views expressed in this book are those of its authors and do not necessarily represent the views of Lumina Foundation, its officers, or its employees.

At the Community College Research Center, Tom Bailey, Lisa Rothman, Sandra Spady, Sarah Phillips, Davis Jenkins, Melinda Mechur Karp, Nikki Edgecombe, Elisabeth Barnett, Shanna Jaggars, Doug Slater, Betsy Yoon, Amy Mazzariello, Wendy Schwartz, Georgia Stacey, Elizabeth Ganga, and Porshea Patterson provided much appreciated support.

We are also very grateful to Kevin Corcoran and Sean Tierney for their encouragement of this project and their support as it went along.

We wish to deeply thank the many people we interviewed who provided us with the main information for this book. Although we cannot name our interviewees for reasons of confidentiality, we wish to acknowledge our deep appreciation of the time and thought they gave us.

We are very grateful as well to Ron Abrams, Elisabeth Barnett, Michael Baumgartner, E. Grady Bogue, Debra Bragg, Kevin Corcoran, Russ Deaton, Nikki Edgecombe, Nicholas Hillman, Robert Holmes, Melanie Hwalek, Davis Jenkins, Nate Johnson, Roger Larocca, Richard Petrick, Martha Snyder, Jeffrey Stanley, David Tandberg, Sean Tierney, and Dustin Weeden for providing very useful data, reports, and advice.

We greatly appreciate the help of those who reviewed drafts of various earlier writings that fed into our book: Ron Abrams, Estela Bensimon, Steven Brint, Charles Clotfelter, Kevin Corcoran, Russ Deaton, Alicia Dowd, William Doyle, Peter Ewell, Alisa H. Fryar, Nicholas Hillman, Davis Jenkins, Nate Johnson, Tiffany Jones, Alison Kadlec, Monica Reid Kerrigan, Marcus Kolb, Michael McLendon, Vanessa Smith Morest, John Muffo, Laura Perna, Richard Petrick, Thomas Rabovsky, Amanda Rutherford, Susan Shelton, Nancy Shulock, Martha Snyder, Jeffrey Stanley, David Tandberg, Sean Tierney, Keith Witham, Lyle Yorks, and William Zumeta. We also wish to thank the editors and the anonymous reviewers for the Association for the Study of Higher Education monographs on higher education, the Russell Sage Foundation, and Johns Hopkins University Press. Needless to say, all remaining errors are the responsibility of the authors.

We also wish to thank the following for invitations to present our findings to their organizations: Julie Bell and Brenda Bautsch of the National Conference of State Legislatures; Travis Reindl and Iris Palmer, then of the National Governors Association; Richard Kazis, Chris Baldwin, and Michael Collins of the Achieving the Dream State Policy Group; and Suzanne Walsh and Michael Collins of Completion by Design.

Finally, we wish to thank our families and friends for their support.

The chapters of this book draw from material found in the following articles: Kevin Dougherty et al., "Looking inside the Black Box of Performance Funding for Higher Education: Policy Instruments, Outcomes, Obstacles, and Unintended Impacts," *RSF: The Russell Sage Foundation Journal of the Social Sciences* 2, no. 1 (2016) © Russell Sage Foundation, 112 East 64th Street, New York, NY 10065, reprinted with permission; and Kevin Dougherty, Sosanya M. Jones, Hana Lahr, Rebecca S. Natow, Lara Pheatt, and Vikash Reddy, "Performance Funding for Higher Education: Forms, Origins, Impacts, and Futures." *The ANNALS of the American Academy of Political and Social Science*, 655 (Sept. 2014), pp. 163–184. Copyright © 2014 by The American Academy of Political and Social Science, reprinted with permission of Sage Publishing.

Portions of appendix A were previously published in Kevin J. Dougherty and Vikash Reddy, *Performance Funding for Higher Education: What Are the Mechanisms? What Are the Impacts?* New York: Wiley, 2013. Copyright © 2013 Wiley Periodicals, Inc., A Wiley Company. All rights reserved.

Performance Funding for Higher Education

CHAPTER 1

Introduction

For several decades, policymakers have been concerned about increasing the efficiency and effectiveness of postsecondary institutions. In recent years, performance funding—which directly connects state funding to an institution's performance on indicators such as student persistence, credit accrual, and college completion—has become a politically attractive way of pursuing better college outcomes (Burke, 2002, 2005; Carey & Aldeman, 2008; Complete College America, 2013; Dougherty & Natow, 2015; Harnisch, 2011; Jones, 2013; Longanecker, 2012a, 2012b; Lumina Foundation, 2009; National Conference of State Legislatures, 2016; Reindl & Jones, 2012; US Office of the President, 2013; Ziskin, 2014).

Higher education financing has historically been driven primarily by enrollments and prior-year funding levels, but performance funding departs significantly from this model (Johnstone, 2011; Jones, 2013; Lingenfelter, 2008; McGuinness, 2011; McKeown-Moak, 2013; McLendon & Hearn, 2013; Richardson et al., 1999; Schmidtlein & Berdahl, 2011; Zumeta & Kinne, 2011). Instead, performance funding ties state funding directly to institutional performance, measured in terms of student outcomes and other outcomes-based metrics (Burke, 2002; Dougherty & Reddy, 2013). These metrics commonly include student persistence, completion of certain gatekeeper courses, degree completion, and job placement (Burke, 2002; Dougherty & Reddy, 2013; Snyder, 2015). As performance funding evolved, certain states, notably Ohio and Tennessee, began tying very large percentages of state appropriations to these performance indicators and embedding the indicators into the base state funding (Dougherty & Natow, 2015).

Performance funding has received broad support from elected officials, appointed policymakers, and various public policy groups at both the state and federal level. The US Department of Education asked states to "embrace performance-based funding of higher education based on progress toward completion and other quality goals" (US Department of Education, 2011, p. 6).

Meanwhile, a report by the National Governors Association praised performance funding for spurring institutional focus on outcomes by changing the incentive structures: "Currently, the prevailing approach for funding public colleges and universities relies on a combination of enrollment numbers and the prior-year funding level. This gives colleges and universities little incentive to focus on retaining and graduating students or meeting state needs. To better drive change at the campus and system levels, performance funding instead provides financial incentives for graduating students and meeting state needs" (Reindl & Reyna, 2011, p. 12). Furthermore, Complete College America, a foundation-funded consortium of states focused on college completion, has called performance funding one of its five "game changers" and outlined mechanisms by which to best accomplish it (Complete College America, 2013; Jones, 2012, 2013). Finally, Lumina Foundation has endorsed performance funding and underwritten state efforts to implement it (Lumina Foundation, 2009; see Dougherty & Natow, 2015).

Widespread Adoption of Performance Funding

These strong endorsements have had an impact. As shown in table 1.1, 33 states were operating performance funding programs as of November 2015, with several more states planning to start one within the next few years (Dougherty & Natow, 2015; National Conference of State Legislatures, 2015; Snyder, 2015). The amount of state funding based on performance indicators ranges greatly, from less than 1% in Illinois to 85%–90% in Tennessee (Davies, 2014; Jones, 2013; National Conference of State Legislatures, 2015; Snyder, 2015).*

Performance funding has also been used extensively abroad. At least 20 European countries and several countries outside Europe use performance outcomes indicators to guide their funding of higher education (Center for Higher Education Policy Studies and University of London, 2010; Claeys-Kulik & Estermann, 2015; de Boer et al., 2012, 2015; European Community / Eurydice Network, 2008; Frolich, Schmidt, & Rosa, 2010; Hicks, 2012; Leisyte, 2012; Organisation for Economic Co-operation and Development, 2012; Santiago et al., 2008). For more on how US performance funding compares to that abroad, see de Boer et al. (2015), Dougherty & Natow (2015), and Kivisto & Kohtamäki (2015).

---

* See Dougherty & Natow (2015) for an analysis of the politics of performance funding which examines why states adopt it, how their performance funding programs change over time, and why these programs often are discontinued.

Table 1.1 States with Performance Funding Programs (as of November 2015)

State	Program type: PF 1.0 or PF 2.0	Institutional coverage		Greater weight for outcomes for certain kinds of students			
		Two-year colleges	Four-year colleges and universities	Under represented minorities	Low-SES students	Less prepared students	Other (STEM, older, etc.)
AZ	1		Yes				Yes
AR	2	Yes	Yes		Yes		Yes
CO	2	Yes	Yes	Yes	Yes		
FL	1,2	Yes	Yes				Yes
HI	1,2	Yes		Yes	Yes		Yes
IL	2	Yes	Yes	Yes	Yes		Yes
IN	1,2	Yes	Yes		Yes		Yes
KS	1	Yes	Yes				
LA	2	Yes	Yes				
ME	2		Yes		Yes		Yes
MA	2	Yes	Yes		Yes		Yes
MI	1	Yes	Yes				Yes
MN	2	Yes	Yes		Yes		Yes
MS	2		Yes		Yes	Yes	Yes
MO	1	Yes	Yes				
MT	2	Yes	Yes				
NV	2	Yes	Yes				Yes
NM	2	Yes	Yes		Yes		Yes
NY	1	Yes	Yes (CUNY)	Yes	Yes		
NC	1	Yes					
ND	1,2	Yes	Yes				
OH	2	Yes	Yes	Yes	Yes		Yes
OK	1	Yes	Yes		Yes		
OR	1		Yes	Yes	Yes		Yes
PA	2		Yes	Yes	Yes		Yes
SD	1	Yes	Yes				Yes
TN	1,2	Yes	Yes		Yes		Yes
TX	2	Yes					Yes
UT	1	Yes	Yes				
VA	1	Yes	Yes				
WA	1	Yes					
WI	2	Yes					Yes
WY	1,2	Yes					

Sources: Dougherty & Natow (2015), table 3.1; Jones (2013); National Conference of State Legislatures (2015); Snyder (2015); D. Weeden (pers. comm.).
Note: Florida, Hawaii, Indiana, North Dakota, and Wyoming have both PF 1.0 and PF 2.0 insofar as their performance funding programs involve both a bonus over and above the regular institutional appropriation and funds that are withheld from that appropriation and paid back according to how well the institution subsequently performs. Tennessee has separate PF 1.0 and PF 2.0 programs.

The Different Forms of Performance Funding

Two kinds of performance funding programs can be usefully distinguished (Dougherty & Natow, 2015; Dougherty & Reddy, 2013; Snyder, 2011, 2015). Performance funding 1.0 (hereafter PF 1.0) takes the form of a bonus, over and above regular state funding for higher education. The typical size of this bonus is between 1% and 5% of state funding for higher education (Burke, 2002; Dougherty & Natow, 2015; Dougherty & Reddy, 2013; Snyder, 2015). Performance funding 2.0 (hereafter PF 2.0) programs—which have also been dubbed "outcomes-based funding"—differ from PF 1.0 programs in that performance funding no longer takes the form of a bonus; rather, these funds are part and parcel of the regular state base funding for higher education. Furthermore, the proportion of state appropriations funding for higher education tied to performance metrics can be much higher, as high as 80%–90%, as in Ohio and Tennessee (Dougherty & Natow, 2015; Dougherty & Reddy, 2013; Snyder, 2015).

With the rise of a sizable number of PF 2.0 programs, distinctions can be made among them according to the proportion of state money subject to performance funding, whether some or all public higher education institutions are included, whether metrics and their weights are differentiated by type of institution, and whether outcomes for underrepresented students are prioritized (Snyder, 2015). The most intensive PF 2.0 programs are ones that not only involve base funding but also are characterized by tying at least 25% of state funding for higher education to performance metrics, covering all public higher education institutions, differentiating the metrics and their weights by type of institution, and prioritizing outcomes for underrepresented students (Snyder, 2015).

Conceptualizing How Performance Funding Works

Advocates of performance funding often describe causal sequences in which such programs will stimulate institutional changes in academic and student services policies, programs, and practices, which, in turn, will generate improvements in student outcomes. Typically, policymakers do not specify particular institutional changes that they are seeking (Dougherty et al., 2014a). These causal sequences involve specific "policy instruments" or "mechanisms that translate substantive policy goals into concrete actions" (McDonnell & Elmore, 1987, p. 134).*

---

* In chapter 2, we discuss in detail the theories of action and policy instruments behind performance funding.

The main policy instrument considered by performance funding advocates is the provision of financial incentives in a way that mimics profits for businesses (Dougherty et al., 2014a; see also Burke, 2005, p. 304; Dougherty & Reddy, 2013; Massy, 2011). This financial-incentives theory of action—which dovetails with resource-dependence theory (Pfeffer & Salancik, 1978) and principal–agent theory (Lane & Kivisto, 2008)—holds that all higher education institutions are revenue maximizers and will make a strong effort to improve their performance if the amount of funding at stake is significant enough (Burke, 2002, pp. 266–72; Dougherty et al., 2014a; Jones, 2012, 2013). A Tennessee state-level higher education official forcefully stated the argument that financial incentives can be a powerful catalyst for action: "Once you get the dollars right and once the financial incentives are properly aligned, that's when I think the campus's attention is focused on completion to a much greater degree than it was previously. . . . I mean, it's really more, again, to try to get the incentives lined up correctly and then let the campus president along with his or her staff figure out how best to go about achieving whatever the end goal is" (as quoted in Dougherty & Natow, 2015).

Using market forces to influence change is not new to education. Several examples from elementary and secondary education illustrate the appeal of using financial incentives to induce institutional change. Consider No Child Left Behind and its state equivalents (Fuhrman & Elmore, 2004; Manna, 2006) and, to a degree, the early twentieth-century "cult of efficiency" in which urban school districts eagerly embraced business models (Callahan, 1962; Tyack, 1974).

Despite the emphasis they put on financial incentives, advocates of performance funding programs have also considered other policy instruments. One is the provision of information to college officials and faculty about the goals and intended methods of performance funding as a means to catalyze institutional change; the aim is to persuade colleges of the importance of improved student outcomes and convince campus actors to reorient their efforts toward success on the identified measures (Dougherty et al., 2014a; Dougherty & Reddy, 2013; Massy, 2011). This policy instrument operates on the premise that once college and university personnel are convinced that a goal is socially valued and legitimate, they will modify their behavior in support of the goal (Ewell, 1999; Rutschow et al., 2011; see also Anderson, 2011; Schneider & Ingram, 1997; Stone, 2012, chap. 14).*

* This persuasive communication theory of action resembles the soft side of the process of "coercive isomorphism" described by DiMaggio and Powell (1991), which may manifest itself as

Another informational policy instrument that advocates of performance funding have used is to make colleges aware of their student outcomes, particularly in comparison to other colleges (Dougherty et al., 2014a). The aim is to leverage, in service of institutional change, colleges' values, curiosity, and feelings of pride and status striving (Burke, 2005; Dougherty et al., 2014a; Dougherty & Reddy, 2013; see also Baldwin et al., 2011; Dowd & Tong, 2007; Witham & Bensimon, 2012).

Financial incentives and information provision receive the most attention from performance funding advocates, but the literature on policy design discusses other policy instruments as well. One such instrument involves improving the capabilities of implementing agencies to do their work by developing their leadership, management systems, and other aspects of organizational capacity (Dowd & Tong, 2007; Kerrigan, 2015; Light, 2004; McDonnell & Elmore, 1987; Witham & Bensimon, 2012). Capacity building has been a major feature of several high-profile, foundation-sponsored initiatives to improve community college performance, including Achieving the Dream and Completion by Design (Nodine, Venezia, & Bracco, 2011; Rutschow et al., 2011; see also Jenkins, 2011). Both programs pair colleges with "coaches" who work with senior administrators and institutional researchers to improve their analysis of student outcomes and decide on institutional changes to improve those outcomes. Though advocates of performance funding have paid little overt attention to capacity building, in this study we examine the degree to which states have used this policy instrument as part of their performance funding programs.

The policy instruments discussed above are intended to have *immediate impacts* on colleges and universities by manipulating their revenues from the state, their attention to and appreciation of the state's priorities for performance funding and higher education, their awareness of their own performance in relation to those state priorities, and their organizational capacities to respond to performance funding. However, to be effective, these immediate impacts must, in turn, stimulate *intermediate institutional changes* involving modifications of institutional policies, programs, and practices, which will presumably lead to the *ultimate intended impacts* that policymakers seek, such as more graduates or increased rates of job placement (Dougherty & Reddy, 2013).

---

pressure from governmental mandates and societal expectations. It also resembles the "hortatory" technique of policy control described by Anderson (2011).

But we should not just focus on intended impacts. We also need to consider the *unintended impacts* of performance funding and how they arise from *obstacles* to its effective functioning (Dougherty & Reddy, 2013; Forsythe, 2001; Heinrich & Marschke, 2010; Moynihan, 2008, 2010). Unintended impacts are results that are not intended by the policy creators but occur as side effects of policy initiatives (Merton, 1968, 1976). Often, these side effects arise as attempts to game accountability programs (Forsythe, 2001; Heinrich & Marschke, 2010; Moynihan, 2008, 2010). In the case of performance funding, unintended impacts may include institutions narrowing their missions to focus on areas that are rewarded by performance funding, restricting their admission of less prepared students who will be harder to graduate, or lowering academic standards for enrolled students (Dougherty & Reddy, 2013; see also Heinrich & Marschke, 2010; Moynihan, 2008, 2010; Rothstein, 2008a, 2008b). As we will explore in chapters 2 and 8, these impacts may be unintended by most state policymakers, but they may be welcomed and even intended by institutional actors and some state policymakers.

Such unintended impacts may arise when public agencies encounter *obstacles* to easily realizing the intended impacts of performance accountability by using legitimate means. Faced with such obstacles, they may resort to less legitimate means to realize the impacts intended by policymakers (Merton, 1968, 1976). For example, in order to boost their performance scores, agencies may lower service delivery standards or restrict the intake of harder-to-serve clients (Forsythe, 2001; Heinrich & Marschke, 2010; Moynihan, 2008, 2010). The obstacles causing these unintended impacts may be characteristics of the performance funding program itself or of the higher education institutions implementing it. Obstacles can take such forms as performance funding metrics that do not align well with college missions or colleges' lack of sufficient organizational capacity to adequately understand their performance problems and to develop feasible and effective solutions (Dougherty & Reddy, 2013; see also Moynihan, 2008; Schick, 2003; Townley, Cooper, & Oakes, 2003).

Chapter Contents and Preview of Findings

Our book is a study of the implementation and impacts (intended and unintended) of performance funding in three leading states: Indiana, Ohio, and Tennessee. To examine these processes in detail, we focus on 18 institutions: three public universities and three community colleges in each state. The institutions vary in their predicted capacity to respond effectively to performance funding, as indexed by expenditures per full-time-equivalent (FTE) student, rated capacity for institutional research (IR), and student-body composition.

In chapter 2, we set the stage for our findings. It describes our research questions and methods and puts them in the context of the research literature on performance funding in higher education and other relevant literatures, including policy design and performance management in government. The chapter delineates our six research questions and the methods we used to answer them. It addresses why we decided to study Indiana, Ohio, and Tennessee, how we chose the 18 public postsecondary institutions we examine in detail, and the positions of the 261 people we interviewed. To explain and contextualize these questions and methods, we review research and theory on performance funding in higher education, performance management in government, policy design, data-driven decision making and organizational learning, policy implementation, and principal–agent relations.

Chapter 3 analyzes the policy instruments our three states used to spur institutions to improve their outcomes, particularly for students. We find that policymakers in all three states relied most heavily on financial incentives to induce change at both community college and university campuses in their respective states. At the same time, officials in all three states made use of other policy instruments as well. They made efforts to educate campus leaders about the new performance funding programs in their states, though such efforts varied in their intensity and their level of campus penetration. We also find evidence of efforts on the part of state officials to inform campus officials about their institution's performance on the state metrics, but again the nature and intensity of these communication efforts varied. Despite statements of intent by state policymakers, we find little evidence of systematic state efforts to enhance campus-level capacity to respond effectively to performance funding demands. For example, we find only minimal efforts by the states to improve institutions' capacity for organizational learning by building up their capacity for IR and effective deliberation. As we will find in chapter 7, insufficient institutional capacity acts as a powerful obstacle to effective institutional responsiveness to performance funding.

Chapter 4 examines the deliberative structures used by colleges and universities to respond to performance funding demands and the factors that aid and hinder their effectiveness. Our study finds that colleges use a variety of deliberative structures—including both general administrative structures and more specialized and evanescent structures such as strategic planning committees and accreditation review committees—to determine how to respond to state performance funding demands. The aids and hindrances to effective deliberation which colleges encounter principally involve the presence or absence of organizational commitment and leadership, effective communication and collaboration, timely and relevant data, and time for deliberation. One of these hindrances—the lack of timely and relevant data—connects back to the insufficient state efforts to build up institutional capacity.

In chapter 5, we examine changes that institutions made in response to performance funding pressures. We consider changes to academic programs, policies, and practices, as well as changes to student services policies, programs, and practices. The two most commonly made campus-level academic changes related to performance funding have involved alterations to developmental (remedial) education and improvements in course articulation and transfer between community colleges and universities. Meanwhile, the two most commonly made campus-level student services changes include revamping advising and counseling services and enhancing tutoring services and supplemental instruction. A major point made by the chapter is that it is difficult to gauge the unique impact of performance funding on these changes, since it has been only one of several concurrent initiatives by states, accrediting associations, and policy groups designed to improve student outcomes.

Chapter 6 reviews the evidence on the impact of performance funding on student outcomes. It begins with reviewing simple descriptive data on changes in graduation numbers in Indiana, Ohio, and Tennessee since the advent of performance funding. The number of graduates in these states increased in the years following the implementation of performance funding programs, and these increases exceeded contemporary increases in enrollments, suggesting a positive impact of performance funding. However, aside from controlling for the size of enrollment increases, these descriptive data do not control for many other factors that might be impacting graduation numbers. These may include the introduction of other reforms and initiatives besides performance funding, shifts in tuition and student aid levels, changes in the state of the economy, social processes commonly affecting states with and without performance funding, and so forth. Careful multivariate analyses that account for many of these other factors largely fail to find a significant positive impact of performance funding on student outcomes. This is true for Indiana, Ohio, and Tennessee, as well as states not covered by our direct sample. The lack of evidence tying performance funding to better outcomes raises this question: Could the lack of impact stem from obstacles institutions encounter in responding effectively to performance funding? This question is taken up in the next chapter.

In chapter 7, we analyze the obstacles that institutions encounter in attempting to respond effectively to performance funding demands. Our respondents most often pointed to the academic and demographic composition of their student bodies (particularly in the cases of community colleges and broad-access public universities), inappropriate performance funding metrics, and insufficient institutional capacity. With regard to student-body composition, many of our respondents perceived that the most difficult obstacle to responding to the performance funding formula is the fact that open-access institutions enroll many students who face academic, social, and economic challenges that make it more difficult for them to graduate. Secondly, particularly at community colleges, respondents often perceived the state performance funding metrics to be poorly matched to their institutions' missions and student-body composition. Respondents frequently argued that many students at community colleges do not intend to get a degree, unlike students at four-year institutions, or will not do so in a timely fashion, because they more often attend part-time. As a result, community colleges will find it more difficult to post good graduation numbers. Finally, many of our respondents pointed to their institutions' insufficient organizational capacity—particularly for effective IR—as a major obstacle to performing well on the state metrics. The presence of these reported obstacles raises the specter that institutions may resort to illegitimate tactics in responding to the pressures of their respective performance funding programs. That is the concern of the next chapter.

Chapter 8 takes its cue from research on policy implementation and on performance management in government which finds that a policy can often produce outcomes that are not intended by policymakers (although they may be intended by institutional actors). As the chapter describes, our respondents principally reported impacts unintended by policymakers such as restrictions in admissions to college and weakening of academic standards. Our institutional respondents frequently noted that their institutions could and sometimes actually have moved to restrict admission of less prepared students by such means as higher admission requirements, selective recruitment, and focusing institutional financial aid on better-prepared students. Our respondents also frequently noted that their institutions could move or already had moved to weaken academic standards by softening academic demands in class (grade inflation) or reducing degree requirements. Because restricting admissions of less prepared students and reducing academic quality are institutionally tempting but societally undesirable approaches for colleges to improve their performance on state metrics, states need to take decided steps to reduce these temptations. We take up this point in our concluding chapter.

The ninth and final chapter summarizes the main findings of the book and draws their implications for policymaking and future research. With regard to policymaking, it addresses how state governments and other public bodies can reduce the obstacles to and unintended impacts of performance funding. The premise is that, however one regards performance funding, such programs are here to stay. The question is how to maximize their beneficial impacts and minimize their negative side effects. With regard to the unintended impacts of performance funding, the chapter addresses how states can counteract the institutional temptation to improve college performance by restricting the admissions of less prepared (and often less advantaged) students and weakening academic standards. It details ways to incentivize efforts to admit and graduate less prepared students and to guard academic standards. But to be fully effective, these state efforts to reduce unintended impacts must also address the obstacles to responding effectively to performance funding which provide the temptation to resort to illegitimate means. Hence, the chapter also details ways in which states can devise performance metrics that better fit college missions, help colleges cope with large numbers of at-risk students, and improve institutions' capacity to engage in effective organizational learning.

CHAPTER 2

Research Perspectives, Questions, and Methods

This chapter lays out our research questions and methods in the context of existing research both on performance funding in higher education and on related subjects. We begin with a review of the existing research on performance funding, noting its main findings and limitations. In order to address those limitations, we draw on research on related subjects, including performance management in government, policy design, data-driven decision making and organizational learning, policy implementation, and principal–agent relations. Drawing on these findings and perspectives, we then lay out our research questions. We finish by outlining our research methods.

Existing Scholarship on the Impacts of Performance Funding and Its Limitations

There is a substantial body of scholarship on the implementation and impacts of performance funding which has been systematically reviewed in Dougherty & Reddy (2013). Since then, subsequent studies of performance funding have largely confirmed the main findings of that review of the literature. Below, we lay out these main findings and, as we go, describe their limitations.

POLICY INSTRUMENTS

The research literature has touched on and analyzed three policy instruments through which performance funding could produce changes in student outcomes: financial incentives operating through changes in institutional funding, provision of information on state goals for performance funding, and provision of information on institutional performance on state performance metrics (Dougherty & Reddy, 2013).

Changes in institutional funding are typically the main policy instrument that policymakers have in mind when they consider performance funding, and they have been the focus of studies of the impact of performance funding on institutional funding (Dougherty & Reddy, 2013; Hillman et al., 2015; Hillman,

Tandberg, & Fryar, 2015; Hillman, Tandberg, & Gross, 2014; Hurtado, 2015; Mc-Kinney & Hagedorn, 2015; Rutherford & Rabovsky, 2014; Tandberg & Hillman, 2014; Tandberg, Hillman, & Barakat, 2014). For the most part, the extant research studies indicate that performance funding has produced only small changes in institutional funding and that the financial incentive has not been powerful (Dougherty et al., 2014b; Dougherty & Reddy, 2013, pp. 36–37). However, we should caution that almost all of these studies are of small PF 1.0 programs and not the much bigger PF 2.0 programs, such as those in Ohio and Tennessee.

Only a handful of studies have examined how state officials go about disseminating information on state goals for performance funding. A larger number of studies have examined whether, with the advent of performance funding, institutional officials do become more aware of state goals. They find that college leaders do become largely aware of the goals and methods of state performance funding programs, though there is also evidence that this awareness is not widely diffused throughout institutions. As one moves down the chain of authority, knowledge of state performance funding programs becomes increasingly superficial (Dougherty & Reddy, 2013, pp. 37–38; see also Ness, Deupree, & Gándara, 2015, pp. 17–18, 34–35).

Virtually no studies examine whether or how states pursue the provision of information on institutional performance on state metrics as a policy instrument that is part of performance funding. Still, there have been numerous studies that show that performance funding programs do lead to greater institutional self-awareness, as colleges have to collect data on their performance and report it to the state (Dougherty & Reddy, 2013, pp. 39–40).

The scholarship on policy instruments could benefit from more studies examining the provision of information, particularly how states go about doing it. Who do state officials communicate with at the colleges? What means do state officials use to communicate, whether high-interaction modalities such as small-group meetings, or impersonal means such as research reports?

The biggest limitation in the research literature's analysis of the policy instruments advancing performance funding is the lack of attention to efforts to improve the organizational capacity of institutions to respond effectively to performance funding. Capacity building has been identified as an important policy instrument in studies of policymaking (Brinkerhoff, 2010; Cohen, 1995; Kezar, 2005; McDonnell & Elmore, 1987; Timmermans & Epstein, 2010; Van Vught, 1994), but the extant research literature on performance funding provides relatively little analysis of whether states make deliberate efforts to build up organizational capacity in colleges to respond to performance funding demands. The main exception is the research by Estela Bensimon, Alicia Dowd, Keith Witham, and their colleagues recounting and analyzing interventions they have conducted in such states as Nevada and Pennsylvania. These interventions were designed to improve state and institutional efforts to deliberate on the best means to realize state goals for performance funding (Bensimon et al., 2012; Dowd & Bensimon, 2015; Lumina Foundation, 2015).

ORGANIZATIONAL CHANGES

The extant research literature shows that performance funding does lead institutional actors to make organizational changes designed to boost their college's student outcomes. Broadly, the organizational changes cited in the research literature can be broken down into four areas: shifts in institutional spending; alterations of academic policies, programs, and practices; changes in developmental education and tutoring; and alterations to student services policies, programs, and practices (Dougherty & Reddy, 2013). There is some evidence that performance funding leads institutions to make small, though statistically significant, increases in their spending on instructional and student services activities. Researchers have employed various statistical controls, including, depending on the study, institutional enrollments, selectivity, student and faculty composition, institutional revenues and expenditures, financial aid characteristics, and state financial and political characteristics (Kelchen & Stedrak, 2015; Rabovsky, 2012). In addition, studies have found that institutions respond to performance funding by making changes in their academic and student services policies and programs. The academic changes include alterations to academic departments and programs of study such as eliminating programs with poor graduation requirements; altering academic curricula and graduation requirements, for example, by removing degree requirements that impede graduation; and altering course content and instructional delivery, perhaps by creating professional development for faculty with high student complaints. Meanwhile, the alterations to student services policies and programs have involved improving services related to registration, financial aid, first-year retention programs, counseling and advising, and job placement services (Dougherty & Reddy, 2013, pp. 45–52).

A major limitation of the existing research on institutional responses to performance funding programs is that the research does not adequately consider or account for contemporaneous and convergent developments. While institutions are being influenced by performance funding to take such steps as revamping their developmental education programs, they are also being pushed in the same direction by other state programs and by various other initiatives such as those championed by the Gates and Lumina Foundations and Complete College America. For example, the Gates and Lumina Foundations have sponsored the Developmental Education Initiative, which works with 15 Achieving the Dream colleges to improve developmental education (Achieving the Dream, 2015a; Boatman, 2012; Complete College America, 2013; Developmental Education Initiative, 2015; Nodine, Venezia, & Bracco, 2011; Ohio Board of Regents, 2012d). We need studies that explore how these other influences intersect with and condition the impact of performance funding.

STUDENT OUTCOMES

The extant research literature has largely found that performance funding has little impact on student outcomes (Dougherty & Reddy, 2013). To be sure, there are studies that find big increases in the number of graduates produced following the advent of performance funding in a given state. But even if student outcomes improve after the introduction of performance funding, these improvements could be influenced by many other factors, such as growing enrollments (which alone could produce more graduates per year), modifications to state tuition and financial aid policies, and other efforts to improve student outcomes (such as recent state initiatives to improve counseling and advising, developmental education, and transfer between institutions). Hence, it is important to conduct multivariate statistical analyses that strive to control for the many factors, apart from the operation of performance funding, that might influence student outcomes. When such studies have been conducted, the predominant finding is that performance funding does not have a significant impact on student outcomes such as retention and graduation from two-year or four-year colleges (Dougherty & Reddy, 2013, pp. 53–56). This surprising finding has been backed up by studies that have come out since the Dougherty & Reddy review (Hillman, Tandberg, & Fryar, 2015; Hillman, Tandberg, & Gross, 2014; Rutherford & Rabovsky, 2014; Tandberg & Hillman, 2014; Tandberg, Hillman, & Barakat, 2014).

While these multivariate studies have been very carefully done, a major limitation is that they are focused on the impact of PF 1.0 programs. We also need research that examines the impact of the more recent and much larger PF 2.0 programs in Tennessee and Ohio. We review such studies in chapter 6.

OBSTACLES TO EFFECTIVE FUNCTIONING

The absence of clear impacts of performance funding on student outcomes suggests that performance funding programs are being inhibited by substantial obstacles to their effectiveness. The extant research on performance funding points particularly to such obstacles as the inappropriateness of many performance measures employed; instability in funding levels, indicators, and measures; the brief duration of many performance funding programs; inadequate funding for performance funding programs; shortfalls in regular state funding for higher education; uneven knowledge and expertise about performance funding within institutions; inequalities in institutional capacity to respond to performance funding; resistance and "game playing" by institutions; and the presence of many students who are less prepared academically and/or need remediation (Dougherty & Reddy, 2013, pp. 57–69; see also Ness, Deupree, & Gándara, 2015, pp. 31–32, 40–43, 47–48, 55; Santiago et al., 2008, pp. 309, 314; Sauder & Espeland, 2009, p. 77).

The extant research notes widespread misgivings about how retention and graduation rates are measured in various performance funding programs. To begin with, a major question is whether colleges should get at least partial credit for students who transfer out and eventually get their degrees elsewhere. Furthermore, some studies note concerns that graduation rates do not account for differences between institutions in the academic preparation or degree ambitions of incoming students, which will strongly affect graduation numbers. In addition, the criticism has been raised that performance funding metrics do not include measures for reducing gaps in college access and attainment by race/ethnicity and social class (Dougherty & Reddy, 2013; Dowd & Bensimon, 2015; Jones, 2014).

Recent research has amplified the finding that the student-body composition of colleges—particularly enrolling high numbers of students who are less prepared academically—will affect how much performance funding the colleges receive. A study of one large Texas community college's experience with the state's performance funding program found that students who enter with a GED degree or need remediation secure significantly lower performance funding for that college than do better-prepared students (McKinney & Hagedorn, 2015). However, if the metric is not institutional performance in a given year but *changes* in institutional performance from one year to the next, then it appears that student-body composition may not be an obstacle to an institution's securing performance funding. Similarly, an analysis of the performance of Washington community colleges on the Student Achievement Initiative has found that changes in institutional performance on state outcomes metrics are not much influenced by student-body composition (Belfield, 2012).

One of the limitations of the existing research on obstacles is that it does not allow us to clearly delineate how those obstacles differ by state and type of college. Performance funding programs differ considerably by state, and different programs are likely to pose different obstacles for colleges. Meanwhile, those colleges—for example, two-year versus four-year colleges and universities—vary greatly in their missions, institutional resources, and student-body composition. Hence, they are likely to experience rather different obstacles in responding to performance funding. However, these state and institutional differences have not been systematically addressed in the extant research on performance funding.

UNINTENDED IMPACTS

Policymakers announce certain goals when adopting performance funding, but as with any policy intervention, there are likely to be consequences that are unintended by the policy framers (see Merton, 1968, 1976; Moynihan, 2008). In fact, the extant research on the impacts of performance funding has uncovered several different impacts not intended by policymakers: restriction of admissions of students less likely to graduate, grade inflation and weakening of academic standards, costs of compliance, and narrowing of institutional missions to those rewarded by the performance funding programs (Dougherty & Reddy, 2013; see also Ness, Deupree, & Gándara, 2015, pp. 25, 47). The compliance costs reported include money and time required to comply with performance funding mandates, such as hiring additional personnel to handle the data collection and reporting required by the state performance funding program (Dougherty & Reddy, 2013, p. 71; see also Stensaker, 2003, p. 155). Reports on narrowing of institutional mission describe cases where colleges de-emphasize missions that are not rewarded or only minimally rewarded by the performance funding program (Barnetson & Cutright, 2000, p. 286). An example would be cutting back training for low-wage jobs because the performance funding program only awards points for placement in jobs with high wages (Dougherty & Reddy, 2013, pp. 72–73). Weakening of academic standards has been reported in such forms as colleges removing academic requirements that hinder students' graduation or pressuring faculty to largely avoid giving out failing grades (Dougherty & Reddy, 2013, pp. 73–75; see also Santiago et al., 2008, pp. 309, 314). Finally, instances of restriction of admission of less prepared students have been found in which colleges—in order to maximize their retention and graduation numbers—cut back their outreach to and admission of less prepared students who are deemed less likely to graduate (Dougherty & Reddy, 2013, pp. 75–76; see also Ness, Deupree, & Gándara, 2015, p. 47). Buttressing this last finding, a recent multivariate study of performance funding in Indiana found that it was associated with highly significant increases in the average ACT scores at both the 25th and 75th percentile for Indiana public four-year colleges (Umbricht, Fernandez, & Ortagus, 2015), indicating that student intake had become more selective by student preparation. Furthermore, a multivariate national study of public institutions found that four-year colleges (but not community colleges) in states with performance funding received somewhat lower Pell Grant revenue than institutions in states without performance funding. This could indicate efforts to change the composition of the student body (Kelchen & Stedrak, 2015).

We note that the extant research on unintended impacts of performance funding should be more careful about delimiting the boundaries of what are considered "unintended" impacts. Certain impacts that are unintended by policy framers may be acceptable to or even intended by others who support or implement performance funding. There may be supporters of performance funding who are not unhappy if it results in reducing college access for less prepared or underrepresented students. For example, there are administrators and faculty at colleges and universities who may happily accept the argument that performance funding pressures require that their broad-access institutions become more selective and less open to less prepared and less advantaged students.*

An additional criticism of the extant research on the unintended impacts of performance funding is that it does not pay sufficient heed to how those impacts are likely to vary by state and type of institution. Performance funding programs differ by state, and different programs are likely to impose somewhat different unintended impacts. Moreover, different kinds of colleges are likely to experience rather different unintended impacts, if only because they may face different obstacles and the unintended impacts are often due to responding to obstacles in illegitimate ways.

---

* We wish to thank Dr. Tiffany Jones of the Southern Education Foundation for her observation that it is important to be careful in how we regard what impacts are indeed "unintended."

OVERALL LIMITATIONS

As we have seen above, the existing research literature is limited on each of the topics that we have covered, from policy instruments to unintended impacts. Two limitations frequently recur.

Almost all the extant research literature—even that on Tennessee and Ohio—is focused on the implementation and impact of PF 1.0 programs rather than the newer and more powerful PF 2.0 programs. This is a major problem because there is reason to believe that the impacts—intended and unintended—of performance funding are likely to be larger for PF 2.0 programs. In particular, the more recently implemented PF 2.0 programs in Tennessee and Ohio involve a much larger proportion of state higher education funding than their PF 1.0 predecessors.

Second, while the research literature has examined performance funding as developed in a variety of states and applied to different kinds of colleges, very few studies have made variation of impacts by state and type of college an organizing principle of their analyses. It is unusual to have studies that examine more than one state at a time, allowing analysis of the impact on institutional and student outcomes of state differences in the design and implementation of performance funding; the structure, governance, and missions of the higher education system; and the nature of the social, economic, and political systems. In addition, the qualitative research literature is also restricted in the scope of institutional contexts it examines. Many qualitative studies investigate just one institution or, occasionally, a number of institutions of the same type, such as community colleges. It is rare to find studies that sample across different kinds of institutions, such as flagship state universities, regional public universities, and community colleges differing in student-body composition and other characteristics. As a result, there is little opportunity to determine how the implementation and impacts of performance funding differ across institutional types. As will be demonstrated below, we have made capturing state and institutional variations in performance funding impacts a central aspect of the design of our own research.

Enlisting Insights from Other Bodies of Literature

To flesh out the insights from existing studies of performance funding, we turn to other bodies of literature that bear on similar issues and have relevant insights. In particular, we draw on research and theory on performance management of government services, policy design, organizational learning, policy implementation, and principal–agent relations.

PERFORMANCE MANAGEMENT IN PUBLIC AGENCIES

Many of the patterns described in the research literature on performance funding implementation mirror patterns described in studies of performance management programs for government and nonprofit agencies operating in policy areas other than higher education (Colyvas, 2012; Forsythe, 2001; Grizzle, 2002; Heckman et al., 2011; Heinrich & Marschke, 2010; Moynihan, 2008, 2010; Radin, 2006; Rothstein, 2008b; Schick, 2002, 2003; Townley, Cooper, & Oakes, 2003). Elected officials and agency heads have widely used policy instruments similar to those employed in performance funding programs, particularly financial incentives, in order to improve the outputs and outcomes of government agencies in such areas as K–12 schooling, workforce development, health care, and social services. Research on those performance management programs has found many of the same obstacles and unintended impacts as those identified to date by studies of performance funding for higher education.

The performance management literature identifies several obstacles encountered by performance management programs in government. One obstacle is difficulty on the part of agencies in interpreting and evaluating the data they collect and devising solutions to problems discovered (Moynihan, 2008, pp. 104–5, 113, 178–79). That difficulty stems from such factors as a lack of sufficient organizational leadership and resources, an organizational culture that promotes defensive responses to organizational problems, and a lack of venues for discussing problems and possible solutions (Moynihan, 2008, pp. 167, 178–85; Schick, 2003, pp. 84–86). A second frequent obstacle is performance metrics that do not capture how well an agency is functioning because they do not align well with the agency's mission (Townley, Cooper, & Oakes, 2003, pp. 1061–62). Yet another obstacle is gaming of the performance metrics by the organizational targets of performance management. Agency officials may attempt to pick easily satisfied metrics or generate deceptive performance scores (for example, through teaching to the test or even fabricating test results in the K–12 education realm) in order to make their agency look like it is truly meeting performance expectations. In such cases, high scores belie a mediocre, or worse, reality. Moreover, in what has been called "the performance paradox," as gaming becomes more common, performance indicators less and less capture real organizational performance (Colyvas, 2012, p. 185; DeBruijn, 2002, pp. 21, 23–32; Grizzle, 2002, pp. 363–65; Heinrich & Marschke, 2010, pp. 195–96; Moynihan, 2010, pp. 288–89; Radin, 2006, pp. 17–19; Van Thiel & Leeuw, 2002, p. 27).

The performance management research literature also turns up unintended impacts similar to those reported for performance funding. Findings of deterioration in service delivery quality and adverse risk selection (or "cream skimming") are reported by studies of K–12 education (Rothstein, 2008a, 2008b), social welfare programs (Wells & Johnson, 2001), workforce-training programs (Heckman et al., 2011; Rothstein, 2008b), health care (Lake, Kvam, & Gold, 2005; Rothstein, 2008b; Stecher & Kirby, 2004), and public services generally (Grizzle, 2002; Heinrich & Marschke, 2010; Moynihan, 2008, 2010). These studies report evidence that, when faced with performance pressures and difficulties in easily responding to them, K–12 schools and other government agencies may resort to focusing on clients easier to help and give less attention to clients who need more help and are less likely to succeed (Grizzle, 2002, p. 365; Heinrich & Marschke, 2010, pp. 199–201; Moynihan, 2010, p. 289; Rothstein, 2008b, pp. 24–29, 40–45; Van Theil & Leeuw, 2002, p. 274). Also, there are reports that agencies have narrowed their missions to focus only on those for which they are rewarded, neglecting missions that are not rewarded. High schools, for example, have cut back their attention to social studies (Colyvas, 2012, pp. 184–85; Moynihan, 2010, p. 289; Rothstein, 2008b, pp. 9–23; Van Theil & Leeuw, 2002, pp. 273–74).

How are we to understand how these obstacles and unintended outcomes arise, under both performance funding in higher education and performance management in government more generally? To gain theoretical purchase on this phenomenon, we turn to studies of policy design, policy implementation, and principal–agent relations.

POLICY DESIGN: POLICY INSTRUMENTS AND THEIR STRENGTHS AND WEAKNESSES

An important stream of policy analysis is devoted to the study of policy design, analyzing the different "policy instruments" that can be used to further policymakers' goals and gauging the relative strengths and weaknesses of those instruments. Policy instruments are the actual "mechanisms that translate substantive policy goals into concrete actions" (McDonnell & Elmore, 1987, p. 134). They are underpinned by "theories of action" as to how they will catalyze changes in the target institutions and, in turn, accomplish the policy's ultimate goals (Argyris & Schön, 1996).* The policy instruments discussed in the policy design

---

* These concepts of policy instruments and theories of action are very similar to the concept of social mechanisms (Elster, 1989; Hedstrom & Swedberg, 1998).

literature are quite varied. They include financial incentives, regulations, mandates, information provision and persuasion, and capacity building (Anderson, 2011; McDonnell & Elmore, 1987; Salamon, 2002; Schneider & Ingram, 1997; Stone, 2012; Van Vught, 1994). We focus here on three that are particularly relevant to performance funding: financial incentives, information provision, and capacity building. They have been mentioned by state policymakers in connection with performance funding (see chapter 3) and are particularly germane to public agencies, such as US higher education institutions, that enjoy considerable autonomy from elected officials (Schmidtlein & Berdahl, 2011).

Financial Incentives. Financial incentives are prominently mentioned in the policy design literature under such terms as "incentives" or "inducements" (Anderson, 2011, pp. 245, 250; McDonnell & Elmore, 1987, pp. 134, 137–38; Schneider & Ingram, 1997; Stone, 2012, chap. 12; Van Vught, 1994, pp. 99–100; see also Etzioni, 1961). Deborah Stone (2012, p. 271) notes, "The idea behind incentives is simple: carrots and sticks. If you promise people a reward or threaten them with a penalty, they will act differently than they otherwise might." This theory of action accords with principal–agent theory, which stresses that there is often a misalignment between the interests of principals and their agents (Lane & Kivisto, 2008). Monetary and other incentives flowing from the principals (government) therefore become a device to bring the interests of the agents (e.g., agency heads) into better alignment with those of the principals. The higher education corollary is the argument that higher education institutions are revenue maximizers. In the past, this has led them to focus on maximizing enrollments (Alexander & Ehrenberg, 2003; Bowen, 1980). However, the argument is made that they can be made to focus on public officials' concern about student outcomes if public funding is no longer focused on student enrollments, but rather on student completions (Burke, 2002; Jones, 2013; Massy, 2011; US Department of Education, 2011).

Financial incentives are so integral to a market economy that we often ignore the fact that they are more complicated and less effective than they appear. The obstacles to their effectiveness are multiple. The receivers of financial incentives may be unaware that they exist or, more often, unaware of their actual size. Moreover, receivers may not be capable of or willing to change their behavior in response to an incentive, because they may not put the same value on it as the giver anticipated, they are being influenced by other factors, or they are unable to determine how to respond effectively to the incentive (see Stone, 2012, chap. 12

for more). We need to keep these impediments in mind as we examine the impact of performance funding on colleges and universities.

These impediments to incentives point to the importance of two other policy instruments that can be very important supplements to financial incentives but are often ignored by the research on performance funding: information provision and attention focusing, and capacity building.

Persuasive Communication. Persuasive communication—involving information provision, attention focusing, and persuasion—is a second instrument that is widely discussed in the policy design literature (Anderson, 2011, pp. 243–44, 261; Schneider & Ingram, 1997; Stone, 2012, chap. 14; see also Barnetson & Cutright, 2000; Espeland & Stevens, 2008; Etzioni, 1961; Townley, Cooper, & Oakes, 2003). As James Anderson states, "Administrative agencies engage in many educational and persuasional activities intended to convince those directly affected, and the public generally, that designated public policies are reasonable, necessary, socially beneficial, or legitimate. . . . The effectiveness of public policies depends considerably on the ability of agencies to promote understanding and consent, thereby reducing violations and minimizing the use of sanctions" (Anderson, 2011, p. 261).

In the context of performance funding, persuasive communication can take two forms. State policymakers can use performance funding to highlight certain outcomes and make the case for prioritizing improvement on those outcomes, thus securing institutional buy-in (Massy, 2011; see also Ewell, 1999; Rutschow et al., 2011).* This instrument operates on the theory of action that once college and university personnel are convinced that a governmental goal is valuable and legitimate, they will modify their behavior. A second way policymakers can use persuasive communication to shape the behavior of others is to set desired performance outcomes, determine how well institutions are meeting them, and make that information available to the institutions and perhaps a wider public. This particular policy instrument relies on a theory of action that the availability of information on organizational performance will trigger feelings of pride and status striving at the local level, even if the information does not explicitly compare institutions to one another (Burke, 2005).

---

* This mechanism closely parallels the soft side of "coercive isomorphism," as discussed in institutional theory, which may manifest itself as persuasion in that pressure from governmental mandates and societal expectations encourage local change (DiMaggio & Powell, 1991).

As with financial incentives, persuasive communication encounters certain obstacles to its effectiveness. Most obviously, the intended receivers of that communication may fail to hear it or hear it in a distorted way. But even if they hear it accurately, they may fail to respond as intended because their reception is shaped by values, cultural norms, stereotypes, and habits that run counter to what the information claims or the actions it is calling for (Golden, 2000; Spillane, Reiser, & Gomez, 2006; Stone, 2012, pp. 320–22).

Capacity Building. The final policy instrument we consider is building up organizational capacity (Brinkerhoff, 2010; Cohen, 1995; Honig, 2006; Light, 2004; McDonnell & Elmore, 1987; Schneider & Ingram, 1997; Van Vught, 1994). A common definition is this: "Capacity building is designed to change some aspect of an organization's existing environment, internal structure, leadership, and management systems, which, in turn, should improve employee morale, expertise, productivity, efficiency, and so forth, which should strengthen an organization's capacity to do its work" (Light, 2004, p. 46). Interest in capacity building has grown as the organizational capacity of implementing agencies has come to be seen as crucial to successful implementation of policies and even the general success and standing of government and nonprofit organizations (Addison, 2009; Light, 2004).

In the context of performance funding, higher education institutions may need help in enlarging their capacity to respond effectively to performance funding (see Kezar, 2005; Witham & Bensimon, 2012). In fact, several major recent interventions in higher education operations intending to improve student outcomes—such as the Achieving the Dream initiative of Lumina Foundation and the Completion by Design initiative of the Gates Foundation—have made building institutional capacity a crucial aspect of their intervention (Nodine, Venezia, & Bracco, 2011; Rutschow et al., 2011). Yet, despite this high potential relevance of capacity building to the implementation of performance funding, it has received little attention in the existing research literature (see above). Because of this, we have made attention to what states are doing to support capacity building a major element of our study of the implementation of performance funding.

As with other policy instruments, capacity building also encounters certain typical obstacles. The main obstacle is that it is too often ignored as a crucial aspect of the implementation of policies designed to change the performance of schools (Dougherty & Reddy, 2013). But even when attempted, policies to build up organizational capacity run into other obstacles. First, efforts to build up organizational capacity may seem to be adding too much fat to public organizations, which are supposed to be lean and not administratively bloated (Light, 2004, p. 123). Another obstacle is that the funding provided is inadequate to really improve facilities, equipment, and personnel (Cohen, 1995; Light, 2004, pp. 126–27). A third obstacle is difficulty finding sufficiently trained personnel to fit new and enlarged capacities, whether in institutional research (IR) or planning (Cohen, 1995; Light, 2004, pp. 129–31). Finally, a crucial but subtle impediment is the inability to develop—even with enough information technology (IT) infrastructure, IR personnel, etc.—the prerequisites for effective and efficient dissemination of and deliberation on information regarding institutional performance. Such prerequisites include effective channels of communication, good professional development in data usage, frequent collaboration among colleagues to improve academic programs, and leadership commitment to and group and institutional norms supportive of a culture of inquiry and data-driven deliberation (Dowd & Tong, 2007; Kerrigan, 2014, 2015; Moynihan, 2008; Schick, 2003; Witham & Bensimon, 2012).

These general remarks about capacity building need to be contextualized in terms of a key demand being put on institutions: the ability to analyze their student outcomes, determine where they are below standard, investigate what might be the causes of those performance gaps, and devise effective solutions. What institutions require in order to meet these demands has been analyzed by the research literature on data-driven decision making and organizational learning, to which we now turn.

DATA-DRIVEN DECISION MAKING AND ORGANIZATIONAL LEARNING IN HIGHER EDUCATION

There is a small body of research literature on data-driven decision making in higher education (Allen & Kazis, 2007; Dowd & Tong, 2007; Kerrigan, 2010, 2014, 2015; Morest & Jenkins, 2007; Rabovsky, 2014a, 2014b; Rutschow et al., 2011; Witham & Bensimon, 2012). It has produced a number of findings about factors that are conducive to the use of data in driving organizational decision making, such as availability of the right kinds of data, a data infrastructure that can produce those data, and an organizational culture supporting effective data usage.*

---

* There is also a larger literature in public administration on the use of information by government agencies. It notes how information collection does not necessarily equal information use (Moynihan & Pandey, 2010; Rabovsky, 2014a, 2014b).

The most immediate factor is the simple availability of the right kinds of data to the right kind of people. The right kinds of data should be disaggregated by student background, address outcomes at key points in the student career, and—if possible—allow a longitudinal, cohort-based analysis of student progress (Allen & Kazis, 2007, pp. 3, 9; Dowd & Tong, 2007, p. 98; Rutschow et al., 2011, pp. 39, 44–45; Witham & Bensimon, 2012, p. 61; see also Moynihan & Pandey, 2010). The right recipients of data should include not just institutional researchers and senior administrators but also faculty and mid-level administrators (Allen & Kazis, 2007, pp. 2, 3, 5–8; Rutschow et al., 2011, p. 39). In fact, the research literature has recommended that faculty and mid-level administrators should be not only data users but also data producers, either deciding on what kind of data they need or being provided with the tools to produce it (Allen & Kazis, 2007, pp. 7–8; Jenkins, 2011, p. 33; Kerrigan, 2014, p. 356; Witham & Bensimon, 2012, p. 60).

The wide availability of the right data requires, in turn, the right organizational infrastructure. Part of this infrastructure involves the presence of an IT system that is capable of producing the right data. The registration systems of many colleges were designed with inputs in mind, and they often cannot support the kind of data capture and reporting needed to produce the data described above (Allen & Kazis, 2007, p. 5; Kerrigan, 2014, p. 356; Morest & Jenkins, 2007, pp. 3, 7, 12–13; Rutschow et al., 2011, pp. 38, 43–44). Another part is the possession by faculty and administrators of the necessary skills to analyze research data and even to produce such data (Allen & Kazis, 2007, p. 6; Kerrigan, 2015; Rutschow et al., 2011, p. 39). A third aspect of the right infrastructure involves the presence of an IR office that has enough personnel skilled in data analysis and is oriented to serving the data needs of various constituencies at a college (Allen & Kazis, 2007, pp. 2, 6–8; Morest & Jenkins, 2007, pp. 3, 7, 12; Rutschow et al., 2011, pp. 39, 42). The IR office needs to seek out the data needs of specific college organizational units, produce data tailored to those needs, and train members of those units in analyzing the data (Allen & Kazis, 2007, pp. 6–7; Rutschow et al., 2011, p. 39). A fourth aspect of organizational infrastructure involves sufficient social capital in the form of regular communication channels within an institution which allow for organized discussions about student success (Kerrigan, 2015; see also Moynihan, 2008). Finally, all these conditions are best met when institutions have ample funding (Rabovsky, 2014b).

All of the above conditions require organizational commitment and cultural support. Organizational commitment—particularly by college leaders, but also by faculty—is important to supporting data-driven decision making. Without it, the data-use prerequisites discussed above either do not develop or do not eventuate in effective use of data (Allen & Kazis, 2007, pp. 2–5, 8; Dowd & Tong, 2007, p. 95; Kerrigan, 2014, pp. 355, 356; Kerrigan, 2015; Morest & Jenkins, 2007, pp. 3, 12–13; Rabovsky, 2014b; see also Moynihan, Pandey, & Wright, 2012). This organizational commitment can take such forms as frequent mention of data by college leaders, a willingness to publicize negative data, and a prominent position of the IR office in the organizational chart of a college (Allen & Kazis, 2007, pp. 5–7). But to make the data usage have real bite, the organizational culture needs to support it. It is easy for the data analysis to fail to critically examine organizational routines and to lead to actions that only tinker with those routines. To more deeply question and change organizational practices, it is necessary that institutions encourage a "culture of inquiry" involving openness to examining how the institution is failing to address or even causing the problems of its students. Such a culture requires an openness to information and perspectives that contradict the image the institution has of how well it is realizing its values and how much it is contributing to student success (Witham & Bensimon, 2012). This distinction between deeper and shallower organizational analysis is basic to the literature on organizational learning, to which we now turn.

Organizational learning has been defined in a variety of ways. Most of these definitions describe processes and practices developed by an organization to identify problems and correct them. For example, Argyris and Schön (1996, p. 2) describe organizational learning as "the detection and correction of error." Somewhat differently, Barnett (n.d., p. 9) describes organizational learning as "an experience-based process through which knowledge about action-outcome relationships develops, is encoded in routines, is embedded in organizational memory, and changes collective behavior."

Argyris and Schön (1996) make a fundamental distinction between "single-loop" and "double-loop" organizational learning. The first does not question organizational goals and basic practices but instead looks for technical solutions to gaps between goals and performance, while the second does question those goals and practices. Argyris and Schön (1996, p. 20) define single-loop learning as "instrumental learning that changes strategies of action or assumptions underlying strategies in ways that leave the values of a theory of action unchanged." As Bess and Dee (2008, p. 675) note, single-loop learning attempts to correct mistakes but doesn't explore why the mistakes occurred to begin with (see also

Witham & Bensimon, 2012, p. 49). Double-loop learning puts organizational goals and fundamental structures and processes into question. According to Argyris and Schön (1996, p. 25), double-loop learning can occur through "organizational inquiry that creates new understandings of the conflicting requirements—their sources, conditions, and consequences—and sets new priorities and weightings of norms, or reframes the norms themselves, together with their associated strategies and assumptions." As Witham and Bensimon (2012, p. 49) note, "a culture that supports 'double-loop' learning is one that focuses on institutional values and practices, brings invisible issues (e.g., racial inequities) to the surface, and considers how conventional problem-solving approaches may themselves contribute to the problem."

The organizational learning literature has much to say about what structural and cultural/psychological factors facilitate or hinder an organization's engagement in effective organizational learning, particularly learning leading to fundamental organizational change. Argyris and Schön (1996, p. 28) state, "An organization's learning system is made of the structures that channel organizational inquiry and the behavioral world of the organization, draped over these structures, that facilitates or inhibits organizational inquiry." They describe the structures of organizational learning as including channels of communication, information systems, and "procedures and routines that guide individual and interactive inquiry; and systems of incentives that influence the will to inquire" (Argyris & Schön, 1996, p. 28; see also Lipshitz, Popper, & Friedman, 2002, p. 82). More specifically, the organizational learning literature points to several key structural elements that include defined channels of communication, such as forums for discussion and debate, and provision for formal and informal patterns of interaction (Argyris & Schön, 1996, p. 28; Kasl, Marsick, & Dechant, 1997, p. 236; see also Yorks, 2005; Yorks et al., 2007). Another important structural element is IR and IT capacity, involving personnel who can analyze data in order to develop and refine strategies (Argyris & Schön, 1996, p. 28; Jenkins, 2011, p. 38; Rutschow et. al., 2011, pp. 38–39, 116, 118).

For Argyris and Schön (1996, p. 29), organizational learning structures need to be supported by a behavioral world that includes "the qualities, meanings, and feelings that habitually condition patterns of interaction among individuals within the organization in such a way as to affect organizational inquiry—for example, the degree to which patterns of interaction are friendly or hostile" (see also Lipshitz, Popper, & Friedman, 2002, pp. 81, 87–90). More specifically, the psychological and cultural factors that facilitate organizational learning include certain specific norms and values. One is a norm of open inquiry and debate. For example, members of the organization "are encouraged to challenge their points of view by becoming critically reflective of the assumptions held in the organization about the content and processes of problem solving that are relevant to performance" (Yorks & Marsick, 2000, p. 274; see also Argyris & Schön, 1996, pp. 82–83, 90–101; Kasl, Marsick, & Dechant, 1997, pp. 230, 240–41; Kerrigan, 2010, pp. 159–61; Lipshitz, Popper, & Friedman, 2002, pp. 85–86). Another norm is a tolerance of error if it is in the service of organizational change. This includes a climate of psychological safety, that is, a "state in which people feel safe to make errors and honestly discuss what they think and how they feel" (Lipshitz, Popper, & Friedman, 2002, p. 87; see also Kerrigan, 2010, pp. 184–86; Yorks et al., 2007, pp. 363–68). Yet another is a commitment to learning and professional development. The organization makes an investment in education and training and provides time and incentives for learning (Jenkins, 2011, pp. 9, 15, 34; Lipshitz, Popper, & Friedman, 2002, pp. 88–89; Rutschow et. al., 2011, pp. 88–91, 98, 105–6).

While the research above clarifies the nature and limits of the policy instruments that are used and could be used by performance funding programs, we still need to know more about what are the obstacles those instruments encounter, what are the causes of those obstacles, and how they lead to unintended impacts. Valuable light is shed on this by research and theory on policy implementation and principal–agent relations.

POLICY IMPLEMENTATION

The policy implementation literature is very useful to exploring why policy instruments do or do not work. It analyzes various obstacles they can encounter and various unintended impacts they can produce.

The policy implementation literature arose out of the attempt to explain why policies as implemented or enforced not infrequently are at sharp variance with the goals of the policy framers (Honig, 2006; Matland, 1995; Mazmanian & Sabatier, 1989; Pressman & Wildavsky, 1973). One of the central divides in this literature has been between a perspective that emphasizes the intentions and actions of policy designers and one that stresses the views and reactions of the target populations and the "street-level bureaucrats" who deliver services to those target populations. The first perspective has been dubbed the "top-down perspective" and dominated the first wave of policy implementation studies. The second perspective has been dubbed the "bottom-up perspective" and has dominated later waves of policy implementation studies (Honig, 2006; Matland, 1995; Mazmanian & Sabatier, 1989; Smith & Larimer, 2009).

The Top-Down Perspective. This perspective focuses on local actors' lack of knowledge about the aims of policy framers as a reason why local instantiations of national programs often deviate from the goals of policy framers. This lack of knowledge is often attributed, in turn, to policy framers failing to fully clarify and effectively communicate the goals of the policy (Matland, 1995, pp. 157, 161; Mazmanian & Sabatier, 1989, p. 41; Smith & Larimer, 2009, pp. 158–62). Another frequent explanation for the mismatch of local outcomes and national goals is a lack of capacity at the local level, whether due to lack of expertise or lack of money and organizational resources (Honig, 2006, pp. 5–6; Matland, 1995, p. 161; Mazmanian & Sabatier, 1989, p. 41; Sunderman & Kim, 2007, pp. 1072, 1077). A third explanation from the top-down perspective focuses on lack of will or good intent on the part of the immediate implementers (Honig, 2006, pp. 5–6; Mazmanian & Sabatier, 1989, p. 41).

The top-down perspective suggests that unintended impacts may arise from the inability of local implementers to meet the goals of higher-level policy designers. Faced with obstacles caused by a lack of resources or knowledge, local actors cope with performance demands by resorting to actions that may deviate from policymakers' intents but allow local actors to apparently meet those performance demands. When institutions cannot successfully use legitimate means, they may resort to illegitimate means to realize socially expected goals (see Merton, 1968, 1976; Mica, Peisert, & Winczorek, 2012).

Bottom-Up Perspective. This perspective arose in reaction to the emphases of the top-down perspective. The bottom-up view stresses the importance of understanding the distinct goals, perceptions, strategies, and activities of local actors. It sees local actors not as ignorant or incompetent but rather as carriers of different goals and understandings. According to this point of view, local divergence from the goals and vision of state and national policy framers is a matter not of implementation failure but rather of mutual adaptation as local implementers attempt to reconcile macrolevel demands with microlevel conditions (Honig, 2006, pp. 6–7; Matland, 1995, pp. 148–49; Smith & Larimer, 2009, pp. 162–69). Bottom-up theorists argue that local implementers may do things differently than intended by policy framers because they have different goals, not because they fail to understand the policymakers' goals. For example, while policy framers may be particularly concerned with organizational efficiency and push merit pay as a solution, local school administrators and teachers may be more concerned about maintaining comity among teachers and therefore prefer common, step-level increments in pay (Loeb & McEwan, 2006, pp. 174–76). The bottom-up perspective also emphasizes that, even when local actors share the same goals as policy framers, they may have different understandings of what those goals entail. Also, local actors may misunderstand new ideas as being the same as those they are already familiar with. These differences in understanding arise from different cognitive schema rooted in different organizational, professional, and cultural backgrounds (Coburn & Stein, 2006, pp. 25–27; Honig, 2006, pp. 16–18; McLaughlin, 2006, pp. 214–15; Spillane, Reiser, & Gomez, 2006, pp. 49–59).

The top-down and bottom-up perspectives should not be seen as mutually exclusive (Matland, 1995; Mazmanian & Sabatier, 1989). Each highlights different ways in which unintended outcomes may crop up in the process of policy implementation. The top-down perspective alerts us to obstacles and unintended impacts that may arise as a result of inadequacies in the actions taken by policy framers, whether failing to communicate their goals well or failing to build up the organizational capacity of local implementers. Meanwhile, the bottom-up perspective alerts us to obstacles and unanticipated impacts that arise from differences in goals and understandings between local implementers and policy framers. We turn to principal–agent theory to further examine what happens when policymakers' goals do not resonate with those responsible for a policy's execution.

PRINCIPAL–AGENT THEORY

Principal–agent theory in economics and political science works well with policy implementation theory to explain the obstacles and unintended impacts encountered by policy instruments, particularly financial incentives (Lane & Kivisto, 2008; McCubbins, Noll, & Weingast, 1987; Miller, 2005; Moe, 1984). Arising originally in the field of economics, principal–agent theory has also become a major theoretical perspective in political science. At its core, it focuses on how principals (for example, elected officials) can ensure the compliance of their agents (such as bureaucrats implementing laws). It holds that while principals and agents do cooperate, they also have separate and often opposing interests that may lead agents to act in ways counter to the interests of principals. As a result, principals must take steps to secure agents' compliance. The first-order step is to specify a more or less explicit contract or agreement, but that agreement must be backed up by oversight, incentives, and, if needed, sanctions. The perennial difficulty with oversight is information asymmetry: agents often have specialized knowledge that principals do not; thus, it is not always easy to determine whether agents are working as hard or as well as principals might wish. Hence, principals typically incur costs to monitor the agents, often by developing methods to extract information about their activities (Lane & Kivisto, 2008; McCubbins et al., 1987; Miller, 2005; Moe, 1984).

Depending on the discipline, the application of principal–agent theory varies quite substantially. Principal–agent theory in economics sees the relationship between the principal and agent as primarily between unitary actors who are motivated by economic self-interest and bound by an explicit contract. Here, any "shirking" by the agent is purposeful and self-interested. In contrast, principal–agent theory in political science allows for multiple principals (such as different regulatory agencies) and even agents. Implicit contracts and definitions of the social good, and not just self-interest, motivate agents to respond to the requests of principals. Further, the tactics of principals might involve not just incentives and sanctions but also appeals to shared values (see Lane & Kivisto, 2008, pp. 150–54). The political science conceptualization better fits the situation of public governance of higher education institutions because (1) the contract between public higher education and government is often implicit, (2) higher education institutions are regulated and otherwise influenced by a host of different principals (including governors, legislators, higher education boards, accrediting and professional associations, students and parents, employers, etc.), and (3) those institutions are influenced not just by financial and other resource flows from principals but also by principals' appeals to shared social and professional values (see Lane, 2007; Lane & Kivisto, 2008).

We find that principal–agent theory is highly compatible with policy implementation theory (Honig, 2006; Mazmanian & Sabatier, 1989). Akin to the top-down perspective in policy implementation, principal–agent theory points to the interest of the principal, in this case state government, in securing compliant behavioral changes in higher education institutions, and its use of monetary incentives to do so. However, to the degree that principal–agent theory (particularly its political science variant) acknowledges conflicting interests and values, it also resonates with the bottom-up perspective. The agents at the institutional levels may resist the demands of the principals because they hold interests and values that conflict with those of the principals. Hence, financial incentives may not be enough to secure the assent of agents.

Conceptual Framework

When we weave together these various empirical and theoretical strands, they suggest that any further study of the implementation and impacts of performance funding needs to go substantially beyond the terms of the extant research literature (as largely summed up in Dougherty & Reddy, 2013).

First, with regard to policy instruments, we need to go beyond focusing on financial incentives and their impacts. We also need to consider persuasive communication and capacity building. Moreover, the analysis of capacity building needs to involve more than simple analyses of how well states build up colleges' IT and IR capacities. We also need to examine how well they foster a culture of inquiry, data-driven decision making, and organizational learning (see Kerrigan, 2014, 2015; Witham & Bensimon, 2012).

Second, with regard to the obstacles and unintended impacts encountered in the process of implementing particular policy instruments, we need to bring to bear the insights of research and theory on performance management, policy design, organizational learning, policy implementation, and principal–agent relations. Performance management theory alerts us to mechanisms and outcomes that occur in policy areas other than higher education but nonetheless may be applicable to it as well. Policy design theory illuminates characteristic strengths and weaknesses of this or that policy instrument, whether financial incentives, information provision, or capacity building. Organizational learning theory and research further illuminate what is required for effective capacity building by analyzing the kinds of capacities organizations need in order to effectively learn and change. Meanwhile, policy implementation theory and principal–agent theory suggest that we should view the obstacles to performance funding in higher education from both a top-down and a bottom-up perspective—that is, as arising on the one hand from inadequacies of communication, expertise, and resources and on the other hand from differences in goals, interests, and understandings within a higher education policy subsystem conceived of as a political system with value and power conflicts. Additionally, since the levers of change are rooted in more than just financial incentives, we must consider how states transmit their messages and how local actors interpret these messages through the filters of their own values and understandings. Hence, it is important that we carefully examine the perspectives of both policy framers and local implementers and that, even among local implementers, we attend to finer divisions of understanding and interest among administrators and faculty at different kinds of institutions.

Research Questions

Drawing on the preceding research, the analysis in this book is organized around six main research questions:

1. What policy instruments have our three states used as a part of their performance funding programs in order to influence the behavior of institutions? What have been the immediate impacts of those instruments?
2. What deliberative processes have colleges and universities used to determine how to respond to performance funding?
3. What have been the intermediate institutional responses of the colleges and universities to performance funding? That is, how have colleges altered their academic and student services policies, programs, and practices in ways that relate to performance funding goals?
4. What have been the impacts of performance funding programs on student outcomes?
5. Have institutions encountered obstacles in trying to effectively respond to the demands of performance funding? What forms have those obstacles taken?
6. Have there been outcomes of performance funding unintended by policymakers? What forms have they taken?

Research Methods

To answer these research questions, we analyzed the performance funding experiences of three community colleges and three public universities within each of three states (Indiana, Ohio, and Tennessee). For purposes of data triangulation, we conducted a large number of interviews in each of the three states with a diverse range of individuals involved with performance funding. We also analyzed available documentary data, including academic research studies (books, journal articles, and doctoral dissertations), public agency reports, newspaper articles, and institutional documents and websites.

Why Indiana, Ohio, and Tennessee? We picked three states that are leaders in performance funding—particularly PF 2.0—but that otherwise differ substantially in the histories of their performance funding programs and in their political and socioeconomic structures, as demonstrated in table 2.1 and discussed in appendix A.

Table 2.1   Programmatic, Political, Social, and Economic Characteristics of the Case Study States

State characteristic	Indiana	Ohio	Tennessee
1. Year performance funding was established[a]			
PF 1.0 program	2007	1995	1979
PF 2.0 program	2009	2009	2010
2. Sectors of public higher education covered by the state's PF 2.0 program			
	Universities and community colleges	Universities and community colleges	Universities and community colleges
3. Proportion of state appropriations based on PF 2.0 indicators			
	6% of state higher education funding (FY 2014–15)	80% of state funding for universities and 100% of funding for community colleges (FY 2014–15)	Approximately 85%–90% of state higher education appropriations; the remainder is accounted for by utilities, major equipment, and similar expenses
4. State's higher education governance structure at the time PF 2.0 was adopted			
Coordinating board for all public higher education in the state	X	X	X
Governing boards for *each* public university or university system in state	X	X	X (for the five University of Tennessee campuses)
Governing board for *all* community colleges	X		X (all public community colleges and universities other than the University of Tennessee)
Governing board for *each* community college		X	
5. State political culture:			
proportion in state dentifying as conservative (1996–2003) (%)	37.9	34.4	39.3
6. Governor's institutional powers on a scale of 1 to 5 (2010)			
	3.25	3.75	2.75

(continued)

Table 2.1   (continued)

State characteristic	Indiana	Ohio	Tennessee
7. Professionalism of the legislature (2009)			
	22nd	5th	37th
8. Index of party competition (2007–11)			
	0.871	0.926	0.913
9. State's population as of 2010			
	6,484,000	11,537,000	6,346,000
10. State's per capita personal income as of 2010 ($)			
	34,943	36,395	35,307
11. Residents over age 24 holding at least a bachelor's degree (2009) (%)			
	22.5	24.1	23.0

Sources: (1, 2) Dougherty & Reddy (2013). (3) Authors' interviews. (4) McGuinness (2003) and authors' interviews. (5) Erikson, Wright, & McIver (2006). (6) Ferguson (2013). Ferguson applies a five-point scale to the following six features: the number of executive branch officials separately elected, the tenure potential of the governor, the governor's powers of appointment, the governor's budgetary power, the governor's veto power, and whether the governor's party controls the legislature. The average for all 50 states across all of these features is 3.3. (7) Hamm & Moncrief (2013). Hamm & Moncrief use rankings on Squire's index (based on legislative salary, the amount of permanent staff, and the length of the legislative session). (8) Holbrook & La Raja (2013). Holbrook & La Raja report the Ranney interparty competition index, with larger numbers meaning more competition, on a 0.5 to 1.0 scale. (9, 10, 11) US Bureau of the Census (2012).

[a] We chose to focus on the date on which performance funding was adopted rather than on a later date of implementation or full phase-in (if applicable). Our reasoning was that performance funding impacts began as soon as institutions realized that performance funding had been adopted.

In terms of policy history, Tennessee established a PF 1.0 program in 1979, the first state to do so. Ohio first adopted performance funding much later, in 1995. Indiana adopted it later still, in 2007. In 2009, Indiana and Ohio adopted new PF 2.0 programs, and Tennessee followed suit in 2010 (Dougherty & Natow, 2015; Dougherty & Reddy, 2013). The Ohio and Tennessee PF 2.0 programs tie a much larger proportion of state appropriations for higher education to performance indicators than the current Indiana program and the earlier Ohio and Tennessee programs. While the PF 1.0 programs in Ohio and Tennessee only tied 1%–5% of state appropriations to performance metrics, the current PF 2.0 programs tie 80%–90% to performance metrics. Meanwhile, the PF 2.0 program in Indiana only ties 6% of state appropriation to performance metrics (Dougherty & Natow, 2015, chap. 5; Indiana Commission for Higher Education, 2013a; Ohio Board of Regents, 2015a, 2015b, 2015c; Tennessee Higher Education Commission, 2015a).

The states also differ in the degree of centralization of their public governance systems for higher education. All but one of Indiana's community college campuses operate under a single governing board (Ivy Tech), and its university campuses operate under five governing boards.* At the other extreme, in Ohio, all 23 of the community colleges and all 13 of the university main campuses have their own governing boards (Education Commission of the States, 2015; McGuiness, 2003).

The states also vary considerably in political culture and structures (Gray, Hanson, & Kousser, 2013). Tennessee and Indiana are above average in the conservatism of their electorates, whereas Ohio is very near the national average (Erikson, Wright, & McIver, 2006). The three states also differ in the characteristics of their political institutions, with Ohio's governor having more institutional power and its legislature a higher degree of legislative professionalism than Indiana's or Tennessee's (Ferguson, 2013; Hamm & Moncrief, 2013). Moreover, Ohio and Tennessee tend to have greater political party competition than Indiana (Holbrook & La Raja, 2013). Finally, the states differ considerably in their social characteristics: population, income, and education. Ohio's population is substantially larger, wealthier, and better educated than those of Indiana and Tennessee, as shown in table 2.1. For more details on the performance funding programs in these three states, see appendix A.

Which Colleges and Universities? This study examines the experiences of 18 public higher education institutions with performance funding: nine community colleges and nine universities. The community colleges and universities differ in their expected capacity to respond effectively to performance funding. Using data from the Integrated Postsecondary Education Data System survey of 2011, we measured expected organizational capacity based on college resources (revenues per FTE student), data-analytic capacity (ratings by two experts in each state), and number of at-risk students (percentage of students receiving Pell Grants and percentage of minority students). We rated the community colleges as being in the top, middle, and bottom third on each of these three dimensions, summed the ratings, and picked one college in each state from each third. We have labeled these colleges as having "high," medium," or "low capacity." For the public universities, we selected two universities that were high and low in their expected

---

* The Ivy Tech system in Indiana operates as a single community college, with the separate campuses reporting to a central office. Only one public two-year college—Vincennes University—is not part of the Ivy Tech system.

capacity to respond to performance funding, using the same capacity measure as for the community colleges. We labeled these universities as "high 2" or "low." The third university in each state is a high-capacity research-intensive institution, which we labeled as "high 1." For our analyses where we compare high- and low-capacity colleges, only the high 1 universities are included in the high-capacity category.*

Data Collection and Analysis. We interviewed 261 state officials, state-level political actors, and institutional administrators and faculty at the 18 institutions (see table 2.2). We also drew on documentary sources such as public agency reports, newspaper articles, and academic research studies (books, journal articles, and doctoral dissertations) to supplement our findings.

At the state level, we interviewed higher education commission officials, gubernatorial advisors, legislators and members of their staff, business leaders, and researchers and consultants. All told, we interviewed 39 state-level officials and political figures, pretty evenly split among our three states.

At the institutional level, our respondents included senior administrators (the president and the main vice presidents reporting to the president), deans and other mid-level academic administrators, nonacademic mid-level administrators such as the director of IR, chairs of different departments representing a range of disciplines and degrees of exposure to outside accountability demands, and the chair of the faculty senate. For the academic deans, we picked one heading up a school of arts and sciences or equivalent and one leading a professional school such as nursing, education, or engineering. Under each dean, we picked two chairs of different kinds of departments. For example, in a school of arts and sciences, we typically chose a chair of a humanities or social science department on the one hand and a chair of a mathematics or natural science department on the other. We relied on the department chairs and the chair of the faculty senate to illuminate the range of faculty opinion. Our expectation was that the dean and faculty of a professional school would likely face much stronger accreditation pressure and therefore have a rather different reaction to state performance funding than would the dean and faculty of a school of arts and sciences. All told, we interviewed 110 community college administrators and faculty and 112

* We did this in order to maintain an equal number of high- and low-capacity colleges and universities. If we had included the high 2 universities, our high-capacity category would have included nine institutions (six universities and three community colleges). However, our low-capacity category would have only six institutions (three universities and three community colleges).

Table 2.2   Interviewees: Categories and Numbers

Category	IN	OH	TN
State-level officials			
State higher education officials	3	5	9
Legislators and staff	4	2	5
Gubernatorial advisors	1	2	3
Business leaders	1	1	0
Other (consultants, researchers, other)	1	1	1
Subtotal	10	11	18
Institutional-level—community colleges			
Senior administrators	10	16	12
Mid-level administrators—nonacademic	5	4	10
Mid-level administrators—academic	11	5	10
Faculty	8	13	6
Subtotal	34	38	38
Institutional-level—universities			
Senior administrators	15	16	11
Mid-level administrators—nonacademic	4	3	9
Mid-level administrators—academic	6	9	6
Faculty	12	13	8
Subtotal	37	41	34
Total	81	90	90

university counterparts. The distribution was quite even across our three states. For more details, see table 2.2.

The interviews were semistructured and lasted approximately one to two hours. While we used a standard protocol, we adapted it to each interviewee and to material that emerged during an interview. All interviewees and their agencies and institutions were promised confidentiality, and we have masked their identities.

The interviews with state officials were mainly conducted in the spring and summer of 2012. However, we also conducted several follow-up interviews in 2013, 2014, and 2015. For these interviews we used a semistructured interview protocol that focused on two main questions. First, how did policymakers envision that the performance funding program would work: what were the policy instruments to be used, the institutional change outcomes to be sought, and the problems and unintended impacts to be anticipated? Secondly, how did the program actually work: what policy instruments were indeed used and what was their perceived impact, what institutional changes and student outcomes actually did occur, and what obstacles and unintended impacts did crop up and how did the state address them? The interview protocol for state officials can be found in appendix B. In addition, to ascertain the historical origins of certain features of the performance funding programs, we also drew on interviews we conducted for an earlier study of the political origins of performance funding (see Dougherty & Natow, 2015).

The interviews with community college administrators and faculty were mainly conducted in the fall and winter of 2012 and spring of 2013. However, our Indiana interviews stretched into summer 2013. In addition, we also conducted follow-up interviews with a senior administrator at most of our community colleges in summer 2014. We used a semistructured interview protocol that focused on how the state performance program affected their college and how it responded: what policy instruments were used by the state, and what were their perceived impacts on the college; what changes did the college make in its academic and student services policies, programs, and practices in response to performance funding; what process did the college use to decide on those changes; what were the eventual impacts on student outcomes; what obstacles did the college encounter in responding effectively to performance funding; and what unintended impacts (if any) did occur? The interviews with university administrators and faculty were mainly conducted in the fall of 2013 and winter of 2014. However, our Indiana interviews stretched into spring 2014. In addition, we also conducted follow-up interviews with a senior administrator at most of our universities in summer 2014. The questions were much the same as those asked of the community college administrators and faculty. However, based on our cross-case analysis of the community college data, we added a number of questions, particularly ones to clarify how the state communicated with universities about the state goals for performance funding, how well the institutions were doing on the state metrics, and how college officials passed on this information to faculty and mid-level administrators. The interview protocol for our university respondents can be found in appendix C. It is essentially the same as the protocol for community college administrators and faculty, with a few questions added.

The interviews were transcribed and coded using the Atlas.ti qualitative data analysis software system. We also coded documentary materials if they were in a format that allowed importation into Atlas. Our coding scheme began with an initial list of "start" or thematic codes drawn from our conceptual framework, but we also operated inductively, adding and altering codes as necessary as we proceeded with data collection and analysis. To analyze the data, we ran queries in Atlas based on our key coding categories. Using this output, we created analytic tables comparing how different interviewees at different kinds of institutions perceived the implementation and impacts of performance funding.

With this background, we turn to our substantive findings. We begin in chapter 3 by examining the nature and impact of the policy instruments used by the performance funding programs in Indiana, Ohio, and Tennessee. In subsequent chapters we examine the deliberative structures colleges used to determine how to respond to performance funding, the changes the colleges made in their policies and practices, the impacts of those changes on student outcomes, the obstacles the colleges encountered, and the unintended impacts that resulted.

CHAPTER 3

Policy Instruments and Their Immediate Impacts

In this chapter, we examine the main policy instruments used by performance funding programs in our three states and their immediate impact on the institutions, as perceived by both our institutional and state-level respondents. We also examine how the use and perceived impacts of these policy instruments differ among the states and by type of institution.

Policymakers in all three states relied most heavily on financial incentives to induce change at both community college and university campuses in their respective states. At the same time, officials in all three states made efforts to educate campus leaders about new programs in their states, though such efforts varied in their intensity and their level of campus penetration. We also find evidence of efforts on the part of state officials to communicate institutional performance on the state metrics back to campus officials, but again the nature and intensity of these efforts varied. However, we find very limited evidence of state efforts to build campus-level capacity for organizational learning. The implications of this important omission will be discussed in greater depth in chapter 7.

Financial Incentives

In all three states, state-level actors—whether elected officials or state higher education agency personnel—made clear that financial incentives were the main policy instrument they sought to use to secure the intended goals of performance funding (authors' interviews; Ohio Board of Regents, 1996, 2008). States used financial incentives because they perceived colleges as often not behaving in optimal ways. As we will see in chapter 7, this not infrequently bred resentment on the part of higher education institutions.

Typical of statements by state-level advocates of the financial theory of action was this comment from a state higher education official in Tennessee: "To say it

Vikash Reddy and Hana Lahr took the lead in writing the report on which this chapter draws (Reddy et al., 2014).

bluntly, when you get the money right, when you get the dollars right, I think that creates proper incentives. . . . I mean, it is now quite clear the production of those outcomes—whether it's degrees or certificates, workforce training, whatever it is— those translate into dollars." Similarly, a state higher education official in Indiana noted, "The state wants higher graduation rates, the state wants more research dollars coming in, the state wants a more efficient higher ed system, and so they would say, 'If you do these things that align with our policies, then we will try and get you some more money for doing that.' It's a simple financial incentive model."

LITTLE INITIAL IMPACT ON INSTITUTIONAL FINANCES

The early years of the new PF 2.0 programs in our three case study states were not marked by huge impacts on the revenues of higher education institutions. From one year to the next, institutions did not experience big shifts in state funding. When one compares shifts in state funding between fiscal year (FY) 2012 and FY 2013—the period that best aligns with when we interviewed our respondents—23 institutions gained in state funding between those two years, and 14 declined in state funding. However, the average shift in state funding for each Ohio institution was only 2.3% in either direction.* Meanwhile, when one compares shifts in state funding between FY 2013 and FY 2014, the average shift in funding for each institution was 3.7% (see table 3.1). It should be noted that the FY 2014 figures were prior to the application of "bridge funding," which would reduce the amplitude even more (Ohio Board of Regents, 2015c).†

Tennessee presents a picture of greater shifts in state funding for each institution. In Tennessee, the average increase or decrease in state funding for each institution was 4.7% between FY 2011 and FY 2012 and 8.1% between FY 2013 and FY 2014 (see table 3.2). Despite the greater volatility in the shifts between FY 2013 and FY 2014 than between FY 2011 and FY 2012, only one Tennessee institution dropped in state funding between FY 2013 and FY 2014. All other cases involved institutions gaining money, with the difference being in how large the gains were. This was made possible by the fact that state spending on higher education in Tennessee rose 7.6% between FY 2013 and FY 2014, whereas it had

---

* This figure is the average of the absolute values. Interestingly, the amplitude for the two-year colleges was slightly higher than that for the universities—2.6% versus 1.8%, despite the fact that only 15% of state funding for community colleges in FY 2013 was driven by performance indicators, compared to 80% for the university main campuses.

† The bridge funding was essentially a hold harmless device.

Table 3.1   Changes in State Appropriations for Ohio Higher Education Institutions

Institution	FY 2012 ($)	FY 2013 ($)	FY 2014 ($)	% Change FY 2012/13	% Change FY 2013/14
Two-year colleges					
Community colleges					
Cuyahoga	56,177,296	57,623,181	59,565,164	2.6	3.4
Eastern Gateway	4,441,204	4,712,349	5,201,388	6.1	10.4
Lorain County	23,704,044	23,206,628	23,474,769	−2.1	1.2
Lakeland	17,621,029	17,564,892	17,594,759	−0.3	0.2
Rio Grande	4,604,017	4,576,734	4,753,629	−0.6	3.9
Sinclair	43,335,227	42,573,655	42,995,103	−1.8	1.0
State colleges					
Clark State	9,404,245	10,137,875	10,810,803	7.8	6.6
Cincinnati State	28,849,500	28,992,889	28,414,628	0.5	−2.0
Columbus State	58,179,006	60,304,099	60,429,175	3.7	0.2
Edison State	6,564,156	6,619,428	6,957,876	0.8	5.1
Northwest State	8,810,941	9,207,167	9,848,420	4.5	7.0
Owens State	36,908,495	35,432,155	34,369,190	−4.0	−3.00
Southern State	7,637,976	7,433,323	7,620,934	−2.7	2.5
Terra State	6,156,312	6,252,763	6,445,349	1.6	3.2
Washington State	5,397,239	5,276,198	5,188,293	−2.2	−1.7
Technical colleges					
Belmont Tech	5,451,398	5,290,341	5,297,532	−3.0	0.1
Central Ohio	10,220,612	10,172,989	10,746,962	−0.5	5.6
Hocking	14,044,597	14,206,775	14,167,392	1.2	−0.3
James Rhodes	9,686,409	9,612,257	9,756,561	−0.8	1.50
Marion Tech	5,391,736	5,455,252	6,014,033	1.2	10.2
Zane State	6,034,654	6,262,563	7,005,025	3.8	11.9
North Central	6,820,280	6,677,774	6,806,799	−2.1	1.9
Stark State	24,559,299	26,066,189	27,793,694	6.1	6.6
Total two-year colleges	400,039,672	403,657,477	411,257,477	0.9	1.9
Four-year colleges					
University main campuses					
Akron	90,578,644	91,008,577	92,257,130	0.5	1.4
Bowling Green	70,040,673	67,239,046	61,040,255	−4.0	−9.2
Cincinnati	153,804,658	156,581,998	162,923,060	1.8	4.1
Cleveland State	64,074,196	64,989,002	68,006,777	1.4	4.6
Central State	6,053,110	6,302,628	6,263,727	4.1	−0.6
Kent State	94,408,730	96,737,165	104,444,944	2.5	8.0

(continued)

Table 3.1   (continued)

Institution	FY 2012 ($)	FY 2013 ($)	FY 2014 ($)	% Change FY 2012/13	% Change FY 2013/14
Miami	54,962,954	55,817,407	57,097,049	1.6	2.3
Neomed	14,950,607	15,146,507	15,809,469	1.3	4.4
Ohio State	329,547,635	331,828,611	334,393,715	0.7	0.8
Ohio University	109,418,758	114,314,913	123,985,906	4.5	8.5
Shawnee State	13,565,627	13,575,997	13,524,638	0.08	−0.4
Toledo	104,216,965	104,450,653	103,356,597	0.2	−1.1
Wright State	75,380,131	74,914,062	75,971,367	−0.6	1.4
Youngstown State	39,347,845	38,480,351	37,712,282	−2.2	−2.00
Total university main campuses	1,220,350,535	1,231,386,916	1,256,786,916	0.9	2.1
Average of absolute values of institutional funding changes				2.3	3.7

Source: Ohio Board of Regents (2012c, 2013c).
Note: The average size of institutional changes is the average of the absolute values.

dropped slightly between FY 2011 and FY 2012 (see table 3.2). If state funding does not continue this rate of growth in subsequent years, the number of institutions losing state funding is likely to increase. As table 3.2 shows, when there was virtually no increase in state funding between FY 2011 and FY 2013, nearly half the institutions received less state funding than the year before.

The lack of big shifts in institutional funding in the early years, particularly in Ohio, is reflected in our interviews. When we asked our institutional respondents to gauge the impact of performance funding on institutional budgets, the modal response—particularly from our Indiana and Ohio respondents—was one of little to no impact on institutional budgets. Of the 141 respondents who felt comfortable assessing the size of annual budget variations,* two-thirds (98 out of 141) indicated that their state's performance funding program had little to no impact on institutional budgets. However, our Tennessee respondents—particularly in community colleges—were more likely to indicate a high or medium impact (see table 3.3).

---

* Many respondents had no idea what the budget was and how it varied over time. Hence, they were unable or unwilling to discuss what impact performance funding had on it.

Table 3.2 Changes in State Appropriations for Tennessee Higher Education Institutions

Institution	FY 2011 ($)	FY 2012 ($)	% Change FY 2011/12	FY 2013 ($)	FY 2014 ($)	% Change FY 2013/14
Community colleges						
Chattanooga	20,166,700	19,970,200	−1.0	21,902,500	26,624,800	21.6
Cleveland State	8,911,100	8,421,200	−5.5	8,672,000	8,997,100	3.7
Columbia State	11,392,300	11,121,800	−2.4	11,294,400	12,339,500	9.3
Dyersburg State	6,131,100	6,484,500	5.8	6,867,800	7,238,900	5.4
Jackson State	10,423,300	10,518,500	0.9	10,821,400	11,510,200	6.4
Motlow State	8,625,000	9,662,900	12.0	10,310,000	11,017,200	6.9
Nashville State	12,554,500	13,794,900	9.9	14,516,500	15,983,500	10.1
Northeast	10,383,600	11,924,900	14.8	12,920,300	13,648,200	5.6
Pellissippi State	17,062,500	18,692,600	9.6	20,819,800	22,913,400	10.1
Roane State	15,620,800	14,750,900	−5.6	15,244,700	16,619,800	9.0
Southwest TN	32,426,900	28,648,100	−11.7	27,953,000	25,739,300	−7.9
Volunteer State	15,345,700	15,281,400	−0.4	15,614,700	16,075,400	3.0
Walters State	15,740,800	15,745,100	0.03	17,043,300	19,866,900	16.6
Subtotal	184,784,300	185,017,000	0.1	193,980,400	208,574,200	7.5

Universities

Austin Peay	25,191,800	26,107,600	3.6	28,537,600	32,995,000	15.6
East TN	44,870,000	44,000,700	−1.9	45,772,200	48,685,000	6.4
Middle TN	70,600,000	73,423,800	4.0	77,193,600	81,024,600	5.0
TN State	28,281,900	29,335,100	3.7	30,810,900	32,610,800	5.8
TN Tech	35,635,400	35,086,300	−1.5	37,288,600	39,559,500	6.1
U of Memphis	91,348,000	85,464,300	−6.4	87,346,700	89,106,400	2.0
UT Chattanooga	33,162,700	33,294,400	0.4	34,601,800	36,128,500	4.4
UT Knoxville	142,165,100	144,150,000	1.4	153,343,900	174,335,300	13.7
UT Martin	23,680,900	23,636,300	−0.2	24,609,100	25,243,000	2.6
Subtotal	494,935,800	494,498,500	−0.09	519,504,400	559,688,100	7.7
Grand total	725,983,600	731,775,800	0.8	767,333,600	825,662,800	7.6
Average of absolute values of institutional funding changes			4.7			8.1

Source: Tennessee Higher Education Commission (2014b, p. 82).

Note: Grand total includes Tennessee Colleges of Applied Technology.

Table 3.3   Perceived Impact of Performance Funding on Institutional Budgets

Level	Total	State			Institutional type		Institutional capacity[a]	
		IN	OH	TN	Community colleges	Universities	High	Low
High	17	5	2	10	9	8	8	4
Medium	26	13	2	11	8	18	3	12
Low/none	98	37	36	25	57	41	27	37
No coded response	81	16	39	26	36	45	38	21
Total	222	71	79	72	110	112	76	74

[a] In this table and subsequent ones, we only report figures for high- and low-capacity institutions. We exclude medium-capacity ones. See text for reasons.

Originally, we asked this as an open-ended question, and we categorized responses as indicating a high, medium, or low impact.* However, after having concluded interviews at the first Ohio and Tennessee community colleges in our sample, we found that not all of the responses we received could be easily categorized as high, medium, or low. Hence, for the remaining colleges and universities, we moved to asking our respondents to rate the impact using a five-point scale and explain their rating. To make an equivalence with our earlier open-ended answers, we treated responses indicating a 1 or 2 as low impact, a 3 as medium impact, and a 4 or 5 as high impact.

In Ohio, the most common response was to state that performance funding has not had much impact on institutional funding. For example, when asked about the program's impacts on college budgets, an Ohio community college administrator told us, "It's really not had much of any impact on our funding. . . . Our state subsidy right now is a little over 10 million dollars. . . . We actually gained a little in our revenue from the change, which meant to me in total that we did a little better than average with the other schools . . . in those different success categories. But it was pretty inconsequential to the total. [*Q: So has it caused any big year-to-year fluctuations in institutional revenues? And what I'm hearing is that it did not.*] It did not."

* Two of our team members independently coded answers and then met to resolve any discrepancies. When they were unable to resolve a disagreement, the tie-breaking vote was cast by the principal investigator.

On the other hand, the following statement was typical of the many responses we received in Tennessee, particularly from our community college respondents, indicating a medium or high impact of performance funding on institutional finances: "We are facing a reduction as a result of the performance-based funding this year. It will amount to around $120,000. . . . I guess the silver lining for me is that it was not as big a hit as some of our colleague community colleges are facing."

EXPLAINING THE LOW INITIAL IMPACT
ON INSTITUTIONAL FINANCES

Several factors help to explain why performance funding did not cause great fluctuations in institutional funding in the early years of the new PF 2.0 programs, particularly in Indiana and Ohio. These relate to the small amount of funding at stake, a protracted phase-in period, devices designed to curb funding fluctuations, and the increasingly important role that college tuition plays in institutional funding.

Small Amount of Money. In Indiana for all institutions and for community colleges in Ohio (until FY 2014), the proportion of state funding tied to performance metrics was quite small. It was 6% in Indiana and 15% or less for Ohio community colleges before FY 2014 (Indiana Commission for Higher Education, 2013a; Ohio Board of Regents, 2011a, 2013a, 2015a).

Protracted Phase-In. In Ohio, the 2009 formula initially had a stop-loss provision limiting how much institutions could lose in a given year. This stop loss did not end until FY 2015 for the universities and perhaps FY 2016 for the community colleges (Ohio Board of Regents, 2009a, 2009b, 2011a, 2011b, 2013a, 2013b, 2015a, 2015b). In addition, for Ohio community colleges, the performance funding proportion of the State Share of Instruction started small and took several years to become quite substantial. It started at 5% in FY 2011 and rose to 7.5% in FY 2012 and 10% in FY 2013. It was only then that it rose rapidly, jumping to 50% in FY 2014 and 100% in FY 2015 (Ohio Board of Regents, 2011a, 2012a, 2013a, 2015a). By that point, the performance funding share of state appropriations for community colleges had caught up with and arguably exceeded that for the state universities. Meanwhile, in Tennessee, the performance funding share of state funding was already quite high by the time of our interviews: around 85%–90% for both two-year and four-year public institutions. However, the system was gradually phased in, roughly in thirds, over FY 2012–FY 2014. It did not take full effect until FY 2014 (Tennessee Higher Education Commission, 2012a, 2012b).

Devices to Curb Fluctuations in Funding. Various mechanisms were put in place to mitigate wild fluctuations from year to year. These features include the use of three-year rolling averages rather than annual statistics and the use of design elements that do not vary greatly from year to year. Rather than relying on one year's worth of data, all three states have implemented systems that include multiple years' worth of data. Indiana's system makes comparisons between blocks of three years, while Tennessee and Ohio have employed a three-year rolling average (Indiana Commission for Higher Education, 2013a; Ohio Board of Regents, 2011a, 2011b; Tennessee Higher Education Commission, 2012a, 2012b). In addition, Tennessee chose performance indicators that would tend not to change greatly from year to year. A senior administrator in Tennessee, in discussing some of the formula's design features, told us, "Actually, it's designed not to make huge jumps. . . . It's basically designed so that nobody would ever gain or lose more than 2 percent in a year."

The Continuing and Growing Role of Tuition. Finally, in all three states, state appropriations for higher education have not kept pace with enrollments, so institutions have continued to rely heavily on tuition funding. This limits the impact of variations in performance on institutional funding. A mid-level administrator in Indiana noted, "[Performance funding] really didn't change my bottom line because I had the same number of students, paying the same amount of tuition." Even in the case of Tennessee, where performance funding accounts for 85%–90% of state funding of public higher education, it only represented 26% of total institutional funding in FY 2013–14 because state funding has lagged and institutions remain very reliant on tuition revenue (Postsecondary Analytics, 2013).

PERCEIVED IMPACT OF FINANCIAL INCENTIVES
ON INSTITUTIONAL BEHAVIOR

Though our respondents tended to perceive only small fluctuations in institutional revenues due to performance funding, they still reported that financial incentives were catalyzing campus-level efforts. As a mid-level administrator in Tennessee told us, "Well, cumulatively . . . it's not a large fluctuation. . . . But it's definitely influenced institutional behavior." Table 3.4 summarizes responses to the question of whether annual variations in funding, such as they are, motivate efforts on campus to improve institutional outcomes.

Most of the respondents who felt that the financial incentive would have a substantial (high or medium) impact in the future stated that performance fund-

Table 3.4 Perceived Impact of Financial Incentive on Institutional Efforts to Improve Outcomes

Level	Total	State			Institutional type		Institutional capacity	
		IN	OH	TN	Community college[a]	University	High	Low
High	61	26	11	24	25	36	10	28
Medium	30	15	10	5	10	20	8	14
Low/none	33	15	15	3	14	19	14	10
No coded response	98	15	43	40	61	37	44	22
Total	222	71	79	72	110	112	76	74

[a] This question about impacts of financial incentives on efforts to improve student outcomes was added to our interview protocol after the interview process had concluded at our first community colleges in Ohio and Tennessee. This is a major reason that the "no coded response" figure is higher for community colleges than for universities.

ing created an incentive for the college to pay closer attention to its efforts to increase student outcomes. As an Indiana community college faculty member explained, "Everything we've been doing really has been targeted at this, and I think that performance funding may raise it to the attention, I guess, this might be a cynical way of thinking. . . . But [student success] certainly has been a concern of ours all along. It's now become maybe a more apparent concern, and different initiatives addressing that get more support and recognition and attention."

A senior university administrator in Ohio mentioned the potential consequences associated with the state's new formula, saying, "I think that just knowing that the change is coming and anticipating that it may at some point have a negative impact [on institutional revenues] has influenced our focus on student success, no doubt."

A mid-level administrator at a university in Tennessee put it this way: "I think it does have a big impact. And I think it establishes sort of officially that this is the business that we're in, and we always should have been in this business. But now we're going to be funded, and anybody who wants to do anything creative, new, expanding whatever, they are going to have to sort of justify it by the funding that comes with these numbers. So yeah, I mean, I think it's a sea change, at least for us on this campus."

Meanwhile, those who believe that the financial incentive has had only a small impact described the incentive as affecting college-level discussions on the importance of graduation rates, without going into specific actions that the colleges have taken. For example, a mid-level academic administrator at a Tennessee community college said that the financial incentives of the Complete College Tennessee Act have created discussions at the college: "How it impacts our funding isn't really discussed down at the level of faculty or really that much at my particular level. We just know that graduation impacts funding, but it does create discussions among faculty about what can they do in their classrooms to help students stay in the class, be successful, and thus lead to higher graduation rates."

While we certainly find evidence backing up the revenue-maximizing theory of action supporting the use of financial incentives as a policy instrument, such incentives also operate by drawing attention to state priorities as policymakers put their money where their mouths are. Let us turn to how else states have tried to focus institutional attention on state priorities.

Communication of State Program Goals and Methods

In addition to drawing attention to state goals and priorities by deciding which performance indicators to use and how much money to tie to each, policymakers can also convey those goals and methods by direct communication with campus administrators and faculty. This constitutes a second policy instrument used by state officials. Below, we discuss the means by which state leaders and their college counterparts communicated the goals and methods of the state performance funding programs, how deeply that information penetrated campuses, and whether increased awareness of state goals affected campus-level efforts to improve institutional performance.

STATE COMMUNICATION

In all three states, state officials informed us that they intended to use the provision of information about the goals and purported methods of performance funding as a means to persuade colleges of the importance of improving student outcomes (authors' interviews; Fingerhut, 2012; Indiana Commission for Higher Education, 2007; Lubbers, 2011; Tennessee Higher Education Commission, 2008). An Indiana state higher education official described how the Indiana Commission for Higher Education saw providing information about the state's goals for its 2009 PF 2.0 program as a means to shape institutional behavior:

We really worked hard to [implement performance funding] in partnership with the institutions. When [the previous commissioner of higher education] was here, he worked with all of the presidents and all the institutions to try to get them to buy into this. We've continued to acknowledge their concerns as we refine the metrics. And even most recently, at the end of the last budget session, [we] met with all the presidents again to talk to them about the formula that we had and how we could make it better in the upcoming session. So we've tried to address their concerns.

The commission stated that it issued a series of PowerPoint presentations, memos, press releases, YouTube videos, and interviews informing the public about the commission's goals for the 2009 performance funding formula (Lubbers, 2011; Stokes, 2011). With support from Lumina Foundation, the commission also employed HCM Strategists, LLC, a consulting firm based in Washington, DC, to publicize and promote many of its initiatives (HCM Strategists, 2011).

In Tennessee, state officials stated that they provided information about the state's goals for the new funding formula prior to and during the implementation of the new funding formula (authors' interviews; Tennessee Higher Education Commission, 2008). Prior to the enactment of the 2010 program, the Tennessee Higher Education Commission was proposing a planning year in which, among other activities, the state would conduct a policy audit that "serves as a diagnostic tool for policies and resources that appear to be misaligned in terms of the stated goal; promotes clear and broad understanding of existing barriers to increased degree production by our public postsecondary institutions; identifies priorities for change; and builds awareness of issues and enthusiasm for change at the system and campus levels" (Tennessee Higher Education Commission, 2008, p. 6). In addition, the commission also proposed a variety of other devices to "ensure buy-in, promote project awareness, and sustain momentum throughout the year" (p. 8). One of them involved communication with university system boards: "We will seek to have MOA-TN [Making Opportunity Affordable–Tennessee] placed as an information item on the regularly-scheduled agendas of the Tennessee Board of Regents, University of Tennessee Board, Tennessee Independent Colleges and Universities Association (TICUA), and THEC [Tennessee Higher Education Commission]. Project leadership will also be available for meetings of presidents' councils and other functional groups, as warranted" (p. 8). During implementation of the 2010 PF 2.0 program, the state supported conferences called "College Completion Academies," during which institutional representatives learned about the state's goals for the new funding formula, as well as recommended practices for increasing retention and completion on their campuses. A state higher education official noted, "Through those strategies [developed at the Completion Academies], we've tried to communicate the goals of the master plan and how the funding formula plays into all of that."

Finally, in Ohio, state officials reported that the chancellor of higher education and the Board of Regents staff consulted extensively with the higher education institutions in developing the new 2009 PF 2.0 program, thus communicating the goals and methods of the new program (authors' interviews; Fingerhut, 2012, p. 10; Ohio Board of Regents, 2008; Petrick, 2012, p. 284). Chancellor of higher education Eric Fingerhut wrote,

> The Board of Regents took a two-pronged approach to garnering the support of college and university leaders for performance-based funding. First, we talked extensively with presidents and their boards of trustees to convince them of the importance of redesigning the formula. . . . Meanwhile, Vice Chancellor of Finance Richard Petrick and his capable staff sat down with the chief financial officers of each institution to work on the technical aspects of the formula. . . . Rich kept revising the formula until the CFOs became confident that they understood the system and that it was as fair as possible given the very different types of institutions that the formula covered. (Fingerhut, 2012, p. 10)

Still, this effort to reach out to and persuade college and university administrators and faculty was not as complete as it could have been. As an Ohio state higher education official noted,

> I would have loved to have sent an email, a three-paragraph email to all of the faculty in the state saying, "Hey, we want to fund student success. We hope everyone does a better job and I hope you can embarrass us with your success to the point where it stretches every resource the state has." But I was not permitted to do that. The Chancellor would not have been able to do that either because of the tradition that the campuses, the institutions, are independent. They have their own board of trustees, they hire the president, and the Board of Regents is a coordinating body, and we generally coordinate macro-level state policies.

To triangulate these statements from state officials, we asked our institutional respondents to whom at the college and through what means the state communicated its goals and intended methods for performance funding. In classifying the means of communication, we follow Büchel & Raub (2001) in distinguishing these means by their richness of communication. Richer communication comprises "(a) the ability to provide rapid feedback, (b) the ability to communicate multiple cues, (c) the ability to convey personal feelings, and (d) the ability to use natural language" (Büchel & Raub, 2001, p. 521). Based on this definition, we distinguish four forms of communication:

1. *Face-to-face, high-interactive,* including face-to-face meetings and informal interactions and group meetings characterized by a high level of potential interaction, such as meetings of the president's cabinet, deans' meetings, department meetings, and faculty senate meetings.
2. *Face-to-face, low-interactive,* including campus-wide gatherings and forums and open-invitation information sessions.
3. *Non-face-to-face, high-interactive,* such as personal e-mails and telephone calls.
4. *Non-face-to-face, low-interactive,* such as websites, reports, newsletters, press releases, and generic e-mail blasts and forwarded messages.

We should note that our data on means of communication do not cover all the colleges. We began asking questions that would shed light on the richness of communication after we had already completed interviews at our community colleges in Ohio and Tennessee. Hence, our data for the community colleges are more limited than our data for the universities. The numbers listed in tables below do not refer to interviewees but rather to examples given, because respondents could cite more than one modality of communication. If, for example, a respondent gave examples of both face-to-face and non-face-to-face communication, he or she would be counted in both rows.

No Communication. Despite the efforts described by state officials, we still received a fair number of responses from college administrators and faculty (particularly the latter) indicating either that the state had not communicated its goals and intended methods or that respondents could not recall receiving any such communication (see table 3.5). A good part of this response pattern may stem from how state and college officials conceived of the flow of communication. State officials often described a classic two-step flow of communication, in which they communicated with senior administrators and the administrators, in turn, communicated with faculty. A Tennessee state higher education official told us, "We never went out of our way to try to speak directly to faculty, though we did if asked. They were not our constituency, and it was probably on balance more

Table 3.5   State Communication of Performance Funding Goals and Methods

Modality	Total	State			Institutional type		Institutional capacity	
		IN	OH	TN	Community colleges	Universities	High	Low
Face-to-face	100	22	32	46	24	76	27	43
Non-face-to-face	80	23	35	22	18	62	25	34
Via upper admin	66	26	26	14	21	45	13	31
None	38	11	18	9	20	18	10	15
Total mentions[a]	284	82	111	91	83	201	75	123

[a] Our respondents sometimes cited more than one modality of communication, so the total number of mentions is not the same as the total number of respondents mentioning communication modalities. Our total mentions are lower for community colleges because we did not systematically ask about communication modalities until we began our university interviews.

effective for faculty to hear about the model from their campus-level administrators rather than those of us at the state level." This perspective was echoed by a community college dean in Tennessee: "I think, and this is just my gut feeling, but I think they have relied on us to take it from them and then diffuse it at our level . . . to the faculty and the staff and so forth that we're working with. So we've gotten it from on high and have filtered down to the next levels."

A similar process may have been at work in Ohio, where a number of reports from university participants also described state communications that filtered down through university channels. A mid-level administrator offered the following thoughts: "They assume that our administration can get this out to the faculty, which is not a weird assumption. But I think what happens is upper administration becomes the messenger. . . . If there had been more active involvement from the state really reaching out to the faculty, I think faculty would have gotten this concept much quicker."

However, many of our respondents did describe direct communication from the state. It took various forms, ranging from face-to-face, high-interactive communication involving meetings with state officials to non-face-to-face, low-interactive communication involving e-mail blasts or information posted on state websites.

Face-to-Face, High-Interactive Communication. Respondents at five community colleges and eight universities mentioned that they heard about the goals and methods of performance funding through their roles on statewide committees that discussed, and in some cases even helped to plan, the performance funding programs. According to a senior administrator at one Tennessee community college, "Because I am in charge of institutional effectiveness and I do serve on committees at the Board of Regents, and my counterparts at the other institutions [and I] meet at the board on a regular basis, we're probably more in-tune with this than the deans would be. Certainly, the chief academic officer, the chief financial officer, and the president are aware of it as well." Similarly, a mid-level academic administrator described the process by which upper level administrators get information in Ohio from statewide meetings: "That was communicated on a little bit higher, more central level. The University of Ohio presidents meet in one forum, and the provosts meet with one forum. And it was through that level. And then we, the deans, heard about it in provost council meetings."

Beyond meetings at which university and college leaders participate, a number of interviewees discussed meetings or workshops at which state officials would discuss details of the performance funding program. One faculty member at a university in Indiana told us, "We even had a meeting in Indianapolis where [multiple] levels of the university administration, including deans, met with one of the commissioners."

Face-to-Face, Low-Interactive Communication. Respondents at seven colleges and eight universities discussed presentations given by representatives from state-level agencies or organizations as mechanisms through which state officials communicated the goals or methods of a particular program. These general forums and presentations were deemed to be less interactive than the committees mentioned in the previous section, though still face-to-face. A major factor in assessing the interactivity of a given venue is whether one would expect it to engender discussion. In Indiana and Tennessee, participants discussed primarily the role played by their respective state commissions in giving presentations that did not involve much, if any, interaction. According to one Tennessee senior administrator, "As the process rolled out, there were several organizations involved in presentations of the formula and communities throughout the state. I know I attended a couple in Knoxville, so sometimes these were presented by folks from THEC [Tennessee Higher Education Commission]. . . . So I do think the state as a whole tried to put in place and let folks know about the changes that were taking place."

Non-Face-to-Face Communication. Participants from eight universities and six community colleges discussed state communication that was not face-to-face. This communication took a variety of forms, including website postings, e-mail blasts, and press releases. An Ohio administrator summed up the state's use of non-face-to-face communication and noted how college personnel required personal motivation to access that information:

> There are websites, there are emails, there's newspaper announcements of, you know, the different things that the state may be doing relative to both K–12 and higher education, but you have to be specifically motivated to spend some time looking at those things. I think a lot of people are getting their news on the web, and so unless you are really connected to something that's going to tweak you when something comes out of the state relative to higher education policy, it might be a fly-by for you that something came out in the paper that said this is news.

One problem, beyond the fact that a person has to be motivated enough to seek out some of this information, has to do with the quality of those resources. One senior administrator at a university in Indiana put it this way: "The commission did put out something. It was a brochure handed out which was about the commission, its priorities, and that kind of thing, and probably was intended to explain performance funding. It was not the kind of piece that is going to encourage a broad public awareness or discussion about it."

COLLEGE COMMUNICATION

In addition to asking about actions taken by the state to better inform campus constituents about the details of their respective programs, we also asked respondents about ways in which their college's leadership had discussed the goals and the mechanics of their state's performance funding formulas. Once again, we examined responses for examples of face-to-face communication and non-face-to-face communication, with responses summarized in table 3.6.

A handful of our participants reported no action on the part of their college leaders to disseminate information about their state's performance funding program. However, we had many more reports of communication efforts by senior administrators to the rest of their colleges. One administrator from a university in Ohio felt that the process for disseminating performance funding information was fairly representative of higher education communications in general:

> It's pretty much through mechanisms that we would use for communicating any important information. It has to sort of reach all the different constituencies. And it could well be, you know, presidents can give sort of town hall

Table 3.6   College Communication of Performance Funding Goals and Methods

Modality	Total	State			Institutional type		Institutional capacity	
		IN	OH	TN	Community colleges	Universities	High	Low
Face-to-face	207	72	67	68	67	140	55	66
Non-face-to-face	59	22	27	10	16	43	17	19
None	16	4	10	2	10	6	5	7
Total mentions[a]	282	98	104	80	93	189	77	92

[a] Our respondents could cite more than one modality of communication, so the total number of mentions is not the same as the total number of respondents mentioning communication modalities. Our total mentions are lower for community colleges because we did not systematically ask about communication modalities until we began our university interviews.

meetings, some distributed by letters from the president or the provost. It's shared by some of the budget people at a number of faculty committees. It's shared at the faculty senate meetings, so the faculty senate is very involved and knowledgeable about it. As deans, we will share it with our department chairs, who in turn make the faculty aware. Our advising officers are very involved in it. So there's many mechanisms.

Face-to-Face, High-Interactive Communication. Participants across the three states related a number of face-to-face, high-interactive communication modes through which performance funding goals and methods could be more deeply discussed within their institutions. Meetings of the president's leadership team came up in interviews at multiple colleges. Meetings for deans were also mentioned as a venue at which upper-level administrators discussed performance funding with faculty and mid-level administrators. A senior administrator at a Tennessee university described the steps of the communication as follows: "We have actually incorporated presentations on the formula into our academic leadership retreat. . . . And we've also made presentations to our council of deans so they can understand how the formula works."

Administrative meetings, in particular those in which budgets or institutional research (IR) are discussed, were mentioned by several university participants, as were administrative committee meetings independent of senior leadership or meetings dedicated to deans and chairs. Indeed, one mid-level nonacademic administrator in Tennessee told us, "There's rarely a meeting that I go to that success and performance funding is not discussed."

A number of participants reported that performance funding was discussed in their faculty or faculty senate meetings. In some instances, this also involved a presentation from a senior administrator. Others related that performance funding matters have been discussed at department meetings. An Ohio community college department chair told us,* "We do lots of discussion in department meetings. Our dean usually comes to our department meetings, but we also do have faculty senate meetings where these things are discussed as well but not as often." Finally, some respondents at community colleges reported that performance funding came up during in-service trainings and workshops for faculty.

Face-to-Face, Low-Interactive Communication. People on campus also pointed to college-wide gatherings, such as state-of-the-college presidential addresses, as venues in which senior administrators might discuss program goals with campus constituents. An administrator from an Ohio college indicated that grappling with the finer details was not a task for such large forums: "to really get down to fine details about it, then that happens in person when we all can sit around the table and talk about it."

Non-Face-to-Face Communication. Participants from all nine community colleges and all nine universities reported receiving e-mails from their institutional leaders related to the goals and methods of their respective states' performance funding programs. Furthermore, respondents at four universities and two community colleges reported the use of institutional websites as a medium through which college leaders put out information.

VARIATIONS IN AWARENESS OF STATE GOALS AND METHODS

As noted, providing local actors with information on the state's goals and the methods by which the state plans on achieving those goals can help motivate those local actors to modify their behavior. This theory of action, however, is dependent on the information penetrating campuses beyond the upper levels of a college's or university's administration. Only a handful of respondents felt that awareness was uniformly high throughout their institution. In fact, we received many responses indicating that awareness is drastically diminished at lower levels in the organizational structure, whether among faculty or mid-level adminis-

---

* Interestingly, though several university-based participants discussed the need for chairs to share information, no participants specifically mentioned department meetings as a venue for information sharing.

trators. Even if there is awareness, it may not involve understanding of any particular depth.* Our sense is that adjunct faculty were particularly unlikely to know much about state goals and methods for performance funding, given their often tenuous connection to institutions.†

A Tennessee administrator characterized the variation in knowledge within colleges by distinguishing between awareness and understanding: "There's a general awareness, obviously, that we're moving to this outcomes-based formula and that we all need to get focused related to our student success measures. And that's driving a lot of work. But . . . I think there's room to grow in terms of a more in-depth understanding of the specifics in the formula, how it works, at the faculty and staff level." This view was shared by an Ohio administrator, who told us, "I would say that there is a minimal understanding of that at those levels. . . . Certainly, senior admin is very cognizant of it, and I don't think that necessarily from a community-wide standard there is the truest understanding of this is it, this is what it's going to mean and how it's going to impact."

Distinctions between awareness and understanding are also recognized by state policymakers. A state higher education official from Tennessee characterized fostering a deep understanding of the state's performance funding program as a goal only for campus leaders, for whom a more developed understanding would yield a greater return on invested time. For the remainder of the college community, a broad but shallow awareness of performance funding would be acceptable.

Our campus interviewees offered five different explanations for why there was variation in awareness between campus actors at different levels of the institution: competing demands on faculty time and attention, differential exposure to performance funding requirements and institutional budgets, the exercise of administrative discretion over what to share and how much to share, communication breakdowns, and program size.

Competing Demands on Faculty Time and Attention. Twenty-three of our respondents stated that more pressing and immediate teaching and research concerns impeded faculty awareness of performance funding. A university faculty member in Ohio stated,

---

* This phenomenon has been observed in other states, for example, Washington (Shulock & Jenkins, 2011).

† We have the impression, but no direct data, that adjunct faculty were rarely involved in faculty meetings to discuss performance funding.

I think a lot of . . . the faculty have, and maybe correctly, decided what they want to do is they want to focus on doing the things that they have trained for: engaging in research, getting students involved in that, and they put a lot of effort into their teaching. I think they're doing a lot of the right things but without perseverating on these concerns coming beyond from the state about what's about [the] funding formula. . . . They should be focusing on doing what they came here to do and want to do, and not getting so mired down in all of these administrative issues.

Similarly, a vice president at a Tennessee community college told us, "I think that for faculty and staff, it seems rather removed from what they do daily, and despite the fact that they've been told that this is how things are working, I think they just sort of turn off at that point, and if you were to ask them a question, they would say, yeah, I heard something about that, but I can't explain it to you."

Differential Exposure to Performance Funding Requirements and Institutional Budgets. While faculty have other concerns that occupy their time and attention, many administrators have jobs that require them to deal with performance funding policies and mandates. Sixteen of our respondents argued that, unlike most faculty members, many administrators are daily engaged in tasks that put them in contact with performance funding requirements and institutional performance on state metrics. According to a senior administrator at a university in Tennessee, "You know, we [vice presidents and deans] are looking at numbers and how many students are progressing through certain [benchmarks]. . . . We look at courses where a high number of students are not successful and look at ways in which we can revise those courses. . . . I was just looking this morning for data on retention rates from one year to another in particular disciplines, and are there any patterns that we ought to be looking at to try to address? So I think at the administrative level, it's very much on people's minds."

Administrative Discretion. Another explanation that 11 of our respondents gave us was that administrators are somewhat cautious in choosing what to share about performance funding and how much detail to include. A senior administrator at a Tennessee university described administrators as wanting to share information somewhat judiciously: "[Administrators] don't sit down and go through the report and say, you know, this, this, and this. Different parts of it may be addressed in faculty meetings where the chancellor or the vice chancellor is speaking . . . and then as that formula funding pertains to a particular area, that piece of it may be discussed. But where they sit down and say, 'Okay, we've got the results, or we've got the standards, and here they all are,' and, you know, do a big communication blast from campus, that's not done. I think it's more of a need-to-know [basis]."

A similar view was expressed by a community college administrator in Ohio, who stated that administrators selectively inform others in the college in order to reduce anxiety and information overload that threaten to distract faculty from doing their job: "We actually tried in Ohio to protect as many of our faculty and staff from the chaos that we have to deal with on a daily basis in Ohio. I mean that very genuinely. . . . In Ohio this has been such a small part of our overall funding that it just is not significant to the level that we would explain in that kind of detail to rank-and-file people. . . . So what I'm trying to say is, faculty are focused on things very different than what we have to deal with."

No doubt these sentiments are largely genuine, but it is also true that they might substantially mischaracterize faculty sentiments. Twenty-eight of our respondents, particularly faculty, felt they did not get enough information about performance funding and wanted more. For example, an Ohio university faculty member stated a clear belief that the administration could do a better job of communicating the nature of the state's performance funding programs:

I think administration needs to talk about the details of this funding—their formulas and the state initiative—better and more to the faculty members. . . . It's not that they are not doing the work required to meet the objective—we are doing quite a bit—but there are a lot of questions at the faculty level as to why certain things are being done and whether these things [that] are being done would be a factor. In other words, there has been less of a participation in terms of formulating the policies to meet those objectives, and much of policy formulation has been done at the upper administration level without much of a faculty participation.

Size of Performance Funding Program. Finally, three of our respondents (two in Indiana and one in Ohio) brought up the small size of their state's performance funding program, suggesting that the payoff was too small to command serious attention at the faculty level. A university faculty member in Indiana stated, "It's 6 percent [of state funding for higher education], and the faculty [members] are focusing on getting their day-to-day job done, and this funding portion that's 6 percent of the overall university budget, they're not spending a lot of time thinking about that. They're thinking about their day-to-day

Table 3.7   Perceived Impact of Awareness of State Performance Funding Goals and Methods on Institutional Efforts to Improve Student Outcomes

Level	Total	State			Institutional type		Institutional capacity	
		IN	OH	TN	Community colleges[a]	Universities	High	Low
High	56	19	10	27	35	21	8	23
Medium	33	19	13	1	10	23	7	16
Low/none	34	17	15	2	16	18	17	8
No coded response	99	16	41	42	49	50	44	28
Total mentions	222	71	79	72	110	112	76	75

[a] This question was not added to our interview protocol until after the interview process had concluded at our first community colleges in Ohio and Tennessee.

operations. . . . I do think that 6 percent is a little low. I don't know that 6 percent will ever have a huge impact, even in good economic times."

PERCEIVED IMPACT OF AWARENESS OF STATE GOALS AND METHODS ON COLLEGE EFFORTS

A common though not universal opinion among our participants was that awareness of their state's goals and methods for performance funding motivated people on campuses to consider ways to improve institutional performance. A majority of those providing a rating viewed awareness of the state's goals and methods for performance funding as having a medium or high impact on their institution's efforts to improve student outcomes (see table 3.7). We began asking our respondents about this after our interviews at the first Ohio and Tennessee community colleges. We asked respondents to rate the impact on a five-point scale. We have rated responses indicating a 1 or 2 on the five-point scale as low impact, a 3 as medium impact, and a 4 or 5 as high impact.*

It is interesting that three-quarters (89 out of 123) of the respondents who gave us an answer responded that awareness of the state's goals and methods for performance funding had a medium or high impact on their college's efforts to improve its student outcomes (see table 3.7). A high-level academic administrator

* This question was not added to our interview protocol until after the interview process had concluded at our first community colleges in Ohio and Tennessee. For those two colleges, two researchers independently coded their open-ended responses as high, medium, and low. In cases of discrepancies, the principal investigator cast a tie-breaking vote.

from a Tennessee community college said that knowledge about the goals and methods of the new funding formula had caused changes because it changed the institutional culture: "It's really changed the culture, from what I understand. Again, you may hear different things from other administrators of this college because they were here when we had the other funding mechanism. But the conversations I've been in with the deans and with faculty, it's really changing the culture in terms of how we're looking at students and what we're considering to be success in terms of completers."

Meanwhile, a dean at an Indiana community college expressed the sentiment that the program had highlighted the need to better serve the student population: "They're really letting people know, 'This is a serious issue.' And again, like I said, it's not all being driven by the fact that its money involved, but there's an awful lot of 'It's the right thing to do. This is a serious problem for the country; we need to see what we can do to solve that problem.'"

Communication of Institutional Performance on the State Metrics

Providing people on campus with information regarding their institution's performance on the state performance funding metrics is a third policy instrument that state officials have used to influence institutional behavior. However, this policy instrument was not wielded as consciously and powerfully as the preceding two.

In Ohio, there was strong evidence that the provision of information about institutional performance was envisioned as a way to spur institutional action. The state chancellor for higher education explicitly stated his interest in using information provision as a policy instrument in the case of the 2009 PF 2.0 program: "It is important to note, however, that we still published the actual results achieved by running the new formula against the available completion data. In this way, everyone would know the completion rates at each school and the impact they would have on funding if the formula were fully and completely implemented. It was always my hope that this information would be as big a spur to reform on campuses as the funding changes themselves" (Fingerhut, 2012, p. 12).

However, in Tennessee, a state higher education official suggested that while publicizing information about institutional performance and catalyzing status competition that would spur colleges to change was not an explicit goal, it was a result state officials would welcome: "We had to be careful, and we had to diplomatically talk about [how] this wasn't intended to pitch one school against the other because it's not that. . . . So we probably never explicitly said it that way, but I don't think there's any doubt that that's what this model represents, and that is on balance a good thing. . . . That's what produces the institutional behavior change we just talked about, the fact that they're competing with one another and the fact that their money has to be re-earned every year."

Finally, in an even more muted vein, Indiana state higher education officials noted that the state did make some efforts to use provision of performance information to catalyze change, but we did not get a sense of urgency. For example, a state higher education official observed, "Graduation data was much, much more important to the commission than it was to anybody else. And so we would put that together and share it with institutions and encourage them to share it with their boards, to share it with their faculty. Some did; some didn't."

While it is clear that the advocates and implementers of performance funding did envision to some degree that data on institutional performance could spur institutional improvement, it is also clear that this policy instrument action was conceived of in limited terms. Reports were issued but, for the most part, were not widely and consistently publicized. Moreover, there is little evidence that there was strong awareness of either the importance or the difficulty of informing faculty and mid-level staffers as well as senior administrators.

Below, we analyze the means by which state and college leaders shared information about campus-level performance on the indicators used in the state formula. Similar to our treatment of communication of program goals and methods, we identify examples of face-to-face and non-face-to-face communication of institutional outcomes. We also asked participants for their perception of how aware college faculty and mid-level administrators were about their college's performance on the state metrics and what impact that awareness had on the institution's efforts to improve student outcomes.

STATE COMMUNICATION OF INSTITUTIONAL PERFORMANCE

Seventy-nine of our respondents, based at eight of our nine community colleges and eight of our universities, told us that the state had not communicated with their institutions regarding how well they were doing on the state performance funding metrics. A university administrator in Indiana noted how state communication around institutional performance was weaker than state communication of goals and methods: "I think they've been less engaged in terms of reporting performance. I mean, they discuss it in their meetings quite a bit, but I don't believe that they've been as much engaged in terms of publicizing at this point. But again, I think that's also a recognition that we're in the early stages of implementation."

Table 3.8   State Communication of Institutional Performance

Modality	Total	State			Institutional type		Institutional capacity	
		IN	OH	TN	Community colleges[a]	Universities	High	Low
Face-to-face	41	19	13	9	25	16	6	11
Non-face-to-face	68	15	27	26	17	51	20	30
Via upper admin	33	6	12	15	14	19	12	17
None	79	30	32	17	34	45	23	26
Total mentions[a]	221	70	84	67	90	131	61	84

[a] Our respondents sometimes cited more than one modality of communication, so the total number of mentions is not the same as the total number of respondents mentioning communication modalities. Our total mentions are lower for community colleges because we did not systematically ask about communication modalities until we began our university interviews.

When our respondents did mention that the state had communicated with their colleges, they mentioned both face-to-face and non-face-to-face communication. The first was more commonly reported by our community college respondents, whereas our university respondents more often reported the latter (see table 3.8).

Face-to-Face Communication. A Tennessee university administrator discussed how the university received information at meetings chaired by the Tennessee Higher Education Commission (THEC) and involving the heads of institutions under the Tennessee Board of Regents (TBR) and the University of Tennessee (UT): "It starts with sort of a meeting at the state level, at THEC, usually with TBR and UT schools together, in a room, with . . . THEC explaining sort of what's been happening [with] the latest data. And then we come back to the campus and disseminate it, sometimes, again sort of in a broad-stroke campus message from the chancellor. Mostly though, it's through the academic chain of command, with me then reporting to the deans, who go to chairs, and the chairs to the faculty."

Non-Face-to-Face Communication. The state governments communicated with institutions through a variety of non-face-to-face means, including e-mail, websites, and print reports. Sixteen respondents, most of whom were administrators, reported receiving e-mails from the state with performance information. Moreover, participants at all nine universities and two community colleges mentioned state websites as a source of information about institutional performance. In Tennessee, the Higher Education Commission's online resources on performance funding include spreadsheets with data for all Tennessee institutions on all formula indicators. Finally, eight respondents told us that the state would report results in the mass media.

Indirect Communication through Campus Leaders. Thirty-three of our respondents observed that the state-level governance agencies, even if they had not communicated with the respondent, were communicating with campus-level higher-ups or, in the case of Indiana, central office personnel. As a mid-level administrator at an Ohio university put it, "I know that I've seen tables in which the graduation rates of all the various public institutions in the state have been compared. And I can't tell you off the top of my head who produced those tables or why they were put in front of me. I think they were put in front of me by the administration in one of our meetings." Several participants noted that the state would send a report to certain people on campus, with responsibility for further dissemination falling to campus leaders.

COLLEGE COMMUNICATION OF INSTITUTIONAL PERFORMANCE

Campus senior administrators are a key means by which state governments can communicate with faculty and mid-level administrators on how colleges are performing on the state metrics. Yet, 24 of our respondents stated that they had not received communications from their college leaders about their institution's standing on the state performance metrics. However, many other respondents mentioned a variety of ways in which their college had communicated to them about how the college was doing on the state performance metrics. Responses are summarized in table 3.9.

Table 3.9   College Communication of Institutional Performance

Modality	Total	State			Institutional type		Institutional capacity	
		IN	OH	TN	Community colleges[a]	Universities	High	Low
Face-to-face	75	15	21	39	27	48	32	25
Non-face-to-face	64	14	23	27	36	28	28	15
None	24	7	10	7	15	9	11	9
Total mentions[a]	163	36	54	73	78	85	71	49

[a] Our respondents sometimes cited more than one modality of communication, so the total number of mentions is not the same as the total number of respondents mentioning communication modalities. Our total mentions are lower for community colleges because we did not systematically ask about communication modalities until we began our university interviews.

Face-to-Face, High-Interactive Communication. A substantial number of participants indicated that performance outcomes had become a part of meeting agendas around the institution, whether for senior staff, other administrators, or faculty. Participants noted that meetings of college or university presidents' senior staff frequently included agenda items pertaining to performance on the state metrics. As a community college administrator in Tennessee told us, "Basically, our president has monthly presidential staff meetings . . . monthly administrative council meetings . . . [and] monthly meetings also with . . . direct staff. So, it's a constant update and review of where we are with our funding formula weights, where we need to be. We're constantly working towards our best outcome. We're constantly looking at outcomes. [The president] makes sure that it's a part of every meeting."

Several participants also mentioned administrative meetings—such as budget meetings, strategic planning meetings, and meetings of deans and department heads—as venues for dissemination and discussion of information about institutional outcomes. As described by a mid-level academic administrator in an Ohio university, "Well, there is our vice president's involvement and we also have institutional research, registrar's office, and associate deans meet monthly . . . and that is one of the topics that they discuss on a pretty regular basis." Participants also brought up meetings of faculty senates or executive committees as places in which performance information is shared on campus.

Face-to-Face, Low-Interactive Communication. College-wide meetings were also brought up by participants at five community colleges and five universities as venues for discussion of performance outcomes. A mid-level administrator at a Tennessee community college discussed the inclusion of performance funding outcomes in the college president's once-per-semester, college-wide meeting: "Well, now they are getting those numbers out fairly quickly, and at each, we have an update or a conference once a semester, and that's when those numbers start to show."

Non-Face-to-Face Communication. Respondents at all nine community colleges and five universities reported that college higher-ups send out information on institutional performance via e-mail. Several respondents also mentioned unspecified memos, reports, or campus newsletters. Only one community college participant mentioned the institution's website, but six respondents from three universities mentioned institutional websites.

VARIATIONS IN AWARENESS OF INSTITUTIONAL PERFORMANCE

Just as awareness of performance funding goals and methods must penetrate a campus if it is to have a substantial impact, a policy instrument predicated on awareness of institutional outcomes can only be expected to be successful if campus personnel are widely aware of their college's or university's performance. However, as with awareness of program goals and methods, we find uneven awareness of institutional performance across personnel within the same college. Here, too, our respondents attributed uneven awareness of institutional performance to the same four causes as for uneven awareness of state goals for performance funding: competing demands on faculty, differential exposure to performance funding requirements and institutional budgets, administrative discretion, and communication breakdowns within the institution.

PERCEIVED IMPACT OF AWARENESS
OF INSTITUTIONAL PERFORMANCE

Our data indicate that, even if it was not uniformly high at the institutions in our sample, awareness of institutional performance nonetheless motivated efforts on campuses. As displayed in table 3.10, roughly half of those respondents for whom we have coded responses (51 out of 101) indicated that awareness of their institution's performance had a high impact on the college's efforts to improve student outcomes.

Table 3.10   Perceived Impact of Awareness of Institutional Performance on Institutional Efforts to Improve Student Outcomes

		State			Institutional type		Institutional capacity	
Level	Total	IN	OH	TN	Community colleges[a]	Universities	High	Low
High	51	12	13	26	27	24	10	26
Medium	27	12	7	8	14	13	8	7
Low/none	23	7	12	4	8	15	11	8
No coded response	121	40	47	34	61	60	47	34
Total mentions	222	71	79	72	110	112	76	75

[a] This question was added to our interview protocol after the interview process had concluded at our first community colleges in Ohio and Tennessee.

While many of these respondents simply indicated an impact, some provided insights into how awareness of performance influenced campus efforts. They pointed to the highlighting of performance weaknesses and the spurring of status competition.

Highlighting Performance Weaknesses. Performance funding programs can identify instances of institutional failure and push colleges to address them. For example, a senior administrator at an Ohio university described the university president's reaction to seeing certain retention numbers: "When the president noticed the retention rate of our entering class—it's really poor; it's one of the poor-performing—he really moved a lot of stakeholders to not only dialoging but to have an action plan of student retention."

Spurring Status Competition. Nine respondents also mentioned how performance information incited status competition among universities and led them to push to improve their student outcomes. A senior administrator of an Ohio university noted, "I'd say the financial impact was completely overshadowed by these other features about this university's reputation and where it really wanted to focus and maintain its status, relative to the other public institutions in the state as well as some of the private schools with whom we know we compete for similar students." A mid-level university administrator in Tennessee also described how performance funding spurred status competition: "It's always been bragging rights, you know, amongst the different campuses. You know, who has the best retention rate? Who has the highest graduation rate?"

Building Up Institutional Capacity to Respond to Performance Funding

Policy scholars have noted that an important policy instrument to effect organizational change is to build the capacity of target institutions to respond effectively to policy initiatives through organizational learning and change (Brinkerhoff, 2010; Cohen, 1995; Light, 2004; McDonnell & Elmore, 1987; Schneider & Ingram, 1997; Van Vught, 1994; Witham & Bensimon, 2012). This instrument takes on greater significance in a context in which state policymakers indicate that they wish to avoid getting involved in day-to-day campus operations and therefore eschew specific prescriptions for campuses (Dougherty et al., 2014a).

We were particularly interested in whether state-level advocates explicitly recognized the importance of state support to build up the capacity of institutions to engage in organizational learning and change, whether through state funds for enhanced institutional research (IR) offices or information technology (IT) capacity, training for college staff in how to analyze student outcomes data, discussion of best practices for improving student outcomes, or seed funds to try out new approaches. However, we found rather limited evidence that state-level advocates envisioned building institutional capacity for organizational learning and change as a means by which performance funding could improve institutional performance.

WHAT STATE OFFICIALS WERE DOING

In the case of Tennessee's 2010 PF 2.0 program, the Tennessee Higher Education Commission, with support from Complete College America, operated "College Completion Academies," which were two-day conferences held by advocates and implementers of the state's new funding formula (authors' interviews; SPEC Associates, 2012a).* Several staff members from each participating institution attended the academies to learn about the state's master plan for higher education and institutional practices recommended by experts in the main areas of concern to the institutions attending. As a state-level higher education official described,

> We invited content experts on things that each institution had told us that it wanted to work on. So if it was advising, we had somebody that we knew of from a campus in the nation that had some kind of an innovation there that they could talk about. If it was approach to learning support, remedial/developmental instruction, we brought those people in. So the institutions had two days of sort of deep introspection with itself, guided by a content expert and an institutional facilitator that was assigned to them to kind of develop these institutional goals and strategies that were aligned with the state master plan, which is called the "public agenda," and the strategic plan for its system.

These conferences aimed to enhance the capacity of institutions to perform well under the new funding formula by assisting them in developing strategies to improve retention and completion. Beyond the Completion Academies, we found no evidence that the new funding formula's supporters envisioned providing institutions with additional funding or any other resources to develop their

---

* The College Completion Academies were sponsored by the Tennessee Higher Education Commission in partnership with the Tennessee Board of Regents, the University of Tennessee system, the governor's office, and the Tennessee Business Roundtable (SPEC Associates, 2012a, p. 4).

capacity to perform well under the formula. For example, we saw no evidence of dedicated state programs to provide financial support to colleges for improving their IR and IT capacity.

In Ohio, the advocates of performance funding also had some vision for capacity building. An Ohio state higher education official described how the state began in 1998 to aid institutions in meeting the data demands of performance funding: "We created this longitudinal data system in 1998 that gave every campus 24/7, 365-day-a-year access to their data, and that helped everybody a lot. . . . We've certainly promoted, on the research side, efficiencies through the creation of the state's ISP system, ONET [Ohio Network for Education Transformation], and the super computer systems, so there were enhancements to centrally design enhancements to both computer capacity and our internet lines that improved communication. So communication improved the sharing of data for research and for other purposes." The emphasis on enlarging institutional access to state-wide data continued into the 2009 performance funding program in Ohio. For example, a state higher education official noted, "We also gave the campuses the SQL [Structured Query Language] that drove those [statewide] data . . . so that they didn't have to hire small armies of programmers to try to do their own specific work to understand what was going on."

In addition, the state has supported the Ohio community colleges in taking part in various curricular innovation and capacity-building initiatives of the Gates and Lumina Foundations, including their Achieving the Dream and Developmental Education Initiatives (Achieving the Dream, 2015a; Developmental Education Initiative, 2015). Though these initiatives were seen as generally helping to improve institutional performance, we have no evidence that they were seen as components of an effort to build institutional capacity to do well specifically on the state performance funding metrics.

In Indiana, when we asked about building institutional capacity, state officials did not indicate that they envisioned it as a component of performance funding which could spur improvements in college performance. In fact, an Indiana legislative official stated, "It's just like any other business—we don't think that we need to give them money to, for example, come up with a plan to do what they ought to already be doing. And so we know they're spending their time trying to develop some kind of a model of how they want all this education process at their institutions to work, so we're just assuming that they're refocusing their mission statements and their goals and objectives so that they can come in compliance with this." Still, there is some evidence that the state has supported sharing information about best practices. As a community college dean explained, "They've encouraged institutions to take a look at best practices. I've not been to the State Commission for Higher Ed's quarterly meetings or anything, but they often are trying to identify or encouraging people to present best practices that's evidence-based." Moreover, the Indiana Commission for Higher Education did state in 2007, "A *statewide forum* should be held each year to allow Indiana's colleges and universities to share strategies, best practices, evaluation and research on persistence and completion efforts" (Indiana Commission for Higher Education, 2007, p. 6). However, there is no evidence that Indiana policymakers envisioned the need to provide support for building up the capacity of colleges in the areas of IR and IT.

As can be seen, the three states have taken some steps to build up the capacity of institutions to meet the demands of performance funding. However, these steps did not seem to arise from a clearly articulated and well-developed espoused theory of action involving capacity building. Although there is certainly some evidence of a view that it is important to build the capacity of institutions to analyze data and identify best practices, we did not see evidence that performance funding advocates clearly and strongly envisioned that performance funding will work in part through state support to build up a college's capacity to engage in organizational learning and change, particularly in the form of enlarged and enhanced IR offices, improved faculty and staff research skills, or enlarged IT capacity.* Furthermore, we saw no discussion of how colleges might need technical assistance and funding to try out new programs and policies to improve their performance.

INSTITUTIONAL OFFICIALS' ASSESSMENT OF THE STATE EFFORT TO BUILD CAPACITY

Regardless of how state officials judged the extent of their capacity building efforts, it is clear that our respondents at both community colleges and four-year institutions overwhelmingly reported that states rarely provided any significant capacity-building assistance to their higher education institutions to help them respond to the demands of performance funding. As can be seen in table 3.11, participants at both community colleges and universities reported very limited capacity-building efforts as part of their state performance funding programs.

---

* However, as we have seen, there was evidence in Ohio of a desire to improve the data analysis capacities of colleges by providing centralized infrastructural support at the state level.

Table 3.11 Perceived Extent of State Capacity-Building Efforts

Level	Total	State			Institutional type		Institutional capacity	
		IN	OH	TN	Community colleges	Universities	High	Low
High	2	2	0	0	2	0	0	2
Medium	6	0	1	5	5	1	1	0
Low/none	165	62	60	43	75	90	53	64
No coded response	49	7	18	24	28	21	23	8
Total mentions	222	71	79	72	110	112	77	74

Of 173 individuals who responded to our queries on the extent of state support, 165 (95%) rated the state capacity-building effort as low or nonexistent. For example, a senior administrator at an Ohio community college stated, "There's not been a specific program or statewide project to direct state funding for increasing capacity in one area or another. . . . There's no programs that measure this is where you are, this is where you need to go, and this is how you need to get there."

Similarly, an Indiana community college administrator noted that the college's president has taken steps to build up IR capacity, but that this has been separate from any state-sponsored efforts: "I know that our current president has built up IR in our regions, and we, we probably have more data examined and forthcoming than we have ever had, as far as I can recall. But to my knowledge, I think that's more internally motivated by our current vice president of administration than it is state-motivated. Now, the state may be the motivating reasons, but, I mean, I don't think they gave you a bunch of money and said, 'Here, figure this out.' If they did, I don't know it."

Meanwhile, our university respondents also reported that the state provided little or no capacity-building assistance. As a mid-level Tennessee university administrator noted, "I just think the state is saying, 'It's up to you to find efficiencies, and it's up to you to do what you need to do to increase outcomes. And if you do a good job, we're going to give you more money.' But they didn't [give] any kind of seed money to start any of these new things. We had to find most of the money ourselves."

Because they saw little or no capacity-building efforts, two university respondents—from Ohio and Indiana—described performance funding as an "unfunded mandate." The first statement comes from a faculty member in Ohio, who described how the lack of state capacity-building efforts was particularly pronounced, given the budget cuts that occurred in 2009, just as the performance funding program was beginning: "I think it's an unfunded mandate, to the best that I know. Maybe you may hear otherwise. I have not heard of anybody saying, here is what the state is going to do to help ease the transition. . . . I'm not aware of any assistance from the state. If there was, we certainly—the faculty center or the union—didn't hear about it." Similarly, a faculty dean from Indiana observed, "It seems like what we get generally from them is unfunded mandates. . . . No, I don't think there's been any big influx of resources to help."

There is reason to believe that institutional actors were not entirely correct that the states were providing virtually no capacity-building assistance. It is clear that the states were providing some support. However, it is also clear that they were providing far less than institutions needed. This discrepancy is troubling. Even if local actors are fully aware of their state's priorities, fully aware of how their institution is performing, and fully motivated to improve, they still need resources and help to identify the necessary changes, determine what solutions might work, and fund those changes, which typically bring added expense. While financial incentives, awareness of goals and methods, and awareness of institutional performance are potent instruments, their power is undercut if they are not supplemented by sufficient efforts to build institutional capacity. We return to this important topic in chapter 7 of this book.

Disaggregating Our Main Patterns

In this section, we disaggregate our responses to examine differences by state and type of institution in how our respondents answered.

DIFFERENCES BY STATE

As we look across our data, we find striking differences between Tennessee on the one hand and Indiana and Ohio on the other. On each of our four policy instruments, our respondents in Tennessee reported stronger impacts than did their counterparts in Indiana and Ohio. Tennessee respondents more often reported that state performance funding had a high impact on institutional budgets and that financial incentives had a high impact on institutional efforts to improve student outcomes (see tables 3.3 and 3.4). These state differences are not surprising, given that at the time of our interviews Tennessee based a greater portion of its state appropriations for public higher education on performance indicators than did Indiana and, until recently, Ohio. Although the proportion of state funding for universities tied to performance metrics was comparable between Tennessee and Ohio, the proportion for community colleges in Ohio was much lower until very recently. It did not reach even 50% until FY 2014.

With regard to communication of information, our Tennessee respondents were less likely to report an absence of state and college efforts to communicate the goals and methods of performance funding and institutional performance on state metrics, and they were more likely to report that the communication efforts had a high impact on institutional efforts to improve student outcomes (see tables 3.5–3.10). Again, this difference by state is not surprising. Tennessee has been particularly known for the extent to which its performance funding system was designed with extensive campus-based input and collaboration (Bogue, 2002; Bogue & Johnson, 2010; Dougherty & Natow, 2015). State officials made extensive efforts to involve institutional leaders in the conceptualization and implementation of the performance funding programs. This is not to say that extensive efforts were not made in Indiana and Ohio, but Tennessee is particularly noteworthy for the extent of consultation between the state and public higher education institutions.

DIFFERENCES BY TYPE OF INSTITUTION:
COMMUNITY COLLEGES AND UNIVERSITIES

We found some noteworthy differences by type of college—in this case, community colleges versus universities—in how the policy instruments reportedly operated. On the whole, we found little difference by type of college in perceptions of whether the financial incentives affected institutional budgets or institutional efforts to improve student outcomes (see tables 3.3 and 3.4). However, in Ohio, our community college respondents much less often reported a high impact of the financial incentives on institutional efforts to improve student outcomes: only 14% (2 out of 14) reported this level of impact, in comparison to 41% of our Ohio university respondents (9 out of 22) (see table 3.4). This large discrepancy is not surprising since in FY 2013—at the time of our community college interviews—the performance funding share of state funding for Ohio community colleges was much lower than that for universities: 10% versus 80% of state funding (Ohio Board of Regents, 2012a, 2012b).

However, with regard to state and college communication of performance funding goals and methods, it is noteworthy that community college respondents much more often mentioned receiving no communication from the state.

Approximately one-quarter (24%) of our community college interviewees reported no communication, while only 9% of our university respondents said the same (see table 3.5). A similar disproportion shows up with regard to communication within colleges, with more reports of no communication from our community college respondents (see table 3.6). However, as table 3.7 indicates, our community college respondents were considerably *more* likely than their university counterparts to state that awareness of state goals and methods had a high impact on their institution's efforts to improve student outcomes: 57% (35 out of 61 who gave us ratings) versus 34% (21 out of 62).

State and college communication of information about institutional outcomes exhibited somewhat the same pattern as above with regard to communication of information about state goals. Compared to university respondents, community college interviewees somewhat more often reported no communication by state or college officials about institutional performance on the state metrics but also more often reported that the state communication had a high impact on their institution's efforts to improve student outcomes (see tables 3.8–3.10).

Finally, with regard to capacity building, there was only a slight difference between university and community college respondents in their tendency to report little or no state effort to build up institutional capacity to respond to performance funding (see table 3.11).

DIFFERENCES BY ESTIMATED ORGANIZATIONAL
CAPACITY OF INSTITUTIONS

Finally, we examine whether respondents at colleges and universities that differed in their expected organizational capacity to respond to performance funding (indexed by revenues per FTE student, data-analytic capacity based on ratings from two experts in each state, and number of at-risk students) viewed the four policy instruments differently.* For the most part, the differences were relatively minimal and scattered. With regard to financial incentives, respondents at high-capacity colleges and universities more often reported than did their

---

* See chapter 2 for the derivation of our measure of expected institutional capacity. We only report differences between high- and low-capacity institutions because we did not have an equal number of medium-capacity institutions. Our high-capacity institutions include three high-capacity community colleges and three high-capacity, research-intensive universities. We exclude the three high-capacity, non-research-intensive universities in order to allow for an equal number of high- and low-capacity institutions.

counterparts at low-capacity colleges that the financial incentives had a high impact on their institutional revenues. But the opposite held true on whether the financial incentives had a high impact on institutional efforts to improve student outcomes (see tables 3.3 and 3.4). With regard to communications, there were no clear differences on communication about state goals and only small differences regarding communication of information on institutional performance on the state metrics. However, respondents at low-organizational-capacity colleges were a bit more likely to report that communication of information on state goals and institutional performance had a high impact on institutional efforts to improve performance (see tables 3.5–3.10). Finally, there was little difference by institutional capacity in the perception that state efforts to build institutional capacity were quite minor (see table 3.11). This was somewhat surprising, in that we expected that the states might expend greater effort helping institutions with lower capacity to improve.

Summary and Conclusions

Our interviews with campus personnel yielded substantial evidence that performance funding programs in Indiana, Ohio, and Tennessee are influencing higher education institutions through financial incentives, awareness of state priorities, and awareness of institutional performance. However, we find little evidence that building up institutional capacity was a significant policy instrument used by the three states.

Financial benefits create incentives for local actors to pursue goals that are determined by policymakers, including retaining more students and producing more graduates. Attaching portions of a college's bottom-line funding to student outcomes did get the attention of campus-level actors, even in cases where they did not perceive that performance funding was yet having a significant impact on institutional revenues.

Providing information as to what are the state priorities for performance funding and just how the performance funding policy is intended to function can further help align the motivations of policymakers and campus personnel through a process of persuasion. State actors in all three states mentioned extensive state and college efforts to discuss with local personnel the goals and methods of their performance funding programs. However, outreach efforts and information penetration varied across the three states. In discussing their state's communication of the goals and methods of performance funding, as many as one-seventh of respondents mentioned that there was no communication. This perception was particularly common among faculty.

Our data indicate that state efforts to mold institutional action by providing information about how the institutions were performing on the state metrics were spottier than their efforts to provide information about state goals. Over one-third (36%) of those respondents discussing state communication of institutional performance mentioned receiving no communication from the state. Moreover, half of our respondents gave us no codable response when we asked them what impact state communication of institutional performance may have had on institutional efforts to improve student outcomes.

We find little evidence that building up organizational capacity—in particular, data-analytic capacity—was an important policy instrument used in the implementation of performance funding. Although our state-level respondents did mention capacity building efforts, our institutional respondents overwhelmingly rated the state efforts as quite minimal. While we did receive some reports of workshops for the sharing of best practices, the broad theme was that this potential policy instrument was not being used to any great degree.

As policymakers consider implementing new programs or revising existing programs, they must carefully consider the ways in which they construct the policy instruments through which performance funding will become operational. We do find evidence to support the notion that tying a greater share of state allocations to performance does catalyze institutional action. However, to be most effective, performance funding should not rely just on financial incentives. There is also an important role to be played by communication of state goals and institutional performance on state metrics. Moreover, if institutions are to successfully engage in the processes required by performance funding programs, states must help them develop sufficient internal capacity to not only conduct analyses but also interpret the results and act on them. Institutions may be on board with the goals espoused by policymakers, as a result of either financial incentives or the communicative efforts of state officials. But if institutions do not have the capacity to figure out *how* and *why* those shortfalls are occurring and the discretionary resources to mount an effective response, they will be hindered in their ability to effectively respond to performance funding. We will return to this point in chapters 4 and 7.

CHAPTER 4

Organizational Learning in Response to Performance Funding

The topic of organizational learning—that is, the processes and practices developed by organizations to identify problems and correct them—is relatively new in higher education (Bensimon, 2005; Bess & Dee, 2008; Kezar, 2005; Witham & Bensimon, 2012). Yet, it has great relevance to the concerns about improving efficiency and outcomes fueling the performance accountability movement in higher education. Lumina Foundation and other funders have been making major efforts to improve college student outcomes, and one of these initiatives—Achieving the Dream—is premised on the idea of assisting colleges with organizational learning:

> Achieving the Dream provided both monetary and technical support to the participating institutions. . . . The colleges were aided by two consultants: a data facilitator, who helped them perform the data collection and analysis and interpret the results, and a coach, who helped them set priorities, build consensus, and implement strategies for improvement. . . . Each institution sent teams of administrators and faculty to these events, where they learned more about the Achieving the Dream process, made plans for their own campuses, and shared ideas and lessons with other colleges on how to help students be more successful. (Rutschow et al., 2011, p. 12)

To date, there has been very little research on how higher education institutions deliberate on how to respond to performance funding demands and what factors aid or hinder those processes of deliberation. In order to bring to the surface the role of organizational learning in response to performance funding, this chapter explores the deliberative processes our 18 institutions utilized to decide how to improve student outcomes and what conditions aided and hindered the operation of those deliberative processes.

Sosanya M. Jones and Kevin J. Dougherty took the lead in writing the report on which this chapter draws (see Jones et al., 2015).

Our research on these issues is guided by our review of the research literature on organizational learning and data-driven decision making (see chapter 2). It is clear from this research that, in order to understand the role of organizational learning in institutions' responses to performance funding, we need to attend to several features of organizational functioning. The literature on data-driven decision making points us toward investigating how well institutions are able to secure, distribute, and deliberate on the right kinds of data. The literature on organizational learning deepens that analysis by pointing to the importance of organizational structure and organizational culture in fostering effective processes of data acquisition, distribution, and usage. Important features of organizational structure are defined channels of organizational communication and well-developed information technology (IT) and institutional research (IR) capacity. And crucial features of organizational culture are norms of open inquiry and tolerance of error, a climate of psychological safety, and a commitment to learning and professional development (see Argyris & Schön, 1996; Dowd & Tong, 2007; Kasl, Marsick, & Dechant, 1997; Kerrigan, 2014, 2015; Lipshitz, Popper, & Friedman, 2002; Witham & Bensimon, 2012; Yorks, 2005; Yorks et al., 2007; Yorks & Marsick, 2000).

In the following, we present our findings on deliberative processes and the aids and hindrances they encounter. Along the way, we examine how the prevalence of those deliberative processes and aids and hindrances varies by state, type of institution (community college or four-year institution), and estimated institutional capacity to respond effectively to performance funding. As we will show, our investigation found that colleges use a variety of deliberative processes—including both their general administrative structures and more specialized and evanescent structures such as strategic planning committees and accreditation review committees—to engage in organizational learning. The aids and hindrances to effective deliberation which colleges encounter principally involve the presence or absence of organizational commitment and leadership, effective communication and collaboration, timely and relevant data, and enough time for deliberation.

Deliberative Processes Used to Respond to Performance Funding

In our interviews, we asked respondents about what kind of deliberative processes their colleges used to decide how to respond to the pressure from the state performance funding program for improved student outcomes. We asked this question in two contexts. First, we picked a particular change in organizational policy and practice which the institution had made to respond to performance funding (see chapter 5), and we asked about what deliberative process the college had used in deciding to make that change. Secondly, we asked about what deliberative process the college used generally to decide how to respond to performance funding.

We discovered that across all 18 institutions in three states, institutions *do* have clear processes for deliberation about how to respond to performance funding demands. Certainly, institutions heavily rely on their established bureaucratic structures to investigate and make decisions about policy and practices in order to improve performance funding outcomes. However, we also found that colleges frequently utilized more temporary and informal organizational structures—such as strategic planning committees, accreditation self-study task forces, and informal discussion groups—in order to monitor their performance on state performance funding metrics and consider how to improve that performance. Hence, we provide an analysis below of the use of not only general administrative deliberative structures but also special-purpose deliberative structures and informal deliberative processes.

We define *general administrative deliberative structures* as ones that have been institutionalized in the central bureaucracy of the institution. They have a long-standing place in the administrative hierarchy, often based on well-established bureaucratic positions or committees, and most likely would continue even if performance funding were to end. They take such forms as regularly constituted groups, such as a president's or dean's council, or a designated position, such as vice president for student effectiveness. Meanwhile, *special-purpose deliberative structures* have been set up for a specific (and usually short-term) goal, are often newer, are not part of the main bureaucratic administrative structure, and are not intended to be permanent. They take such forms as strategic planning committees or accreditation self-study task forces. Finally, *informal deliberative structures* take such forms as groupings of like-minded people who on their own assemble to address student outcomes issues arising because of performance funding.

Our data show that, generally, across all 18 institutions, respondents reported general administrative structures and special-purpose structures equally often (see table 4.1). However, as we shall see, the relative balance between them varied across types of institutions (see below). Informal deliberative processes were the least often reported.

GENERAL ADMINISTRATIVE DELIBERATIVE PROCESSES

Several types of general administrative deliberative processes emerged from our data, including designated staff positions in charge of improving student outcomes and standing committees that review data on student outcomes and

Table 4.1   Structures for Deliberating on Responses to Performance Funding

Type of structure	Total	Number of community colleges with mentions (out of 9)	Number of universities with mentions (out of 9)
General administrative structures	127	5	9
Special-purpose structures	121	8	9
Informal deliberative structures	40	6	7
Total reports	288		

Note: The unit of analysis is reports and not individuals. An interviewee may have mentioned more than one deliberative structure. We only counted an institution as having one or the other type of deliberative structure if two or more respondents at that institution mentioned that type of structure.

decide how to respond. For example, a senior administrator at an Ohio community college described such a designated staff position: "We also created a position that's focused on planning, and so that has allowed us to go back to your capacity question, that has allowed us to have someone who is focused on this 24/7. . . . This individual is very gifted in facilitating discussions and so a number of divisions will call her in to help facilitate a conversation around a specific issue. She then can come in and say 'Here's the research. Here's the results that institutions have realized in this area or that area.'"

The standing committees can take several forms: executive meetings involving presidents and their vice presidents, general administrative meetings run by provosts or deans, departmental meetings, and college-wide standing committees. A dean at a Tennessee community college noted a variety of general-purpose structures being used:

> There's a vice president's council which makes some decisions and then we have a learning council which is more the academic deans and the directors of financial aid and admissions . . . all those folks who are the support for the academic side of the house. And so, yes, we come together and we talk about what performance funding indicators . . . what we want those to be, what we think we can reach, how much we want to put into this particular indicator and how much we want to put into that one. And then we, as deans, take it back to our departments for conversations and get inputs from our departments.

Similarly, a dean at an Indiana community college described the use of two kinds of standing committees: "I do know that in each region we have a vice chancellor of academic affairs. All of those people meet once a month and they do review the statistical data. In addition to that, the curriculum committees that meet in the fall and the spring review the statistical data. . . . The curriculum committees are really the groups [that are] charged with looking at the data and then deciding what worked and what didn't work and making changes."

SPECIAL-PURPOSE DELIBERATIVE STRUCTURES

We found several types of special-purpose structures used for deliberating about how to respond to performance funding pressure. They include the following: accreditation planning committees; strategic planning committees; and special task forces, councils, and committees dedicated to specific areas of concern such as retention, curriculum realignment, tutoring, and advising (see table 4.2).

Special-purpose structures were often described by respondents as more inclusive than the general-purpose structures, drawing in more faculty and mid-level administrators and sometimes students. A senior administrator at an Ohio community college noted, "The president's advisor to the dean's council [creates these projects] and that includes faculty representation, administrative representation, staff representation. So it's a somewhat formalized committee. And then it reaches out into the general faculty or staff for administration who aren't on that committee to join in especially if they have the expertise for the project that's moving forward."

Many of the special-purpose structures were not primarily created to engage in deliberations about performance funding. They were developed to address

Table 4.2 Types of Special-Purpose Deliberative Structures

Type of structure	Total	Number of community colleges with mentions (out of 9)	Number of universities with mentions (out of 9)
Special task forces, councils, and committees	77	7	9
Strategic planning committees	32	4	6
Accreditation planning committee	12	2	0
Total reports	121		

Note: The unit of analysis is reports and not individuals. An interviewee may have mentioned more than one special-purpose deliberative structure. We only counted an institution as having one or the other type of special-purpose deliberative structure if two or more respondents at that institution mentioned that type of structure.

other concerns but then became a college's device for deliberating on its responses to state performance funding demands. In Ohio, special-purpose structures sometimes originated as devices for conducting accreditation self-studies and then became vehicles for responding to performance funding. For example, an Ohio community college used its involvement with the Academic Quality Improvement Program (AQIP) initiative of the North Central Association of Colleges and Schools as one of its main vehicles to address the state's performance funding demands. Similarly, in Indiana, special-purpose structures arose in response to community colleges' involvement with the Achieving the Dream (ATD) initiative, and then those structures became devices for responding to performance funding. A senior administrator at an Indiana community college noted how its Achieving the Dream committee became the college's vehicle for deliberation on how to respond to performance funding:

> Once we joined Achieving the Dream . . . we convened panels of faculty and staff from the various regions to address individual issues like student orientation, individual academic plans, and these groups of faculty and staff came up with several proposals. . . . We have not to my knowledge had any meetings specifically for performance funding. We do have meetings on a regular basis though on, again, the Achieving the Dream goals. But . . . like I say, the performance funding has just kind of fallen [into a] one-to-one relationship with our Achieving the Dream efforts.

Respondents often described special-purpose structures as being used in conjunction with general administrative structures. For example, a special task force for reviewing retention strategies and outcomes may be convened as a result of an executive administrative order, and it reports its findings and recommendations to senior administrators who have final say on which recommendations will be implemented. This process allows a number of ways for including faculty and mid-level administrators in deliberations about institutional changes to improve student outcomes.

INFORMAL DELIBERATIVE STRUCTURES

Some deliberations took place outside of any formal structure. Respondents described informal discussions about addressing performance funding as occurring spontaneously, usually in response to an immediate or pressing need. They were not connected to any formal general administrative or special-purpose structures, but often they were led by one or two persons who were committed to addressing the issue with like-minded individuals who were in the units connected to the area of concern. A senior administrator at an Indiana university described this type of informal deliberative structure:

> I was in a position where I was seeing lots of students who were high risk and vulnerable . . . I also had a call center that reported to me. I asked them to do an informal student [report] . . . there had been a background of complaining, but no one had taken it on as a primary issue. I took it on as a primary issue, I said let's get some data; I waved the data in everybody's faces. Our chancellor who is relatively new, he saw the data and it made him cringe so he has become a little bit of a nag too.

Variations in Deliberative Processes

Having explored the general patterns, here we examine how the patterns vary by state, type of institution (community college versus university), and differences in expected institutional capacity to respond effectively to performance funding. We find noteworthy differences along the first two dimensions but not the third.

VARIATIONS BY STATE

As can be seen in table 4.3, our Tennessee respondents were somewhat more likely to mention informal deliberative structures. We have no ready explanation

Table 4.3   Differences by State in Reports on Deliberative Structures

Type of structure	Indiana		Ohio		Tennessee	
	Number of reports	Percentage of all reports	Number of reports	Percentage of all reports	Number of reports	Percentage of all reports
General administrative structures	51	47	40	41	36	43
Special-purpose structures	45	42	45	46	31	37
Informal deliberative structures	12	11	12	12	16	19
Total reports	108	100	97	100	83	100

Note: The unit of analysis is reports and not individuals. An interviewee may have mentioned more than one deliberative structure.

Table 4.4   Differences by Type of College in Reports on Deliberative Structures

Type of structure	Community colleges			Universities			Total number of reports
	Number of reports	As % of community college responses	Number of colleges with mentions (out of 9)	Number of reports	As % of university responses	Number of universities with mentions (out of 9)	
General administrative structures	40	34	5	87	51	9	127
Special-purpose structures	56	47	8	65	38	9	121
Informal deliberative structures	22	19	6	18	11	7	40
Total reports	118	100		170	100		288

for this pattern, since it runs counter to our expectation. We would have thought that the fact that Tennessee has had a much longer experience with performance funding than the other two states would result in greater institutionalization of deliberative processes and less use of informal deliberation. However, it could be argued that Tennessee's long history with performance funding might mean that Tennessee institutions had already tackled the more difficult organizational issues posed by performance funding and were more comfortable using less formal structures to address the remaining issues.

VARIATION BY TYPE OF INSTITUTION

Our university respondents more often reported the use of general-purpose administrative structures than did their community college counterparts (see table 4.4). On the other hand, our respondents at community colleges were relatively more likely to mention the use of special-purpose administrative structures.

One of the reasons that community colleges may have more often used special-purpose structures than universities is that they seem to participate more often in reform initiatives that have aims parallel to those of performance funding.* For example, the entire Indiana state community college system joined the

---

* This greater tendency of community colleges to participate in such initiatives may reflect the greater need of community colleges for external validation and new sources of funding, given

Table 4.5 Differences by Institutional Capacity in Reports of Deliberative Structures

Type of structure	High-capacity institutions		Low-capacity institutions	
	Number of reports	Percentage of all reports	Number of reports	Percentage of all reports
General administrative structures	40	47	42	44
Special-purpose structures	34	40	37	39
Informal deliberative structures	11	13	17	18
Total reports	85	100	96	100

Note: We only report figures for high- and low-capacity institutions. We exclude medium-capacity ones. See chapter 2 and note 4 in this chapter for the reasons.

Achieving the Dream initiative of Lumina Foundation, which is directed only to community colleges. As a condition of participating in Achieving the Dream, institutions have to establish a college-wide steering committee to consider how to improve student outcomes. As we have seen, those steering committees can then become structures the colleges use to deliberate on how to respond to performance funding.

VARIATIONS BY EXPECTED INSTITUTIONAL CAPACITY

We next analyze how the reported use of deliberative structures varies according to the estimated organizational capacity of institutions to respond effectively to performance funding (see chapter 2 for how we measured this). We focus on differences between our six high-capacity universities and community colleges and our six low-capacity universities and community colleges (see table 4.5).* We found little difference between high- and low-capacity institutions in the distribution of reports about deliberative structures.

Regardless of which deliberative structures colleges have used, what factors affected how well they worked? What factors aided effective deliberation, and which ones hindered it? We now turn to these questions.

---

their still subordinate role within the higher education prestige and funding hierarchies (Brint & Karabel, 1989; Dougherty, 1994; Dowd & Shieh, 2013).

* We only report differences between high- and low-capacity institutions because we did not have an equal number of medium-capacity institutions. Our high-capacity institutions include three high-capacity community colleges and three high-capacity, research-intensive universities. We exclude the three high-capacity, non-research-intensive universities in order to allow for an equal number of high- and low-capacity institutions.

Aids and Hindrances to Deliberation

Our interviews revealed particular conditions that aid and hinder colleges' deliberations on how to respond to performance funding. In this section, we review the general patterns. In the next section, we examine how they differ by state, type of college, and expected institutional capacity.

Respondents identified several factors that aid and hinder effective deliberation on how best to improve student outcomes in the face of pressure from the state performance funding program. Using axial coding, we grouped these factors into themes. Our university and community college respondents identified the following as the most important aids: organizational commitment and leadership, communication and collaboration, time and opportunity to implement changes, and timely and relevant data (see table 4.6). The absence of these aforementioned aids emerged as hindrances. For example, many respondents felt that the absence of accurate data operated as a hindrance.

ORGANIZATIONAL COMMITMENT AND LEADERSHIP

Institutional respondents in all three states often indicated that successful deliberation required commitment and leadership from both senior administration and faculty. We coded several factors identified by respondents in this category: leadership, commitment to improving institutional effectiveness, getting on the agenda for college discussion, capable staff, and professional development. Respondents who identified these factors generally expressed that it was important for senior administration not only to take initiative to focus discussions and actions on performance funding outcomes but also to keep these conversations and actions on the institutional agenda and have them carried out by

Table 4.6   Aids and Hindrances to Effective Deliberation

Type	As aid	As hindrance	Total reports
Organizational commitment and leadership	26	14	40
Communication and collaboration	58	39	97
Time and opportunity to implement changes	6	52	58
Timely and relevant data	26	14	40
Total reports	116	119	235

Note: The figures above constitute the number of reports, not the number of individuals who reported. An interviewee may have reported more than one aid or hindrance.

competent and committed staff.* A senior administrator at an Indiana community college explained, "I think it's been the chair of that committee [that] means everything I think . . . and the other thing is the participation of the provost. And in the first year there was a fairly strong chair and the provost was involved. And I think a number of things got done." A Tennessee university senior administrator echoed that perception: "I have these six committees reporting out to [the] chancellor every single month. What have you done, what [are] your top two or three priorities, and how are you going to measure it? . . . Our staff meets Monday mornings for a couple of hours, for a couple of hours every Monday for as long as someone is watching it. If we stop watching it, it will fall by the wayside."

When deliberations did not go well or did not take place at all, institutional respondents often cited a lack of commitment and leadership. For instance, an Indiana university senior administrator explained, "I think that an inability to understand how to manage that resistance from leadership [presents a major obstacle]. So, corporate America has a whole . . . industry called change management. We don't have that, we need that. We need somebody to say change is going to happen, it's inevitable, and here's what we need to do to make it happen smoothly at our campus. . . . I think there is just an inability to know how to facilitate change in an organization of this size."

However, this lack of commitment and leadership was not solely placed at the feet of senior administration. As a department chair at an Ohio university noted, the lack of commitment could also come from faculty: "A lot of [the faculty] felt . . . they wanted to keep it the old way right. So it just took time to convince them. So I basically did it without the full support."

COMMUNICATION AND COLLABORATION

Communication and collaboration were the most frequently mentioned aids or hindrances to deliberation, which are closely associated with organizational commitment and leadership. Communication and collaboration were usually expressed as necessary not only for identifying needs and problems across the institution but also for gaining buy-in. When asked about aids or hindrances to deliberation on how to respond to performance funding, the head of the faculty

---

* There is a substantial literature in public administration which points to the importance of institutional and agency leadership and culture in determining how performance information is used in organizational decision making (Lavertu & Moynihan, 2012; Moynihan & Pandey, 2010; Moynihan, Pandey, & Wright, 2012; Rabovsky, 2014a, 2014b).

senate at an Ohio university stated, "One, the fact that we involved a lot of people and have tried to get a broad-base of support. But then also the fact that the leadership—the president, the provost, and the Board of Trustees—were willing to work with us in a very cooperative conversational kind of way, not telling what it had to be, but in discussion helping us agree on what those objectives should be. So the broad-based nature of it and then secondly the fact that the leaders allowed that to happen and participated in it."

This sentiment was echoed by a senior administrator at an Indiana community college: "I think the piece that makes it effective is the cross-sharing in the department. The people will bring it back, the senior leadership will bring it back from Central [Office] to the regions, and they work within their team to implement. But then they give a higher level of cross-sharing in our senior leadership team. So we all have an idea of what is happening . . . and we are doing much better at seeing how that impacts the other areas as well."

Respondents who mentioned communication and collaboration as aids often conveyed a sense of greater inclusiveness of all sectors at a college. The way communication and collaboration engendered inclusiveness can be seen in the following statement by a senior administrator at an Ohio community college:

> The Policy Advisory Council [is] broadly representative and I have really stressed with the members that their role is to bring ideas from their constituents, their fellow department members, into the group and communicate in the other direction. So I think we have a good vehicle for communication and I'm also looking to that as a means of helping to educate faculty and others who may not be receiving all of this email, may not be attending the types of meetings that I am, where they hear about these things. So I don't think that we'll be able to make meaningful change unless we infuse knowledge about what's going on throughout our academic and student affairs areas, and so that's what we're looking to this group to do and help that way.

While communication and collaboration were identified as aids, those who felt that the deliberative processes were dysfunctional or nonexistent often cited the absence of communication and collaboration as a hindrance. As a senior administrator at an Indiana university explained, "I think it would be more effective if the people who we are relying on to actually change the way they think about education are at the table. When you just have a lot of big heads at the table, all you can do is boss people around. We can't change minds. . . . I would like to see more of those conversations with faculty."

Others also felt that the failure to communicate led directly to a lack of buy-in and participation necessary for successful deliberations. As a Tennessee university senior administrator stated, "I think programs that don't have the kind of cross-institutional participation, dialog, communications tend to be less likely to succeed, unless they are very targeted to a specific population."

TIME AND THE OPPORTUNITY TO DELIBERATE
ON NEW POLICIES AND PRACTICES

Having enough time to gather the necessary data and the opportunity to use it in the deliberative process was a prominent theme, especially for our Indiana interviewees. Interestingly, when time and opportunity to deliberate were mentioned as aids to deliberation, they were often linked to having a small-size mid-level staff, allowing easy communication. As a senior administrator at an Indiana university explained, "Well in our particular case it's that we have a very small administrative staff that's physically collocated right next to each other. We see each other every waking moment of every day, so . . . it's not like I've got to walk across campus or schedule a meeting. There's a lot of informal, incidental communication that keeps the pathways of information flowing."

This view about the benefits of a small staff was echoed by a department chair at an Ohio university: "In instances that don't require a lot of broad discussion or things that maybe don't have such a huge financial impact, keeping the participants small and allowing it to move forward in a timely fashion is one way that it makes it work effectively."

While time and opportunity to implement changes were the least mentioned aids, the lack of both of these factors was the most frequently cited hindrance. A departmental chair at an Indiana community college noted, "I think sometimes, from my level and my perspective, we'd like a little bit more time to kind of get comfortable and do more research. Sometimes the timeline is pretty short from when we hear about a change to when we have to implement the change. . . . There have been a couple of other changes or initiatives that have seemed to come more quickly, you know, with a quick time frame for us to implement those changes. So that's been a little bit of a challenge." An Ohio university academic dean echoed the previous comment:

> What is harder is really the timing issue. . . . I think the change in the formula—
> even though we were probably aware this is happening—but it changed pretty
> rapidly this last year. We could see that if we were not improving quickly we

will lose a lot of the state funding. So everything had to be done very quickly. And I think that was very stressful for a lot of people. Now we have to change a lot of things, a lot of procedures, how we address some of the students. The timing issue is really making it . . . I don't know if it made it harder, but definitely more stressful for a lot of people.

TIMELY AND RELEVANT DATA

The time pressures described above make it important that the individuals making decisions receive the right data when they need it. Many of our institutional respondents indicated that an important aid to deliberation was to receive *timely* and *relevant* data.

Respondents complained of having old data that gave them little insight into what types of needs they should be discussing. A Tennessee mid-level community college administrator explained, "We have one institutional researcher who actually spends part of her time doing something else. Going to her and asking for data, we get the data as quickly as she can produce it, but often it's too late to implement it for that semester or for that funding realm. We could use some help there." A mid-level administrator at an Indiana university echoed that point: "The latest data we have is for the 2009 cohort. Okay, so for that first target year, we're going to be looking at a group that's already been here for two years. That's kind of a hard group to effect a change with if they've already been here for two years. You know, we may have already lost the bulk of those students."

Respondents also indicated that they needed data that were specific to their particular situation in order to make good decisions, as a Tennessee university senior administrator explained:

Our various councils have looked at what are the clusters of questions in which we seem to be challenged with our students. The problem has been to take those institution-wide data . . . and how do you drill down with any kind of face validity to a departmental level? . . . All right, to what extent is what's happening in the English department as opposed to the math department contributing to what those outcomes were? Since you couldn't do that, I think it led to . . . not being able to determine exact cause-and-effect factors associated with [outcomes].

Our interviews indicate that the following factors are important to creating capacity for producing timely and relevant data: the size and skills of the IR office, IR office outreach to potential data users, and IR office efforts to build up the research skills of faculty and staff. These issues about insufficient capacity again underscore the importance of our finding in chapter 3 about the limited efforts of the states to build up institutional capacity to respond effectively to performance funding.

Many of our respondents noted that although their institutions wanted to do more to provide data, the IR staff was limited in size and capacity to do more. A faculty member at an Ohio community college noted the limitations of the college's IR capacity: "He's only one guy. There's been an increase in the amount of work that he's putting out to show us, but there's been no increase in other people coming in to help."

While many respondents indicated that the IR office at their college was responsive in providing data when it was requested, only a few respondents indicated that IR offices *proactively* reached out to determine their data needs and offer data reports tailored to their particular information needs. According to a department chair at an Ohio university, "The main IR areas are in the [campus central] offices and they do not reach out to us. We have to ask them for information, and we're often at the end of the line to get it." Similarly, a prominent faculty member at an Indiana university noted, "There's very little exchange between institutional research and the department level. I know that when data [are] required or requested, typically, those requests [are] process[ed] through a dean's office and then provided from a dean's office, maybe through the help of a chair. But very rarely is it a direct contact between institutional research and a chair or a program coordinator."

Finally, another way that faculty and staff can get access to data on student outcomes at their institutions is to conduct analyses of their own. Several of our respondents noted that their IR offices were helpful in providing training in data analysis. Still, many of our respondents—particularly at community colleges—reported that they had not seen or been made aware of efforts to help faculty and mid-level administrators better understand and analyze student outcomes data. When asked, "Have there been any efforts at the college to help improve the ability of faculty and staff to analyze and interpret some of the data?" a mid-level administrator at a Tennessee community college replied, "No. I've sat in on some committees where I'm confused about some of the data. You know, there's been an effort when I'm in a meeting and I ask a pointed question, but not overall just general, 'Let us help you interpret and understand.' No."

Variations in Aids and Hindrances

Having explored the general patterns, here we examine how our reports about aid and hindrances to deliberation vary by state, type of institution, and differences in expected institutional capacity to respond effectively to performance funding. We find noteworthy differences along all three dimensions.

DIFFERENCES BY STATE

Table 4.7 shows the distribution by each state of the various aids and hindrances to deliberation which were mentioned by our respondents. The most noticeable differences were that organizational commitment and leadership were more often mentioned by our Ohio respondents, while timely and relevant data were more often mentioned by our Tennessee respondents. We have no ready explanation for the first difference. However, the difference with regard to timely and relevant data could reflect greater effort by Tennessee to provide the colleges with data on their performance on state funding metrics (see chapter 3).

Table 4.7   Differences by State in Reports of Aids and Hindrances

Type	Indiana		Ohio		Tennessee	
	Number of reports	Percentage of all reports	Number of reports	Percentage of all reports	Number of reports	Percentage of all reports
Organizational commitment and leadership	13	15	19	22	8	13
Communication and collaboration	35	41	39	44	23	38
Time and opportunity to implement changes	25	29	20	23	13	21
Timely and relevant data	13	15	10	11	17	28
Total reports	86	100	88	100	61	100

Note: The figures above constitute the number of reports, not the number of individuals who reported. An interviewee may have reported more than one aid or hindrance.

Table 4.8   Aids and Hindrances by Type of Institution

Aids and hindrances	Community colleges		Universities		
	Number of reports	Percentage of all reports	Number of reports	Percentage of all reports	Total responses
Organizational commitment and leadership	8	9	32	22	40
Communication and collaboration	39	43	58	40	97
Time and opportunity to implement changes	22	24	36	25	58
Timely and relevant data	21	23	19	13	40
Total reports	90	100	145	100	235

DIFFERENCES BY TYPE OF INSTITUTION

There were also some noteworthy differences between community colleges and universities regarding aids and hindrances to deliberation. One of the most striking differences is the response rate. University respondents were considerably more likely to answer our questions about aids and hindrances (see table 4.8). We do not know what accounts for this gap.

In addition, our university and community college respondents differed in how often they mentioned organizational commitment and leadership and timely and relevant data. A greater proportion of university respondents mentioned the former, while a greater proportion of community college respondents mentioned the latter. The greater university mention of organizational commitment and leadership may reflect the greater importance it has for moving large, complex organizations with many different subunits with different data demands at their institutions. We are not clear on how to explain the greater community college mention of timely and relevant data, especially when most of the community college mentions involve having been aided by access to such data rather than facing hindrances due to lack of such data.

DIFFERENCES BY INSTITUTIONAL CAPACITY

We found differences in reports of aids and hindrances by estimated institutional capacity (see table 4.9). Our respondents at low-capacity institutions more often mentioned organizational commitment and leadership, while their

Table 4.9   Variation in Aids and Hindrances by Institutional Capacity

Institutional changes	High-capacity institutions		Low-capacity institutions	
	Number of reports	Percentage of all reports	Number of reports	Percentage of all reports
Organizational commitment and leadership	5	8	18	23
Communication and collaboration	24	40	37	48
Time and opportunity to implement changes	16	27	16	21
Timely and relevant data	15	25	6	8
Total reports	60	100	77	100

Note: We only report figures for high- and low-capacity institutions. We exclude medium-capacity ones. See chapter 2 and note 4 in this chapter for the reasons.

counterparts at high-capacity institutions more often cited timely and relevant data. In both cases, the preponderance of mentions involved aids rather than hindrances. High-capacity institutions seemed to have an advantage in timely and relevant data, while low-capacity institutions had an advantage in organizational commitment and leadership.

Summary and Conclusions

If the goal of performance funding is to encourage institutional change that will promote more efficient and successful practices that result in better student outcomes, organizational learning is an important component of improvement efforts. To respond effectively to performance funding demands, colleges and universities need to carefully deliberate on their educational processes, determine where improvements are needed, devise solutions, and evaluate those solutions.

We distinguish among three types of structures our 18 institutions used to deliberate on how to improve student outcomes: general administrative structures such as designated positions in charge of improving student outcomes, special-purpose deliberative structures such as strategic planning and accreditation self-study committees, and informal deliberative structures outside of any particular formal structure. Each of the 18 institutions typically used all three kinds of deliberative processes, but general- and special-purpose structures were about equally common and much more often used than informal structures.

Our respondents in Tennessee were somewhat more likely than their counterparts in Indiana and Ohio to note the use of informal deliberative structures, something that ran counter to our expectations. There was a strong tendency for community colleges to rely more heavily on special-purpose structures than did universities. We attribute this to the greater involvement of community colleges in initiatives to improve student outcomes, such as Achieving the Dream and Completion by Design, which are restricted to community colleges. We found virtually no difference by estimated organizational capacity in the use of one or the other deliberative structure.

Institutional respondents cited many factors that contributed to aiding or hindering the deliberative processes necessary for addressing performance funding demands. We grouped these factors into the following broad themes: organizational commitment and leadership, communication and collaboration, time and opportunity to implement changes, and timely and relevant data. The most commonly noted factor affecting deliberative processes was the presence or absence of communication and collaboration.

Underlying this general pattern were some interesting differences by state, type of college, and estimated institutional capacity. Organizational commitment and leadership were more often mentioned by our Ohio respondents, while timely and relevant data were more often mentioned by our Tennessee respondents. The difference with regard to timely and relevant data could reflect greater effort by the state of Tennessee to provide the colleges with data on their performance on state funding metrics (see chapter 3). University respondents more often cited organizational commitment and leadership than did community college respondents, but the opposite held for timely and relevant data. The greater university mention of organizational commitment and leadership may reflect the greater importance it has for moving large, complex organizations with many different subunits with different data demands. We are not clear on how to explain the greater community college mention of timely and relevant data, especially when most of the community college mentions involve having been aided by access to such data rather than facing hindrances due to lack of such data. Finally, our respondents at low-capacity institutions more often mentioned organizational commitment and leadership, while their counterparts at high-capacity institutions more often mentioned timely and relevant data. The latter finding may reflect greater resources to invest in systems and personnel for data acquisition, analysis, and communication.

With these deliberative structures and their vicissitudes in mind, we move to a consideration in chapter 5 of what decisions institutions made. What changes in their policies, programs, and practices did they make in response to performance funding?

Changes to Institutional Policies, Programs, and Practices

A key stage of the implementation of performance funding is when institutions take steps to revise their campus policies, practices, and programs in order to improve their performance on the outcomes for which they are now being funded. Our study posed the following questions concerning this stage: How are institutions altering their academic and student services policies, practices, and programs following the adoption of performance funding programs in ways that relate to performance funding goals? To what extent do institutional actors believe that these changes are the result of performance funding as opposed to other factors, such as accreditation demands, reform initiatives supported by states and foundations, or simply the desire to increase institutional standing and reputation? How do the institutional changes differ by state, institutional status (whether community colleges or universities), and expected organizational capacity to respond to performance funding demands?

Other researchers have recently found relationships, even if small, between performance funding policies and shifts in institutional spending allocations toward instruction and student services (Kelchen & Stedrak, 2015; Rabovsky, 2012). Meanwhile, our study focused on analyzing the specific academic and student services changes that campuses have made with the goal of improving student outcomes, as well as the extent to which institutional actors attribute those changes to performance funding. In this chapter, we present our findings about the ways that 18 public universities and community colleges in Indiana, Ohio, and Tennessee have altered their academic and student services policies, practices, and programs following the adoption of performance funding in each state.*

Rebecca S. Natow and Lara Pheatt took the lead on writing the report on which this chapter is based (Natow et al., 2014).

* In addition to academic and student services changes, some institutions were also making changes to their admission criteria to enroll better-prepared students. This phenomenon is discussed in chapter 8, which examines the unintended consequences of performance funding.

Perceptions about the Impact of Performance Funding

Before we identify the campus-level changes that followed the adoption of performance funding for higher education, we examine the extent to which our respondents believed that campus-level changes were being made in response to performance funding, as opposed to other external forces. Higher education institutions experience a variety of demands for accountability from both internal and external constituents, and these compete with the impact of performance funding programs (Harcleroad & Eaton, 2011; Olivas & Baez, 2011; Schmidtlein & Berdahl, 2011).

RATINGS OF THE IMPACT OF PERFORMANCE FUNDING ON INSTITUTIONAL CHANGES

We asked our institutional actors their perception about the extent to which performance funding motivated the institutional changes they were observing. During data analysis, we categorized these perceptions as involving a high, medium, or low (meaning little to no) impact of performance funding. Table 5.1 charts the distribution of these perceptions across our interviewees.*

As table 5.1 shows, almost one-fifth of our 198 respondents who commented on this question rated the influence of performance funding as high. For example, a senior administrator at an Ohio community college noted,

> We're going to be in the midst [this year] of 50 percent of our [state] funding [being] based on performance, and we're going to be heading into the next year where it's going to be a hundred percent of our funding. So a little more than a year from now we are going to have to make some major, major changes in the way we operate. . . . So there's no doubt in my mind that we and all of our sister institutions will be looking at the way we operate and will be assessing whether or not our policies, practices, procedures, whatever, are contributing toward completion.

* The total number of respondents whose statements are reflected in this section is fewer than the total number of institutional actors we interviewed owing to the evolving and semistructured nature of our interview protocol, the fact that some interviewees had more knowledge about performance funding (or particular performance funding programs) than others, and the fact that, on occasion, questions about the extent to which performance funding influenced institutional changes were not asked or answered. Nonetheless, the majority of our interviewees provided data with regard to this issue.

Table 5.1   Number of Respondents Who Indicated That
Performance Funding Has Had a High, Medium, or Low
Influence on Institutional Changes to Academics
and Student Services

Influence	Number
High	38
Medium	86
Low	60
Unsure	14

Note: Some respondents indicated that more than one of the performance funding programs in the state had the same level of influence; in these cases, the respondent's perceptions are reflected in this table as one count under that level of influence. When respondents indicated that different performance funding programs in the state had different levels of influence, the respondents' perceptions are reflected in this table as one count under each level of influence indicated.

However, more statements were made about performance funding having either a medium- or low-level influence than a high-level one.* This finding points to the fact that most of the time respondents felt that forces other than performance funding at least factored into institutional decision making about changes in academic and student services policies, programs, and practices.

REASONS GIVEN FOR NOT RATING THE IMPACT OF PERFORMANCE FUNDING "HIGH"

Our respondents gave a variety of reasons for why the impact of performance funding on their institution's actions was not high. They included the following:

* In chapter 3, we find that the modal response from our interviewees about the impact of various performance funding policy instruments on efforts to improve student outcomes was "high." How, then, do we account for the fact that the modal response about the influence of performance funding on institutional academic and student services changes was "medium"? The influence of performance funding may have been high with regard to institutional efforts to improve student outcomes when construed broadly, which may include such factors as enhancing institutional research capacity, forming task forces and special committees, taking steps to analyze how and why students succeed, etc. Making changes to academic and student services policies and practices is but one facet of institutional efforts to improve student outcomes. Additionally, as discussed in this chapter, external sources other than performance funding also exerted influence on institutional decisions to make certain academic or student services changes. Thus, while the policy instruments of performance funding may have had a relatively high influence on institutional efforts to improve student outcomes, the actual influence of performance funding specifically on academic and student services changes may have been more muted.

performance funding had little financial impact, the institution was already performing well or was already motivated to seek better performance, or other external initiatives were also leading institutions to pursue improvements in student outcomes.

Performance Funding Had Little Financial Impact. Ratings of a small impact of performance funding on institutional changes sometimes were rooted in a perception that performance funding does not have much financial impact on institutional revenues.* For example, a faculty member at an Indiana university said, "Money matters. . . . It's not unimportant, but its impact is pretty marginal. Again, our primary driver and the reason why I want to do this is because I want to serve my students, not because the state is saying that it's important to me."

The Institution Was Already Performing Well. Sometimes respondents discounted the impact of performance funding because they perceived their institutions as already performing well on the outcomes being measured by performance funding. A mid-level administrator at an Ohio university stated, "We were already doing really well on the performance metrics. . . . We really saw it as being a very positive change for us that we would do well under the system as is. [Q: *Without having to make any major changes?*] Right."

The Institution Was Already Committed to Improving. Other times respondents did not give performance funding great weight because, even if their performance needed improvement, they believed that their institutions were already committed to improving student outcomes, regardless of performance funding. As a senior administrator at an Indiana community college argued,

> Regardless of the funding, we have determined that students require a higher level of customer service or maybe more structure. So internally, even without the funding change, I would hope that we would still be moving towards the same levels that we're working on right now. We have really done a lot of restructuring service-wise, curriculum-wise, and I don't believe that it's totally driven by the funding. I think that it's the right thing to do, and it strengthens the college's ability and capacity to . . . offer a strong educational system to students. So I'm believing that we would have made these changes and gone in that direction anyway, but I think that this is a further incentive with the funding model change.

* The performance funding share of state support for higher education was small in Indiana. It only accounted for 6%, a much lower figure than in Ohio and, especially, Tennessee (see appendix A for more details).

Similarly, when asked to what extent the institution would have made changes to improve student outcomes regardless of performance funding, a department chair at an Ohio university replied, "I think they would have taken place without pressure from the state . . . we've been trying to boost our standing in the public domain, so I think there was a lot of pressure on to get more national recognition."

No doubt there is a degree of defensiveness to these responses. As professionals committed to the ideals of higher education, college administrators and faculty are loath to acknowledge that the lash of possible funding loss may have spurred them to action. However, we should not discount the role of professional ideals. Professional values are very important motivators, and as we will note below, it is possible to observe the impact of performance funding and yet also acknowledge that other springs to action also operate. Before we turn to that point, we should examine external factors other than performance funding which also influenced programmatic changes at public colleges and universities.

Other External Initiatives Driving Improvements. Our respondents pointed to several initiatives that were operating around the same time as the state performance funding programs and were also affecting their programmatic decisions (see also Ness, Deupree, & Gándara, 2015). These included accreditation demands, foundation initiatives such as Achieving the Dream and Complete College America, and state policy initiatives pushing changes in institutional policies and programs.

Accreditation Demands. Particularly in Ohio and Tennessee, respondents frequently noted that pressure from accrediting associations played an important role in the development of new academic and student services policies. For example, a senior administrator of an Ohio community college described the impacts of the college's involvement with the Academic Quality Improvement Program (AQIP) of the North Central Association of Colleges and Schools: "When we started the AQIP process—I think it was seven years ago now [in 2006]—the issues regarding student success came to the forefront. We started on these initiatives of mandatory testing of students and mandatory placement into developmental classes and now we're working on mandatory orientation. So all of those are student success initiatives that if we're being graded on our performance probably it would help us. [Q: *But from your perception, these have been independent efforts that the college has been doing?*] From my perception, yes."

Similarly, in Tennessee, a community college was influenced by its involvement with the Quality Enhancement Plan (QEP) of the Southern Association of

Colleges and Schools (SACS). A faculty leader at the community college noted, "When we worked on our QEP . . . probably eight years ago for our SACS accreditation five years ago, we were looking at various strengths and weaknesses in academics as well as other offices that could help our students and what we might focus on . . . out of some of those conversations, we saw that our students really need counseling services."

Achieving the Dream. This initiative was started by Lumina Foundation and now exists in over 30 states, including Ohio and Indiana. The initiative focuses on enhancing student outcomes at community colleges, and its central strategies involved improving developmental education and student advising (Achieving the Dream, 2015a, 2015b). A goodly number of our Indiana community college respondents indicated that Achieving the Dream had influenced their college's actions. An academic dean at an Indiana community college described this influence:

> We were also part of the Achieving the Dream project. So, as part of that initiative, we have made a lot of changes in how we react to retention. We've hired new advisors so that we have a larger advising staff. . . . We've instituted more tutoring in order to help these students along the way to be successful. We have a lot of supplemental programs in place to identify people earlier in their educational process so that we can help them to be successful beginning at an earlier date. We've just purchased the Starfish software, which will allow us to make students more aware when they are having difficulty in the classes and help them become aware of how they can get help. So, in that way, we have sort of geared up to be responsive to performance-based funding.

Complete College America. This organization seeks to improve college completion rates and promotes a number of changes in college policies, including revamping developmental education and advising practices (Complete College America, 2013). Its main impact has been on state policymakers (Dougherty & Natow, 2015), but there is some evidence that its recommendations have influenced institutional actions as well. For example, a community college faculty member in Ohio told us, "There is going to be a conversation about . . . whether or not to combine developmental students with college-level ready students. . . . [The college] works with Complete College America. We got their emails suggesting the changes and we were told that there would be a meeting this semester to discuss how we wanted to implement those changes."

State Policy Initiatives. Across all three of our case study states, state governments were also pushing for changes in academic and student services policies which paralleled the goals of performance funding. In Tennessee, the 2010 Complete College Tennessee Act that gave rise to the new performance funding program also established initiatives to revamp the process of student transfer from community colleges to universities and to reform developmental education (Boatman, 2012; Complete College Tennessee Act, 2010). In Ohio, the state has also made efforts to smooth student transfer and articulation pathways (Ohio Board of Regents, 2007). Moreover, the Board of Regents convened a "Complete College Ohio" task force that made numerous recommendations for campus-level changes designed to increase college completion, including providing more opportunities for dual enrollment, reforming developmental education, enhancing first-year orientation, improving course transfer and articulation, and adopting more rigorous student advising practices (Ohio Board of Regents, 2012d). And in Indiana, the state mandated a 120-credit limit on baccalaureate degrees, took steps to improve the transferability of general education courses from community colleges to universities, and required colleges to provide new students with degree maps that show them what steps to take in order to complete a baccalaureate program in four years (Indiana Commission for Higher Education, 2013b; Indiana State Senate, 2013).

These initiatives clearly joined with pressure from performance funding to affect institutional efforts.* A senior administrator at a Tennessee university mentioned how these state policy initiatives had influenced his institution's actions:

> You know the one thing we haven't talked about, which is not formula-related, it's Complete College [Tennessee Act] related . . . is all of the work on the core, on the transfer pathways, on some of the course numbering stuff. I think the policy aspects of Complete College are going to have a greater impact on moving the needle than just simply the [performance funding] formula. The state put in place transfer pathways. The state put in place a block core of courses that all institutions have to take across . . . both the TBR [Tennessee Board of Regents] and UT [University of Tennessee] system. If there were 20 policies, the [performance funding] formula is just one out of 20. There's more to this than just the formula.

---

* Ness, Deupree, and Gándara (2015, pp. 17, 26) similarly found that parallel initiatives in Tennessee, including the governor's "Drive to 55" goal (aimed at increasing to 55% the proportion of state adult residents with college degrees), likely influenced campus-level changes separately but around the same time as the state's performance funding reform.

THE JOINT INFLUENCE OF SEVERAL DIFFERENT FACTORS

In sum, most respondents perceived that performance funding had at least some impact on institutional changes, but more often than not, they suggested that the impact was not high. Moreover, many respondents believed that, although performance funding was certainly driving institutional changes, there were other factors (such as a quest for institutional prestige, accreditation requirements, participation in initiatives such as Achieving the Dream, and state mandates) driving these changes as well. As a result, it often was difficult for respondents to determine what was the unique impact of performance funding. For example, a senior administrator at a Tennessee university observed,

> Well I think part of the challenge with your question is that the things that I'm walking through [with you] are not just simply because of the new formula or the old formula. They are the result of policy directives from the board. They are the results of questions from regional and professional accrediting entities. They are the result of public pressures. So it's not just simply the formula, it's a national mood and a national conversation around the importance of completion. You know a lot of this is triggered by the realization that students are covering the reported costs of going to college and they are going in debt to do so, so morally there's an imperative to ensure that students who are making personal investments in post-secondary education are realizing a return on that investment. So I think these two policy mechanisms—the funding formula and the old performance funding—are just part of a broader national conversation and dialog around student success and academic performance.

Not surprisingly, then, several of our respondents viewed the situation as one of joint causation. Sometimes, this was seen as a matter of alignment in which actions taken in response to one program (whether performance funding or another initiative) also served the aims of another program. A senior administrator at an Indiana community college observed,

> You're probably aware that we're an Achieving the Dream member, and a number of statewide initiatives [are] happening at the same time. I really think it's a nice alignment of the stars, if you will. We've got the state pushing for it; we've got Lumina pushing for it through Achieving the Dream. Our strategic plan that we have in place focuses very much on student success, so I think the timing is right. . . . What, if any, particular changes in college policies

or practices was performance funding expected to stimulate? Well again, a lot of our changes would be captured in what we're doing with the Achieve the Dream initiative. And if you look at how our strategic plan is aligned with the Achieving the Dream initiative, I think that there again, the alignment is really kind of a key point for us.

Other times, performance funding was regarded as accelerating the impact of preexisting motivations and initiatives. For example, a senior administrator at an Indiana university noted,

> Unfortunately, even though in theory we want all of us to believe that students graduating from college is what we should all be striving for, it's easy for us to get lazy and, if the state thinks we are doing okay, to not worry about it. I think even though retention has been on everyone's mind for many years, it's elevated because of the performance funding. And in that respect it's probably a good thing and necessary thing, because sometimes you got to get the state to light a fire under you to do the right thing. I think the conversations were happening, but I do think the performance funding added a sense of urgency.

Similarly, a senior administrator at an Ohio university said that institutional changes "would have happened anyway, . . . but I think that having the state metrics come in at this time probably increased the speed as far as these changes happening."

Changes in Academic Policies, Practices, and Programs

In this section, we discuss the changes in academic policies, practices, and programs made by institutions which came after the adoption of performance funding and relate to performance funding goals (for example, changes that promote persistence, degree completion, job placement, and other performance funding objectives). As shown above, it was difficult if not impossible for respondents (and for us) to disentangle the influence on institutions' decisions of performance funding, on the one hand, and other external forces pushing for improved institutional outcomes, on the other. In some cases, these changes were specifically mandated by the government as part of a policy initiative that is separate from performance funding (for example, the Tennessee Transfer Pathways initiative), yet the changes were often seen as benefiting college performance on the state performance funding metrics. We therefore include these reforms in our analysis, with the caveat that performance funding may not have been the sole or even primary reason for the adoption of these campus-level changes.

Table 5.2   Total Institutional Changes to Academic Policies, Practices, and Programs Related to Performance Funding Objectives

Institutional changes	Number of institutions that adopted changes
Developmental education changes	10
STEM-field academic changes	6
Curricular changes and revisions to graduation requirements:	
Better course articulation / easier transfer	8
Cohorts / block scheduling	6
Adding programs/courses	5
Changing number of credits required for completion of degree or part of program (e.g., core curriculum)	5
Concurrent enrollment	3
Curricular changes based on student test scores	2
Credit for life experience	2
Changes in major declaration procedures	1
Grade forgiveness	1
Elimination of programs/courses	1
Emphasis on summer courses	1
Instructional techniques:	
Instructional technology / online instruction	3
Changes to academic departments and academic personnel issues:	
Program review	1
Follow-up on program review results	1

Note: Some institutional changes fall under more than one category. Developmental education and STEM-field academic changes were of both curricular and instructional nature and are therefore reported in those categories as well in tables 5.3–5.9. Institutional changes mentioned by interviewees were only included in those tables when responses were corroborated by either another interviewee at the same institution or documentary evidence.

Academic changes across all of the institutions included in our analysis are presented in table 5.2. They generally fall into five categories: developmental education changes; changes in science, technology, engineering, and mathematics (STEM) courses; general curricular changes and revisions to graduation requirements; changes to instructional techniques; and changes to academic departments and academic personnel. Below we discuss the first four of these categories.

DEVELOPMENTAL EDUCATION CHANGES

Changes to developmental education were identified in more of our case study institutions than any other academic change. Developmental education changes were made at ten of our institutions (almost all of them community colleges) around the time of, or following, performance funding adoption. The connection to performance funding is clear in that all three of our states made developmental education completion a funding metric for community colleges. But at the same time, performance funding was just one of many forces shaping remediation reform in these states. In all three states, developmental education changes were promoted not only by performance funding but also by separate statewide initiatives, including the Developmental Education Initiative in Ohio (Quint et al., 2013), the Developmental Course Redesign Initiative in Tennessee (Boatman, 2012), and a statewide mandate regarding course sequencing in Indiana (Ivy Tech Community College, 2014).

Changes to developmental education involved both curricular and instructional changes.* A way that one Tennessee community college restructured its developmental education was through "pre-term remediation," in which students could enroll in remedial classes during the summer before their first fall term. A senior administrator at this institution told us, "We got, I guess, 30 percent or so of our new applicants through their remediation requirements in the summer, and so they were ready for college level in the fall."

In other instances, students enrolled in developmental courses at the same time as college-level courses. In Indiana, this "corequisite" model is a statewide mandate for community colleges separate from the performance funding component (Ivy Tech Community College, 2014). A high-level administrator at an Indiana community college described the corequisite model as one in which students "take the academic skills course along with the program-level course." Corequisites have been strongly promoted by Complete College America (2013, p. 10).

Instructional changes in developmental education provision in the classroom have also been adopted, both in title and in substance. For example, a nonacademic administrator at one Tennessee community college explained that, at that institution, "instead of calling it remedial and developmental courses now, we call it learning support. And the way those classes are offered has changed as well. They're offered in a lab type setting with instructional support there, but they're pretty much self-paced."

STEM-FIELD ACADEMIC CHANGES

Some institutions have implemented academic changes specifically affecting science, technology, engineering, and mathematics (STEM) courses. We address these

---

* As we explain later in the chapter, instructional changes at the institutions in our sample involved use of technology in learning.

changes as a separate category because, like the changes made to developmental education, STEM-field course changes involved both curricular and instructional changes. STEM-field changes were made at six institutions in our sample.

Oftentimes, STEM instructional changes were made in conjunction with changes to developmental education instruction. As one Ohio university faculty member told us, "We have changed the delivery of our remedial math course to a mathematics emporium model which is a computer assisted instruction model . . . in the library so students work at their own pace through a series of 14 modules. This is a national model that has been in use around the country for over a decade."

Some institutions were also making changes to science instruction. A high-level administrator described the following reform at a Tennessee university: "We've also done something with Chemistry XX, which is many years, the most-failed-class on our campus. . . . And what we now do, if you're a student in the middle of the semester and you're failing Chemistry XX . . . you have the option of dropping that class, but then jumping right into Chemistry YY, . . . you're going to spend the second half of the semester slowly building a foundation from which we think, when you repeat [the more advanced Chemistry class] the next year, you can pass it." In other words, students deemed to be unprepared for a difficult science course were given a different form of science instruction—essentially developmental science training—to teach them at their own level of academic preparedness, with the possibility of returning to the more difficult science course in the future.

GENERAL CURRICULAR CHANGES

Besides academic changes specific to developmental education and STEM, institutions also made more general curricular changes following performance funding adoption. These curricular changes fell into a number of different categories, including better course articulation and transfer, the use of cohorts and/or block scheduling, the addition of programs or courses, changes in the number of credits required to complete a program (or part of a program, such as the core curriculum), concurrent (dual) enrollment, curricular changes based on student standardized test scores, the granting of credit for life experience, changes in procedures for major declaration, modification of grade forgiveness policies, elimination of programs or courses, and expansion of summer programs. Below we discuss the most common of these curricular changes.

Better Course Articulation and Transfer. The most common subcategory of general curricular changes was the enhancement of course articulation across campuses (the goal of which is to promote easier student transfer), with eight institutions adopting such changes. All three of our states had a transfer incentive as part of their performance funding programs.*

For example, Tennessee's performance-based funding formula included metrics for numbers transferring out of two-year and four-year institutions with 12 or more credits (Tennessee Higher Education Commission, 2011b). However, Tennessee also passed a state mandate to improve articulation which was part of the same legislation that revamped the higher education funding formula but was separate from performance funding (Complete College Tennessee Act, 2010). In any case, in 2011 the University of Tennessee and the Tennessee Board of Regents announced a "Guaranteed Transfer Pathways" program, designed to make transfer between the state's community colleges and most public universities much easier (University of Tennessee, 2011).

Cohorts and Block Scheduling. Another common curricular change made by colleges was the creation of cohorts and block schedules, occurring at 6 out of our 18 case study institutions (see also Ness, Deupree, & Gándara, 2015). A cohort approach involves having a largely similar group of students progress through a number of courses together. Block scheduling refers to the scheduling of courses in such a way that students with certain program requirements can take the courses they need in the same semester without scheduling conflicts. Both of these changes are designed to enhance retention and graduation by allowing for easier course scheduling and for groups of students to take courses together.† An academic administrator at a Tennessee community college told us the following: "There's more of an emphasis on cohorts. Trying to get as many programs as would be practical to set their courses up and set their sequencing up and cohorts rather than just drop-ins like that. I think one of the things we learned out of this is that students and cohorts tend to . . . complete at a higher rate than people who were just doing it on their own or something like that."

The Addition of Programs or Courses. The addition of programs or courses often involved the creation of new certificate programs. This was particularly

---

* Indiana had a transfer incentive in place only for the 2009–11 biennium (Indiana Commission for Higher Education, 2013a).

† Some evidence of the effectiveness of the use of cohorts and block scheduling comes from an evaluation of Accelerated Study in Associate Programs (ASAP) in community colleges at the City University of New York. A random control trial of ASAP—which included a number of other interventions in addition to the use of cohorts and block scheduling—found that, by the end of the study period, 40% of the program group had received a degree and 25% were enrolled in a four-year school, compared with 22% and 17%, respectively, of the control group (Scrivener et al., 2015).

the case in Tennessee, where the 2010 outcomes-based funding formula began to reward institutions for certificate program completions (Tennessee Higher Education Commission, 2011a; see also Ness, Deupree, & Gándara, 2015). A senior administrator at one of the state's community colleges explained, "The one thing we have done as a system is to embrace general education certificates which are shorter term certificates for students to complete their general ed., and those were all approved at system level. We've also approved a couple of other additional certificates and programs that are consortial programs that we've done through the Tennessee Board of Regents."

A Change in the Number of Credits Required. A change that was seen at five of the institutions we examined is altering the number of credits required for completion of a program or part of a program. This change included a reduction in the number of credits required for a bachelor's degree to 120, a reduction in the number of credits required for an associate's degree to 60, and a reduction in the number of credits that constitute a "core curriculum" requirement. Reducing the number of required credits can help students complete their programs more quickly. In the words of a senior administrator at an Indiana university, "If you take 30 credits a year, after four years, you're done."*

Other Curricular Changes. Some curricular changes were observed at only a few institutions. Three institutions in our sample engaged in concurrent or dual enrollment, which sometimes refers to the enrollment of current high school students in college courses and sometimes involves the concurrent enrollment of community college students in university courses. Dual enrollment is a performance metric in Tennessee's higher education funding formula and was a metric in an early iteration of Indiana's performance funding program (Indiana Commission for Higher Education, 2013a; Tennessee Higher Education Commission, 2011a). Two institutions—both community colleges—began awarding college credit for life experience of some nontraditional students.

CHANGES TO INSTRUCTIONAL TECHNIQUES: TECHNOLOGY / ONLINE EDUCATION

The only change to instructional techniques we identified in our sample was the increased or improved use of technology in instruction, which frequently

---

* In Indiana, an external force other than performance funding was influential with respect to this institutional change: a statewide policy mandated that universities reduce bachelor's degree credits to 120 (Clark, 2012; Indiana Commission for Higher Education, 2013b).

involved online learning. This trend was observed at three institutions. An academic advisor at a Tennessee university said, with respect to a particular program, "We . . . made some changes and are continuing to make changes and brought that program from an in-class to an online program to streamline it so that it would be appealing to . . . [students] who were working different schedules, different shifts." An academic administrator at an Ohio university mentioned that changes made to "e-learning" at that institution were about "finding ways as we are doing within the college to handle a significant increase in enrollment with no significant increase in faculty or staff." Online learning can help nontraditional students, who are not always able to attend face-to-face classes that meet at inflexible times, at particular locations, to complete their programs of study. Under Tennessee's performance-based funding formula, institutions can receive "a premium of 40 percent for progression and undergraduate degree production data attributable to low-income and adult students" (Tennessee Higher Education Commission, 2011b, p. 1). Although such enhancements in online learning may not always be a direct response to new performance funding demands, it is instructive that these changes—which are specifically identified as ways to increase both enrollment and efficiency—are being developed around the same time that these institutions are facing new performance funding pressures.

Student Services Changes

As displayed in table 5.3, ten different categories of changes in student services policies, practices, and programs were identified at institutions in our sample.

Table 5.3   Total Institutional Changes to Student Services Policies, Practices, and Programs Related to Performance Funding Objectives

Institutional changes	Number of institutions that adopted changes
Advising/counseling	18
Tutoring / supplemental instruction	13
Orientation / first-year programs	8
Tuition / financial aid	7
Registration/graduation procedures	6
Student services department/staffing	6
Residence life	3
Job placement services	3
Mentoring	2
Enhanced student organizations	1

The one student services change that was observed in some form at all 18 institutions involved changes to advising and counseling. Changes to tutoring and supplemental instruction were also commonly adopted, having been observed at more than two-thirds of our case study institutions.

ADVISING AND COUNSELING

Changes to student advising were observed at all of the campuses we studied. This finding is corroborated by Ness, Deupree, and Gándara (2015), who note in their analysis of changes on Tennessee campuses aimed at improving college graduation that "advising seems to be a major mechanism for encouraging completion" (p. 24). Changes to advising and counseling included adding more academic advisors or counselors, creating online advising systems, asking faculty members to play more of a role in student advising, and employing retention programs known as "early alert" or "early warning" systems that notify advisors of students who are in danger of dropping out. All of the institutions in our sample adopted some form of advisement or counseling change. One common change was the use of early warning systems. A senior administrator at an Indiana university described "an early warning system" as follows: "a whole enterprise-wide system that is for the entire university, which faculty and advisors ultimately have in place [to be used] at a very early date when students are struggling so that we can really do our best to help."

The concept of "intrusive advising" often goes hand in hand with early warning programs (Complete College America, 2013). As a senior administrator at a Tennessee university explained, "If you're an engineer and you don't take calculus the first semester you're here, you cannot pre-register without seeing an advisor. That advisor would say something like this, 'You're an engineering major, you should have taken calculus first semester. Why didn't you? You take it next semester. And oh, by the way, we suggest you go to summer school next summer to take Calculus II so you take Calculus III in your first semester as a sophomore because that's what keeps you on track to get a degree.' So that's intrusive advising."

Another advising change that was mentioned by our respondents was the increased use of "degree maps." In Indiana, this device was strongly pushed by the state's higher education commission (Indiana Commission for Higher Education, 2013b). A faculty member at an Indiana university described what is involved: "A degree map . . . shows [first-year students] step-by-step how they can complete the program in four years. And to the extent that if we say the four-year map includes taking course x this semester, and course x for some reason isn't offered, then the student has to be given that course for free. And it has to include certain milestones so students know what they should be doing, when."

Sometimes, institutions implemented multiple types of advising changes. A respondent from an Ohio community college described the following changes to advising at that institution: "We have educated our academic advisors. The first-year students have the academic advisors. The second-year students have faculty advisors. The academic advisors with the first-year students have undergone intensive training to learn about intrusive advising and they have also learned and we're implementing virtual advising."

These advising changes could certainly help institutions respond to performance funding pressures by improving retention, transfer, and graduation, and several respondents did indicate that performance funding had at least some relationship with these changes. However, advising reforms were also recommended by such organizations as Complete College America (2013) and the Complete College Ohio task force (Ohio Board of Regents, 2012d), and some institutions may have been moving in the direction of making advising changes regardless of performance funding. An administrator at a university in Indiana explained, "I think there's been this realization that advising is so important to student success and I think that's something that's kind of going on anyway," but adding that performance funding "probably hurried up the process." And a faculty member at a different Indiana university said, "I think ultimately whether we called it performance funding formula or if we called it anything else, that funding was and is going to be tied to productivity of the university. And the only way to increase your productivity is to, you know, do these things. Advise the students, give them maps, degree maps, give them a core that's more manageable. So, again I'm hem-hawing around was it a result of performance funding, but I think these things would have happened anyway ultimately. But for the same reasons, money."

TUTORING AND SUPPLEMENTAL INSTRUCTION

Another widely adopted institutional change involved tutoring and the provision of supplemental instruction with the aim of enhancing student retention and credit progression, which are rewarded by the performance funding programs. Tutoring changes consisted of creating new tutoring centers, requiring faculty to meet personally with students, and even providing tutoring online. As one senior administrator at an Ohio community college told us, "We give free tutoring to all students in anything they want it in related to their courses. And so that's a great benefit. We have an online tutoring system as well as face-to-face, one-on-one."

For at least one community college in our sample, tutoring was particularly important for developmental education students. As a nonacademic administrator at that institution said, "We are putting a lot of resources into helping students get up to college level because so many of our students come in not ready for college level." In some cases, supplemental instruction allowed students to attend an extra academic session after their regular classes. For example, an academic administrator at an Ohio university explained, "In terms of tutoring, we have this thing called Supplemental Instruction where undergraduate students sit in on the class and . . . [run] a session after class on a voluntary basis. They do these in a lot of math classes and a lot of other high enrollment, low performing classes."

ORIENTATION AND FIRST-YEAR PROGRAMS

Another popular student services change involved reconstructing orientation and other programs for first-year students with the aim of enhancing retention (see also Ness, Deupree, & Gándara, 2015). Such changes were observed at eight of our case study institutions. A senior administrator at one Tennessee community college described some of the first-year program changes at that institution as follows: "I know one of the big pushes we have is in the student's first year. I know they've done some studies that really tie in a success rate of a student with their first year into college. So, [we've] started a number of first-year programs to help orient the students and to help develop various study habits among the students that will carry them through their college career. . . . The first year college focus, that came as a result of the [outcomes-based funding] formula plus the Complete College Tennessee Act."

In a study of Tennessee institutions specifically, Ness, Deupree, and Gándara (2015) likewise found that efforts to encourage college completion included changes to orientation such as enhanced advising and student workshops focused on college completion.

TUITION AND FINANCIAL AID POLICIES

Seven of our institutions also adopted changes to their tuition and financial aid policies following the adoption of performance funding in their states (see also Ness, Deupree, & Gándara, 2015). Tuition and financial aid changes involved creating new scholarships (for example, for special student populations) and providing tuition discounts. Students who were close to graduating were sometimes specifically targeted for financial assistance. An administrator at a Tennessee community college said that, following the adoption of the performance-based funding formula, "there was a real emphasis made to look for those students who were close to graduating, and contacting them to make them aware that, 'Did you know that if you got a couple of more credit hours you'd have your degree?' And then we also did some scholarships to help students who were in that position actually finish and get their degrees." And at one Ohio university, a faculty leader said, "A lot of our students . . . being first-time students, working class, first-generation, need to work a lot. So the more we can do to help them financially with their college education then the more time in theory they ought to be spending on their studies and the more successful they will have been."

REGISTRATION AND GRADUATION PROCEDURES

Six institutions in our sample changed registration procedures and nonacademic requirements for graduation.* These changes included such measures as simplifying the graduation application process, eliminating the graduation fee, prohibiting late registration, and shortening the course withdrawal period. The aims were to make it easier for students to graduate and, in the case of the course withdrawal change, to discourage registration by students with weaker academic commitments and therefore lesser likelihood of graduating.

In response to a question that asked how the college had altered polices or practices in order to improve its performance on the state performance funding indicators, a faculty leader said that "one thing that they did was they got rid of late registration," and that the purpose of this change was "to improve student success, which faculty had been saying for a long time, 'They can't miss the first week . . . and be successful.'" Likewise, an institutional research director at an Ohio university identified a prohibition on late course registration in response to a question about the impacts of the state's 2009 performance funding program. Finally, a nonacademic administrator at a Tennessee university told us,

> We . . . changed our drop policy, so that students only have the opportunity to withdraw from classes four times during their academic career. Again, this is

---

* Ness, Deupree, and Gándara (2015) found similar changes to registration and graduation policies as a campus response to Tennessee's new funding formula.

directly related to keeping them on track. What we learned was that students will take classes over and over and over again, and recognize that those credits don't count for graduation. So, they have [spun] their wheels, taking these courses without the outcome that they had hoped for. And so, making sure they understand how to spend those withdrawals, sort of in a way that makes sense, and understanding that you can't just do that every semester.

RESTRUCTURING STUDENT SERVICES DEPARTMENTS AND STAFFING

One-third of the institutions in our sample restructured their student services departments and/or staffing. The department restructuring often involved either creating new departments designed to manage enrollment issues or reorganizing student services into one large department, thereby creating what was frequently described as a "one-stop shop" for student services (see also Ness, Deupree, & Gándara, 2015, pp. 26–27). A high-level administrator at a Tennessee university identified "one-stop student services" as a means to improve student outcomes under the new funding formula. Another academic administrator at that university further described this one-stop shop: "We created a one-stop, which you know is a place that any student can walk in and really get advice or issues with registration or really just helping them along the way. And that's in our library, staffed you know, many hours a day and just a real easy way."

Student services staffing changes often involved adding new staff to specialize in student retention and success. Such changes also sometimes involved hiring new high-level student services administrators to oversee enrollment management.

OTHER STUDENT SERVICES CHANGES

Some student services changes were not widely adopted among the institutions in our sample but are still worth noting. Three institutions enhanced their job placement services program. Three institutions made changes to residence life, including the development of living-learning communities and increasing the number of students required to live on campus. New or enhanced mentoring programs were implemented at two case study institutions, and one institution focused on improving its student organizations.*

---

* Similarly, Ness, Deupree, and Gándara (2015) found mentoring programs as one campus-level response to the new funding formula in Tennessee.

Isomorphism and the Institutionalization of Campus Changes

Our findings demonstrate that several types of campus changes made following the adoption of higher education performance funding policies are on their way to becoming institutionalized, if they are not already institutionalized. They include changes to developmental education, course articulation, advising and counseling services, tutoring and supplemental instruction, and orientation and first-year programs. All of them were observed in at least eight institutions in our sample and were consistently identified (with a few notable exceptions) across states and institutions differing in institutional type and capacity level.

Higher education institutions that have adopted these policy, program, and practice changes are becoming *isomorphic* (DiMaggio & Powell, 1991). That is, they become more similar in their academic and student services structures and practices to improve student outcomes. How can we understand the sources of this isomorphism?

When government entities incentivize or mandate that higher education institutions adopt certain practices, *coercive isomorphism* takes effect. Clearly, performance funding is a source of coercive isomorphism insofar as it puts pressure on institutions to make changes that will improve their student outcomes and therefore their state funding. Coercive isomorphism is also seen in the enactment of statewide mandates, such as statewide transfer and articulation reform in all three states (Indiana State Senate, 2013; Ohio Board of Regents, 2007; University of Tennessee, 2011).

But as we have seen in our discussion of various policy instruments in chapter 3, states also influence institutions through communication and persuasion. This points us toward another source of isomorphism: the influence of social and professional norms, or *normative isomorphism* (DiMaggio & Powell, 1991). Many of the changes frequently adopted by colleges and universities in our sample are similar to institutional changes promoted by Complete College America (2013) and Achieving the Dream (2015b). Interestingly, some of the words used by our respondents are found in Complete College America's (2013) list of "Game Changers." For example, Complete College America (2013) discusses specific types of advising such as "early warning systems" (p. 22), "degree maps" (p. 23), and "intrusive advising" (pp. 20, 23). These exact phrases appeared frequently in our respondents' statements about advising changes on their campuses. In addition, many of the commonly adopted institutional changes also appear in Vincent

Tinto's (2012) analysis of campus-level changes that can promote college persistence. Tinto (2012) specifically describes the enhancement of first-year programs, advising, tutoring, and developmental education, as well as the elimination of late registration, as campus-level changes that could help promote college persistence. Some other commonly adopted institutional changes—such as cohorts, block scheduling, and the creation of "one-stop shops" for student services—are reflected in Tinto's (2012) discussions of learning communities, course schedule improvement, and the centralization of student services departments. To the extent that research on college persistence influenced institutional personnel—some of whom may have studied higher education in graduate school— to adopt particular practices on their campuses, normative isomorphism may have played a role.

Disaggregating Our Main Patterns

In this section, we disaggregate our data to examine differences by state and by type of institution in how our respondents described institutional changes. We examine two types of institutional differences. One is between community colleges and universities. The other is among institutions differing in their expected organizational capacity to respond effectively to performance funding.

DIFFERENCES BY STATE

It is important to understand how changes to institutions' academic and student services practices differ by state, because each state's performance funding program has unique features and may therefore provoke different types of institutional changes. Table 5.4 charts how many institutions in each state made one or another change in academic policies, programs, and practices. Meanwhile, table 5.5 displays differences by state in number of institutions reporting changes in student services policies, programs, and practices.

A noteworthy difference can be observed in institutional efforts to improve course articulation and ease transfer. While all six of the Tennessee institutions in our sample reportedly made such changes, we have no such reports for any of our Ohio case study institutions. One reason for this may be that course articulation and transfer had been reformed in Ohio a few years earlier (see Ohio Board of Regents, 2007), so there was little need to make further revisions with the advent of the new 2009 performance funding program. Another is that the Tennessee system is more centralized and colleges were required to make articulation

Table 5.4   Number of Institutions That Made Changes to Academic Policies, Practices, and Programs Related to Performance Funding Objectives, by State

Institutional changes	Indiana (out of 6)	Ohio (out of 6)	Tennessee (out of 6)
Developmental education changes	3	4	3
STEM-field academic changes	2	2	2
Curricular and graduation changes:			
Better course articulation / easier transfer	2	0	6
Cohorts / block scheduling	2	1	3
Addition of programs/courses	1	1	3
Change in number of credits required for			
completion of degree or part of program	4	1	0
Concurrent enrollment	1	0	2
Curricular changes based on student test scores	0	0	2
Credit for life experience	0	1	1
Instructional techniques:			
Instructional technology / online instruction	0	1	2
Changes to academic departments and personnel:			
Program review	0	0	1
Follow-up on program review results	0	0	1

and transfer changes at the behest of the Tennessee Board of Regents and the University of Tennessee board.

There was also a substantial difference by state in reduction of the number of credits required for a degree or for part of a degree program. No Tennessee institutions and only one Ohio institution reported doing this, but four of six Indiana institutions reported such reductions. Indiana's reductions likely responded to a statewide mandate separate from performance funding (see Clark, 2012; Indiana Commission for Higher Education, 2013b) which the other states did not experience.

Three Tennessee institutions added courses or programs, while only one institution each in Indiana and Ohio did so. Tennessee's additions may be due to the fact that the state's new funding formula rewards community colleges for awarding postsecondary certificates. After it was implemented, several Tennessee institutions began offering more certificate programs.

Table 5.5 displays the campus-level student services changes by state. One striking difference is that no changes to registration or graduation procedures were observed in our Indiana institutions following the adoption of performance funding in that state, although such changes were reported for multiple institutions in Ohio and Tennessee. Furthermore, Tennessee institutions were more

Table 5.5   Number of Institutions That Made Changes to Student Services Policies, Practices, and Programs Related to Performance Funding Objectives, by State

Institutional changes	Indiana (out of 6)	Ohio (out of 6)	Tennessee (out of 6)
Advising/counseling	6	6	6
Tutoring / supplemental instruction	3	4	6
Orientation / first-year programs	4	2	2
Tuition / financial aid	3	2	2
Registration/graduation procedures	0	3	3
Student services department/staffing	3	1	2
Residence life	0	2	1
Job placement services	1	0	2
Mentoring	0	1	1

likely to report changes in tutoring and supplemental instruction than were Ohio and Indiana institutions.

DIFFERENCES BY TYPE OF INSTITUTION

Because universities and community colleges are subject to rather different performance funding metrics, the institutional changes made in response to performance funding are likely to differ by institutional type. In this section we analyze how universities and community colleges differ in the number reporting academic and student services changes. Table 5.6 displays academic changes and table 5.7 charts student services changes by institutional type.

Academically, developmental education changes were observed much more frequently at community colleges than at universities, occurring at eight out of the nine community colleges in our sample but at only two out of nine universities. This makes sense, given that a major role of community colleges is to provide college access and remedial education to underprepared college students and that the universities in Indiana were barred from providing developmental education (Bailey, 2009; Cohen, Brawer, & Kisker, 2014; Hughes & Scott-Clayton, 2011). Moreover, developmental education success was a performance metric for community colleges but not universities in all three states, and it has been an object of several major state and national policy initiatives (see Achieving the Dream, 2015a, 2015b; Complete College America, 2013).

Adding programs and courses was also observed more frequently at the community colleges in our sample, possibly because this change often involved the

Table 5.6 Number of Institutions That Made Changes to Academic Policies, Practices, and Programs Related to Performance Funding Objectives, by Institution Type

Institutional changes	Universities (out of 9)	Community colleges (out of 9)
Developmental education changes	2	8
STEM-field academic changes	4	2
Curricular and graduation changes:		
Better course articulation / easier transfer	5	3
Cohorts / block scheduling	2	4
Addition of programs/courses	1	4
Change in the number of credits required for completion of degree or part of program	4	1
Concurrent enrollment	1	2
Curricular changes based on student test scores	1	1
Credit for life experience	0	2
Instructional techniques:		
Instructional technology / online instruction	2	1
Changes to academic departments and academic personnel:		
Program review	1	0
Follow-up on program review results	1	0

Table 5.7 Number of Institutions That Made Changes to Student Services Policies, Practices, and Programs Related to Performance Funding Objectives, by Institution Type

Institutional changes	Universities (out of 9)	Community colleges (out of 9)
Advising/counseling	9	9
Tutoring / supplemental instruction	6	7
Orientation / first-year programs	3	5
Tuition / financial aid	4	3
Registration/graduation procedures	3	3
Student services department/staffing	3	3
Residence life	3	0
Job placement services	2	1
Mentoring	1	1

addition of certificate programs in Tennessee community colleges and because the new funding formula for higher education in that state rewards two-year colleges for certificate completions (Tennessee Higher Education Commission, 2011a). Moreover, community colleges more often reported introducing the use of student cohorts and block scheduling.

In contrast, changes in the number of credits required to complete a program or part of a program were observed more frequently at the universities in our sample. Also, universities more often reported STEM-field academic changes and changes in course articulation and transfer.

Regarding student services changes (see table 5.7), there were few differences of importance between universities and community colleges. However, we did observe residence life changes at three universities but at no community colleges. This difference is expected, given that community colleges are considered "commuter institutions" and frequently do not have student residence halls. Also, community colleges were somewhat more likely to make changes in orientation and first-year programs.

DIFFERENCES BY INSTITUTIONAL CAPACITY

We next analyze how academic and student services changes differed according to the estimated organizational capacity of institutions to respond effectively to performance funding (see chapter 2 for how we measured this). Given that institutions with varying levels of capacity have different resources, priorities, and needs, one might assume that the campus-level changes may vary by institutional capacity level. Tables 5.8 and 5.9 show the academic and student services changes, respectively, made by institutions of different capacity levels in our sample. We focus on differences between our six high-capacity universities and community colleges and our six low-capacity universities and community colleges.

One interesting difference across institutions in academic changes is that we observed changes in online instruction only at high-capacity institutions, possibly because they are more likely to have greater resources to support online learning than lower-capacity institutions. Conversely, we observed changes in the number of credits required for completion of a degree or part of a program more often at low-capacity institutions. This raises the possibility that these institutions, because they face greater challenges to responding effectively to performance funding, are reducing their academic quality. We return to this point in the next section.

Table 5.8 Number of Institutions Making Changes to Academic Policies, Practices, and Programs Related to Performance Funding Objectives, by Institutional Capacity

Institutional changes	High-capacity institutions (out of 6)	Low-capacity institutions (out of 6)
Developmental education changes	3	4
STEM-field academic changes	1	2
Curricular and graduation changes:		
Better course articulation / easier transfer	2	3
Cohorts / block scheduling	2	2
Addition of programs/courses	1	1
Change in the number of credits required for completion of degree or part of program	1	3
Concurrent enrollment	1	1
Curricular changes based on student test scores	1	1
Credit for life experience	0	1
Instructional techniques:		
Instructional technology / online instruction	3	0
Changes to academic departments and academic personnel:		
Program review	0	0
Follow-up on program review results	0	0

Table 5.9 Number of Institutions Making Changes to Student Services Policies, Practices, and Programs Related to Performance Funding Objectives, by Institutional Capacity

Institutional changes	High-capacity institutions (out of 6)	Low-capacity institutions (out of 6)
Advising/counseling	6	6
Tutoring / supplemental instruction	4	4
Orientation / first-year programs	2	3
Tuition / financial aid	2	3
Registration/graduation procedures	2	2
Student services department/staffing	3	2
Residence life	1	1
Job placement services	2	0
Mentoring	1	1

There was little difference by institutional capacity in the number of institutions reporting changes in student services policies, programs, or practices (see table 5.9). However, only high-capacity institutions made changes to job placement services.

Summary and Conclusions

Performance funding clearly has had an impact on institutional academic and student services policies, programs, and practices. The most commonly made campus-level academic change that occurred around the time of performance funding adoption was the altering of developmental education. This was particularly true at community colleges but also occurred at some universities. Performance funding provided an incentive for changing developmental education insofar as the program's success was a performance metric for community colleges in Indiana, Ohio, and Tennessee. However, in all three states, developmental education reform was also mandated or incentivized by legislation or other initiatives separate from performance funding. For example, Ohio and Tennessee participated in privately sponsored developmental education reform initiatives (Boatman, 2012; Quint et al., 2013), and changes to developmental education were required under a statewide policy in Indiana (Ivy Tech Community College, 2014).

Another common academic change was improvement in course articulation and transfer (see also Ness, Deupree, & Gándara, 2015). Transfer numbers constitute a performance funding metric in Ohio and Tennessee and did so for a while in Indiana as well. But again, in all three states, changes in course articulation and transfer were also mandated statewide through policies separate from performance funding. Other commonly adopted academic practices include the use of cohorts and block scheduling, adding programs and courses, and changing the manner in which courses in the STEM fields are taught.

The most commonly made campus-level student services change occurring around the time of performance funding adoption has been the altering of advising and counseling services (including the use of early warning systems, degree maps and audits, and involving more faculty in advising). Changes in these services were clearly seen as helping to improve institutional outcomes on performance funding metrics for credit accrual and degree completion. However, some components of student advising (for example, degree maps in Indiana) were also mandated by a statewide policy independent of performance funding. Other commonly adopted student services practices included revamping tutoring and supplemental instruction, changes to tuition and financial aid policies, modifications of registration and graduation procedures, and the restructuring of student services departments and staffing (including creating a "one-stop shop" for many student services).

While there were great commonalities across our three states in changes made in academic and student services policies, there were also some noteworthy divergences. In terms of academic policies, we find noticeable differences by state in the number of institutions modifying course articulation and transfer, changing the number of credits required for completion of degrees or parts of degree programs, and adding courses and programs. With regard to student services policies, we observed differences between states in the number of institutions reporting changes to registration or graduation procedures and to tutoring and supplemental instruction programs.

Looking at differences between types of institutions, the most noteworthy differences in changes in academic policy involved more community colleges reporting that they had changed developmental education, added programs and courses, and introduced cohorts and block scheduling, while more universities reported changes in STEM-field academic policies, course articulation and transfer, and number of credits required to complete a program or part of a program. In terms of student services policies, there were few differences by type of institution beyond universities more often reporting changes in residence life and community colleges more often reporting changes in orientation and first-year programs.

Finally, looking across institutions differing in expected organizational capacity to respond effectively to performance funding policies, we find some noteworthy differences in numbers of institutions making changes in academic and student services policies. With regard to student services policies, the only difference of any size was that more high-capacity institutions made changes to job placement services. However, with regard to academic policies, high-capacity institutions were more likely to change online instruction, while low-capacity institutions were somewhat more likely to change the number of credits required for completion of a degree or part of a program. This second pattern is troubling. It raises the possibility that institutions facing greater difficulty in responding to performance funding pressures may be resorting to reducing their academic quality. As it happens, we find in chapter 8 that we received more reports of potential or observed weakening of academic quality from our respondents at low-capacity institutions than their counterparts at high-capacity institutions.

Clearly, performance funding has prompted institutions to make changes to their academic and student services programming and policies, with the goal of improving student outcomes. These findings are consistent with other recent research that has found that institutions subject to performance-based funding policies tend to allocate more funding toward instruction and student services than do comparable institutions in states without performance funding (Kelchen & Stedrak, 2015; Rabovsky, 2012).

At the same time, performance funding is but one of several concurrent external influences that seek to improve higher education institutional outcomes. States have legislatively mandated such institutional changes as enhancing course articulation and transfer, reforming developmental education, using degree maps, and lowering the number of credits required for a degree. Institutions are also influenced by accreditors, foundations, and other nonprofit associations that fund or otherwise advocate for particular reforms. In light of all of these concurrent influences, it is difficult (if not impossible) to disentangle the unique influence of performance funding from the influence of other external factors on institutions' decisions to make particular campus-level changes. Perhaps for this reason, the modal assessment of our respondents of the impact of performance funding on academic and student services changes was medium. Respondents rating the impact of performance funding as medium or low often observed that performance funding was frequently only one force among many that factored into institutional decisions.

CHAPTER 6

Student Outcomes

Our colleges and universities have made extensive changes in their academic and student support policies in part in response to performance funding. But has this resulted in a significant improvement in student outcomes? As it happens, we have no research definitively establishing that it has, and answering that question is trickier than one might imagine.

Determining the impact of performance funding on student outcomes in college is difficult. Even if student outcomes improve after the introduction of performance funding, these improvements could be influenced by many other factors, such as growing enrollments (which alone could produce rising graduation numbers), and various efforts to improve student outcomes—such as recent state initiatives to improve counseling and advising, developmental education, and course articulation and transfer—other than performance funding (Hearn, 2015; see also chapter 5 in this book). Conversely, a lack of improvement in student outcomes following the advent of performance funding could be due to obstacles it is encountering in its implementation. Hence, it is important to conduct multivariate statistical analyses that strive to control for all the possible factors that might account for improvements or lack of improvements in student outcomes apart from the operation of performance funding. Before we move to examining the multivariate studies, we should first establish whether there are any simple descriptive data indicating that student outcomes have improved in our three states.

Descriptive Data

Simple descriptive data do suggest that the arrival of performance funding is associated with an improvement in student outcomes. We pay particular attention to changes in graduation numbers, since they have been the principal concern of state performance funding programs. Across all three states, we consistently find that—following the advent of the PF 2.0 program in our three states—graduation numbers increased by a larger amount than enrollment numbers, possibly indicating an increasing effectiveness of the higher education system.

INDIANA

In Indiana the number of undergraduate and graduate degrees and certificates awarded by public universities rose 16.1% from 39,932 in academic year (AY) 2008–9 to 46,366 in AY 2012–13 (Townsley, 2014). At the same time, fall enrollments of full-time and part-time students rose only 8.9% from 214,536 in fall 2008 to 233,497 in fall 2012 (National Center for Education Statistics, 2011, table 223; National Center for Education Statistics, 2014, table 304.60). For community colleges, the number of degrees and certificates awarded doubled, from 9,100 in AY 2008–9 to 18,129 in AY 2012–13 (Townsley, 2014). Meanwhile, enrollments increased much less: 21.7%, from 82,414 in fall 2008 to 100,272 in fall 2012 (National Center for Education Statistics, 2011, table 223; National Center for Education Statistics, 2014, table 304.60).

OHIO

In Ohio, the number of degrees and certificates awarded by the main and regional campuses of Ohio public universities rose 16.6%, from 61,090 in 2009 to 71,201 in 2012. Meanwhile, fall headcount enrollments did not increase as much, 10.9%, from 306,261 to 339,760 (Ohio Board of Regents, 2013e, 2013f). Or using a related metric, the number of degrees awarded per FTE rose from 0.219 to 0.254 between 2010 and 2013 (Ohio Board of Regents, 2014).

Meanwhile, the number of performance funding Success Points* generated by community colleges rose 5.8%, from 163,471 in FY 2009 to 172,878 in FY 2013. However, this increase was smaller than the 7.4% increase in fall headcount enrollments during the same period (Ohio Board of Regents, 2013d).

TENNESSEE

In Tennessee, there is also evidence of rises in graduation numbers which exceeded increases in enrollment counts. For the universities, the number of graduates rose 12.6%, from 26,152 in 2010 to 29,443 in 2013, while enrollments only went up 2.6%, from 139,568 in fall 2009 to 143,228 in fall 2012 (Tennessee

---

* For FY 2015, the Success Points were based on the number of students completing developmental education or reaching certain credit thresholds. They drove 25% of the State Share of Instruction funding formula for community colleges (Ohio Board of Regents, 2015a).

Higher Education Commission, 2011c, 2014b). Meanwhile, the number of students receiving degrees and certificates from community colleges jumped by 57%, from 9,750 in 2010 to 15,312 in 2013, while enrollments barely budged, from 92,226 to 92,742. Most of the increase for community colleges was in certificates, which tripled in number, but the number of associate's degrees granted still went up by one-quarter (Tennessee Higher Education Commission, 2011c, 2014b).* In addition, the number of bachelor's degrees and associate's degrees awarded by universities and community colleges rose faster in the years following the introduction in 2010 of the outcomes-based formula than in the years previous. For example, the number of bachelor's degrees rose 3.4% annually between 2010 and 2014, whereas the average annual rate of increase from 2001 to 2010 had been 2.5% (Johnson & Yanagiura, 2015; Postsecondary Analytics, 2013). However, the number of associate's degrees rose more sharply: 6.3% a year between 2010 and 2014, versus 2.8% a year in the preceding nine years (Johnson & Yanagiura, 2015; Postsecondary Analytics, 2013).

While these data on Indiana, Ohio, and Tennessee are of interest, we cannot in any way conclude that performance funding in these three states is producing higher student outcomes. Except for controlling for enrollment changes, the comparisons above do not control for a host of other influences that could be driving student outcomes. This caution is driven strongly by the results of multivariate analyses that have been conducted on the impact of performance funding programs. Most of these programs are of the PF 1.0 variety and not PF 2.0 programs, but the results of these studies are sobering.

Multivariate Study Findings

Most of these multivariate analyses focus on graduation from public four-year colleges, although some also consider graduation from community colleges and retention in both two-year and four-year colleges. The studies compare states with performance funding to states without any performance funding, using a variety of multivariate statistical techniques (e.g., difference-in-differences or hierarchical linear modeling) and controlling for a variety of institutional characteristics (e.g., median test scores, student income and racial composition, and institutional spending on instruction), state policies (e.g., average tuition for

---

* The greater rise in certificates has been explained as being due to the fact that they are easier to produce than associate's degrees but they counted just as much toward student completion in the Tennessee performance funding program (Postsecondary Analytics, 2013).

two-year and four-year colleges, state financial aid per student, and state appropriations per student), and state socioeconomic characteristics and conditions (e.g., population size and state unemployment rate) (see table 6.1 for details on these studies). We will begin by reviewing the findings specific to our three states, but then, to provide context and greater depth, we review findings from other bodies of research: studies of performance funding for higher education in all states, and performance funding in fields such as K–12 education, workforce training, and social work.

STUDIES SPECIFIC TO OUR THREE STATES

Three multivariate studies have been conducted on our three states. One is specific to Indiana (Umbricht, Fernandez, & Ortagus, 2015). Another is specific to Tennessee (Sanford & Hunter, 2011). The third covers all three states (Hillman et al., 2015).

Umbricht, Fernandez, and Ortagus (2015) examine the impact of Indiana's PF 1.0 and PF 2.0 programs on three-year averages of the numbers graduating from Indiana public four-year institutions during the years 2003–12. Nine different models were estimated involving three different lag times and three different comparison groups. Differences between earlier and later graduation numbers were calculated, allowing for no lag, a one-year lag, or a two-year lag between policy implementation and institutional response. Three comparison groups were used: 29 public four-year institutions in three states similar to Indiana (Kentucky, Missouri, and Wisconsin) but without performance funding in the years 2003–12; 21 private four-year institutions in Indiana, which were not subject to performance funding; and 55 public four-year institutions in six surrounding states also without performance funding (Iowa, Illinois, Kentucky, Missouri, Minnesota, and Wisconsin). A difference-in-differences analysis was used with year and institutional fixed effects and the following control variables: FTE enrollments for the entering class in each year, state appropriations for the public institutions, and state-level unemployment rate. The study found that—across all nine models—performance funding in Indiana did not lead to increases in the three-year average number of four-year graduates. In fact, the impacts found—although none was significant—were negative (Umbricht, Fernandez, & Ortagus, 2015).

Sanford and Hunter (2011) examine the impact of the PF 1.0 program Tennessee established in 1979 on the one-year institutional retention rates and six-year graduation rates of its public universities over the years 1995–2009 (the precise end points varied by which dependent variable was being examined). Each

Table 6.1   Multivariate Analyses of Impacts of Performance

Study characteristics	Hillman et al. (2015)	Hillman, Tandberg, & Fryar (2015)	Hillman, Tandberg, & Gross (2014)	Larocca & Carr (2012)
Institution type focused on	Public four years in IN, OH, TN	Public two years in WA	Public four years in PA	Public two and four years in US
Data set	IPEDS, etc.		NCES Delta Cost Project	IPEDS, etc.
Methods	Difference-in-differences	Difference-in-differences	Difference-in-differences	Cross-sectional time series with fixed effects
Dependent variables				
Retention rate (institutional)		One year		One year
AA or certificate completion		AA and certificates: Number in given year		Rate
BA graduation: Rate or number	Number graduating in given year		Number graduating in given year	Rate graduating in six years
ACT scores				
Admission rate				
Change in number of FTE incoming minority students				
Change in number of incoming FTE federal aid recipients				
PF impact				
Positive, statistically significant	Graduation number (1 out of 12 models)	Graduation numbers: Short-term certificates (2 of 6 models)	Graduation number (3 of 10 models)	Retention two-year colleges
Positive, not statistically significant	Graduation numbers and rates (7 out of 12 models)	Graduation numbers: Associate's (4 of 6 models); short-term certificates (3 of 6 models)	Graduation numbers: (7 of 10 models)	Graduation rate two-year colleges; retention four-year colleges

Rutherford & Rabovsky (2014)	Sanford & Hunter (2011)	Shin (2010)	Tandberg & Hillman (2014)	Tandberg, Hillman, & Barakat (2014)	Umbricht, Fernandez, & Ortagus (2015)
Public four years in US	Public four years in TN	Public four years in US	Public four years in US	Public two years in US	Public four years in Indiana
IPEDS, etc.	Tennessee data	IPEDS, etc.	IPEDS, etc.	IPEDS, etc.	IPEDS, etc.
Cross-sectional time series with fixed effects	Spline linear mixed model	Hierarchical linear modeling	Difference-in-differences	Difference-in-differences	Difference-in-differences
One year	One year				
				AA: Number in given year	
Number and rate graduating in six years	Rate: Change in six-year graduation rate	Rate graduating in six years	Number graduating in given year		Number graduating (three-year average)
					25th and 75th percentiles
					X
					X
					X
					ACT scores at 25th and 75th percentile (18 of 18 models); number of incoming federal aid recipients (2 of 9 models)
Graduation rate (5 of 6 models); retention rate (3 of 6 models)	Retention rate	Graduation rate	Graduation numbers: BAs (6 of 6 models)		Number of incoming federal aid recipients (2 of 9 models)

(continued)

135

Table 6.1   (*continued*)

Study characteristics	Hillman et al. (2015)	Hillman, Tandberg, & Fryar (2015)	Hillman, Tandberg, & Gross (2014)	Larocca & Carr (2012)
Negative, statistically significant	Graduation numbers and rates (1 out of 12 models)	Graduation: Long-term certificates (4 of 6 models)		
Negative, not statistically significant	Graduation numbers and rates (3 out of 12 models)	Graduation numbers: Long-term certificates (2 of 6 models); retention (6 of 6 models)		Graduation four-year colleges
Performance accountability measures: Performance funding (PF), performance budgeting (PB)				
PF or not	X	X	X	X
PB or not				
Years since PF adoption	X	X		X
PF indicators mandated or not				
Institutional characteristic control variables				
Enrollments	X undergrad	X		X undergrad
Control	Public	Public	Public	Public
Mission (e.g., Carnegie class)				X two year or four year
Student aid $ per student			X	
Students % Pell				X
Students % minority	X	X	X	X
Students % undergraduates				
HBCU or not				
Students % PT	X	X		X
Selectivity (e.g., mean SAT/ACT)				
Operating revenues	X			

Rutherford & Rabovsky (2014)	Sanford & Hunter (2011)	Shin (2010)	Tandberg & Hillman (2014)	Tandberg, Hillman, & Barakat (2014)	Umbricht, Fernandez, & Ortagus (2015)
Graduation numbers (2 of 6 models)					Number of incoming minority FTE students (2 of 9 models); admission rate (9 of 9 models)
Graduation rate (1 of 6 models); graduation numbers (4 of 6 models); retention rate (3 of 6 models)	Graduation rate			Graduation numbers: AAs (6 of 6 models)	Graduation numbers (9 of 9 models); number of incoming federal aid recipients (5 of 9 models); incoming minority FTE students (7 of 9 models)
X	X	X	X	X	X
		X			
X		X		X	
		X			
X	X				X
Public	Public	Public	Public	Public	
X	X	X			
	X				
X	X				
X					
X					
X	X				
X		X			

(continued)

Table 6.1   (continued)

Study characteristics	Hillman et al. (2015)	Hillman, Tandberg, & Fryar (2015)	Hillman, Tandberg, & Gross (2014)	Larocca & Carr (2012)
State appropriations				
Revenues from state: %	X	X	X	X
Revenues from tuition: %		X		
Tuition level	X	X		X
Federal and state grant aid per FTE		X	X	
Expenditures on instruction			X	
Dorm beds				
Faculty/student ratio				
Faculty % FT				
State or local characteristics control variables				
Public higher education enrollments				
Enrollment in community college sector				
Governance arrangements				
State higher education appropriations				
Average tuition public four years				
Average tuition public two years				
State student aid per FTE				
Average SAT score freshmen				
State population				
Education level of adult population				
State political culture				
State GDP				
Poverty rate				
State or local unemployment rate	X	X		
Labor force size		X		

Note: IPEDS = the Integrated Postsecondary Education Data System survey.

Rutherford & Rabovsky (2014)	Sanford & Hunter (2011)	Shin (2010)	Tandberg & Hillman (2014)	Tandberg, Hillman, & Barakat (2014)	Umbricht, Fernandez, & Ortagus (2015)
					X
X					
	X				
X		X			
X	X	X			
		X			
		X			
X					
			X		
				X	
X					
X		X	X	X	
			X	X	
			X	X	
			X	X	
		X			
			X	X	
			X		
X					
			X		
			X	X	
X		X	X	X	X

Tennessee public university is compared to 12 peer institutions in other states. The analytic technique is a spline linear mixed model that takes into account the nested nature of the data and allows the slope to vary year by year. The control variables are several institutional characteristics: enrollments, Carnegie classification, proportion of students receiving Pell Grants, proportion of students of minority background, proportion part-time, proportion of institutional revenues coming from tuition, and expenditures on instruction. Using a variety of tests, the study finds that performance funding does not have an impact on either one-year retention rates or six-year graduation rates.* One of the key limitations of the Sanford and Hunter (2011) study is that it applies only to Tennessee's original performance funding program, which is much smaller than the PF 2.0 outcomes-based funding program enacted in 2010. That newer program has been analyzed by a third study of our three states.

Hillman et al. (2015) examine the impacts of performance funding in Indiana, Ohio, and Tennessee on baccalaureate graduation numbers through FY 2013 using a difference-in-differences analysis, with year and institution fixed effects and controlling for the local unemployment rate and the following institutional characteristics: enrollment, proportion of students who are white, proportion part-time, tuition level, operating revenue per FTE student, and share of operating expenditure covered by the state. Hillman et al. estimate four models for each state involving different comparison groups. The first involves public four-year institutions in other states in the same geographic region which did not adopt performance funding for public four-year institutions during the same period. The second comparison group involves public four-year institutions in any state that did not adopt performance funding during the same period. The third comparison group includes four-year colleges from other states with performance funding. And the final comparison group involves colleges—from states that never adopted performance funding—that are matched to colleges in Indiana, Ohio, and Tennessee via propensity scores on the pretreatment trend in bachelor's degree production. In 10 out of 12 models (four models for each state), they find that performance funding had no multiyear average impact on graduation numbers.† However, when the authors examine performance on outcomes year

---

* States have mostly shifted toward focusing on graduation numbers rather than graduation rates because the former are more easily calculated and perceived as less easily gamed.

† There was a statistically significant impact in one model for Indiana and a statistically significant negative impact in one model for Ohio. The positive impact for Indiana comes in an equation that compares it to other states that are also members of the Midwest Higher Education

by year, significant impacts begin appearing three or four years after the state PF 2.0 programs were established, particularly in the case of Indiana. This raises the possibility that the performance funding programs—particularly in Indiana and Tennessee—may have lagged effects that would become increasingly pronounced after the programs had fully phased in by FY 2014 or 2015 (see below for more on this point).

STUDIES OF PERFORMANCE FUNDING
OUTSIDE OUR THREE STATES

The relative paucity of multivariate studies of performance funding in our three states prevents us from reaching final conclusions about the impacts of performance funding on student outcomes in Indiana, Ohio, and Tennessee. However, it is clear that the performance funding programs have failed so far to demonstrate that they are effective. Moreover, it is instructive to review the findings from studies of performance funding in other states. For the most part, they find no impact of performance funding. However, there is some scattered evidence of impacts which deserves following up.

Hillman, Tandberg, and Gross (2014) investigate the PF 2.0 program in Pennsylvania. As with the program in our three states, this program—which has operated since 2002—applies to the base state funding for higher education, rather than being a bonus. Hillman et al. (2015) used a difference-in-differences design to compare the change in number of bachelor's degrees conferred by Pennsylvania public four-year institutions with the change in baccalaureate conferrals by similar institutions in non–performance funding states. The authors estimated ten models involving five different comparison groups with lagged and nonlagged variables in each case. Besides controlling for state unemployment rate, they also controlled for several institutional variables: percentage of the student body of minority background, federal and state grants and scholarships per FTE student (as a measure of socioeconomic composition), educational and general expenditures per FTE student, and percentage of operating revenues from state appropriations. They found positive and significant impacts of performance funding in three of their ten models. However, they decided that these three models are not

---

Compact but did not operate performance funding at the time. Hillman et al. (2015) attribute this positive finding to Indiana having a dip in graduation numbers prior to the advent of performance funding; its subsequent rebound would therefore appear to be an effect of performance funding. Hillman et al. (2015) do not provide an explanation of the negative impact for Ohio.

as definitive as four others they had estimated using institutions matched on pretreatment-year patterns. Because performance funding had no impact in those four models, Hillman, Tandberg, and Gross (2014) concluded that PF 2.0 in Pennsylvania has had no impact.

These findings are echoed by other studies that examine the impact of performance funding on public university outcomes in states that—at least for the years covered by the studies—almost all had PF 1.0 programs. The predominant finding is that performance funding does not have a significant impact on four-year graduation numbers and rates for institutions and states (Fryar 2011; Larocca & Carr 2012; Rutherford & Rabovsky, 2014; Shin 2010; Shin & Milton 2004; Tandberg & Hillman, 2014). For example, Rutherford and Rabovsky (2014) examined the impact of performance funding on three institutional outcomes for a national sample of public institutions. Their dependent variables were one-year institutional retention, rate of baccalaureate graduation within six years, and number of baccalaureate graduates divided by number of FTE students. They used a cross-state panel study model with state and year fixed effects. Their control variables included both institutional and state characteristics. The institutional characteristics were total enrollments, the minority percentage of the student body, whether the institution was a historically black college or university, the proportion of students attending part-time, the proportion of all students who were undergraduates, instructional expenditures per student, in-state tuition and fees, proportion of revenues from state appropriations, proportion full-time of the faculty, and institutional selectivity. The state-level variables were state appropriations for higher education per FTE student, state governance structure, state unemployment rate, and state political culture. Rutherford and Rabovsky (2014) found virtually no impacts of performance funding. The only statistically significant impact was for presence of performance funding on number of baccalaureate degrees produced (two of six models), but that impact was negative and disappeared when they added state fixed effects.

Although the multivariate analyses of four-year graduation have not found that performance funding has an impact when one examines average impacts over several years, there is a question about whether performance funding may have a delayed impact, beginning several years after enactment. Tandberg & Hillman (2014) found that performance funding began to have a positive impact on bachelor's degree production seven years after the performance funding programs were established in the few states that had programs lasting that long. They argue that this could be due to the fact that institutions need enough time to react to performance funding demands and make necessary changes and enough time to see students pass on to graduation, which often comes five or six years after college entrance (Tandberg & Hillman, 2014). However, it should be noted that Rutherford and Rabovsky (2014) found that length of time with performance funding has a *negative* impact on graduation rates and numbers which is statistically significant in 5 of 12 models.*

Community college outcomes have not received as much attention as university outcomes, but there are two multivariate studies that estimate the impact of performance funding on student completions at community colleges (Hillman, Tandberg, & Fryar, 2015; Tandberg, Hillman, & Barakat, 2014). Tandberg, Hillman, and Barakat (2014) control for state conditions by including in their regression equations percentage of students enrolled in the community college sector, in-state tuition at public two-year colleges, state aid per public FTE student, state appropriations per public FTE student, state population, poverty rate, and unemployment rate. For the Hillman, Tandberg, and Fryar (2015) study, the controls included two county-level variables (size of county labor force and county unemployment rate) and several institutional variables: percentage enrolled part-time, percentage of students who are white, percentage of revenues from state appropriations, tuition and fees, and federal and state grant aid per FTE student. Using a difference-in-differences fixed effects analysis comparing institutions in states with performance funding to those in various combinations of neighboring states without performance funding,† both Hillman, Tandberg, and Fryar (2015) and Tandberg, Hillman, and Barakat (2014) found that performance funding has no impact, on average, on associate's degree completions. However, both studies did find more localized impacts of interest. Tandberg, Hillman, and Barakat (2014) found that—across six separate equations—four states evidence a significant positive impact of performance funding on associate's degree completion, though they find evidence of a negative impact in six states, mixed impacts in three states, and no impact in six states. Moreover, Hillman, Tandberg, and Fryar (2015) found that performance funding for community colleges in Washington had a delayed impact on associate's degree completion beginning four years after the establishment of the program in 2007. Hillman, Tandberg, and Fryar

* This analysis of length of time was separate from their analysis of the average impact of performance funding.

† Tandberg, Hillman, & Barakat (2014) also included states with state coordinating or planning boards as a comparison group.

(2015) also found a positive impact of Washington's Student Achievement Initiative on short-term certificate awards (less than one year) in comparisons of Washington to three different combinations of states. However, they found a negative impact on the awarding of long-term certificates.

Finally, a few multivariate studies have also been conducted of retention rates, and almost without exception they found no impact of performance funding (Hillman, Tandberg, & Fryar, 2015; Larocca & Carr, 2012; Rutherford & Rabovsky, 2014). Larocca and Carr (2012) found that two-year colleges in states with performance funding had higher one-year retention rates than their counterparts in states without performance funding. However, Hillman, Tandberg, and Fryar (2015) found no impact of performance funding on community college retention in Washington. Moreover, three other studies found no effect of performance funding on retention in public four-year colleges (Larocca & Carr 2012; Rutherford & Rabovsky, 2014; Sanford & Hunter, 2011).

In sum, the multivariate studies conducted to date largely fail to find evidence that performance funding improves retention and graduation. However, there are some interesting findings of more localized effects involving delayed effects on four-year college graduation, impacts on short-term community college certificates, and, in some states, impacts on community college associate's degrees.

It should be noted that these multivariate studies primarily examined PF 1.0 programs, which do not tie much state funding to performance indicators. While PF 2.0 programs have now become much more common, only a few existed before 2007 (see Dougherty & Natow, 2015). Hence, only a few PF 2.0 programs are captured by the existing studies of performance funding impacts through 2010, and they are captured very early in their development. We have only two studies that examine PF 2.0 programs in any depth (Hillman et al., 2015; Hillman, Tandberg, & Gross, 2014). Nonetheless, it is instructive that both find that PF 2.0 programs do not have a significant impact, on average, on student outcomes, although there is some evidence—in time-specific analyses—of delayed effects.

US PERFORMANCE FUNDING OUTCOMES OUTSIDE OF HIGHER EDUCATION

Studies of the impact of performance accountability programs in other US policy areas besides higher education have arrived at mixed results (Heckman et al., 2011; James, 2015; Rothstein, 2008b). Studies of the federal No Child Left Behind program and of similar state K–12 accountability programs in Florida and Texas have found evidence of significant impacts on student achievement, although these impacts are not uniform across subjects and grades (Dee & Jacob, 2011; Deming et al., 2013; Rouse et al., 2007). On the other hand, a study of the impact of the Schoolwide Performance Bonus Program in New York City found no impact on student achievement (Marsh et al., 2011).

Similarly, studies of the performance standards attached to the Job Training Partnership Program have also yielded mixed findings. They find that the program did lead training centers to produce the intended results in terms of improvements in immediate employment and short-term earnings. However, those immediate results are very weakly correlated with earnings and employment 18 and 30 months after completing training (Cragg, 1997; Heckman, Heinrich, & Smith, 2011).

Finally, studies of health care have found that report cards and other performance incentives do spur efforts by hospitals to improve patient outcomes. However, there is also evidence that these efforts may result in adverse selection, where health providers avoid patients less likely to thrive and survive (James, 2015, pp. 3–4; Lake, Kvam, & Gold, 2005, pp. 21–25).

Summary and Conclusions

The descriptive statistics and reports we examined at the beginning of this chapter at first blush present a rosy picture of the impact of performance funding in our three states. Following the initiation of PF 2.0 programs in 2009 and 2010, graduation numbers increased at higher rates than enrollments.

However, these descriptive data do not control for many other factors that might be increasing graduation numbers apart from performance funding. Multivariate analyses allow us to compare student outcomes in our three states with those in other states without performance funding, while also controlling for a host of factors affecting student completion other than performance funding. These include variations in enrollments, changes in tuition and student aid levels, changes in the state of the economy, and so forth.* When these factors are in good part accounted for in careful multivariate analyses, the researchers largely fail to find a significant positive impact of performance funding in higher education.

To be sure, most of these multivariate studies are predominantly analyzing PF 1.0 programs rather than the potentially more powerful PF 2.0 programs in our

---

* What these studies do not control for, however, is the impact of state and foundation initiatives to improve retention and graduation through reform of developmental education, course articulation and transfer, and so forth. For more on these companion efforts, see chapter 5.

three states. Still, three recent multivariate studies of PF 2.0 programs (Hillman et al., 2015; Hillman, Tandberg, & Gross, 2014; Umbricht, Fernandez, & Ortagus, 2015) fail to find significant impacts. However, some of these studies (Hillman et al., 2015; Hillman & Tandberg, 2014) do find that performance funding may have delayed impacts that do not appear for several years.

The lack of evidence clearly tying performance funding to better outcomes raises the question whether the lack of impact stems from obstacles institutions and campus personnel encounter in responding effectively to performance funding (Dougherty & Reddy, 2013; Hillman, Tandberg, & Gross, 2014; Tandberg, Hillman, & Barakat, 2014). If so, what forms would such obstacles take? In chapter 7 we turn to analyzing the obstacles higher education institutions may encounter in effectively responding to the demands of performance funding programs.

Obstacles to Effective Response

A s with any policy, policymakers must be concerned with whether there are obstacles that may hinder performance funding from being successfully implemented.* As seen in the previous chapter, even the most careful multivariate analyses of the impacts of performance funding find little or no impact (see chapter 6). This suggests that colleges may be encountering major obstacles to responding effectively to performance funding (Dougherty & Reddy, 2013; Hillman, Tandberg, & Gross, 2014; Tandberg, Hillman, & Barakat, 2014).

This chapter examines the obstacles respondents at 18 colleges and universities in Ohio, Tennessee, and Indiana reported as interfering with the capacity of their institutions to respond effectively to the performance funding programs. We first discuss the obstacles our respondents most often mentioned: student-body composition, inappropriate performance funding metrics, and insufficient institutional capacity, among others. Then, we evaluate how perceptions of these obstacles vary across states and types of institutions.

To illuminate the potential obstacles institutions might encounter during the implementation of performance funding, we draw on the research literature on performance funding implementation and impacts, performance management in government agencies, policy design theory, policy implementation theory, and principal–agent theory (see chapter 2). The research literature on performance funding in higher education and performance management in government alerts us immediately to certain possible obstacles to the effective operation of perfor-

---

Lara Pheatt and Hana Lahr took the lead in writing the report on which this chapter draws (see Pheatt et al., 2014).

* There may be instances when the successful implementation of performance funding is not of concern to policymakers. If they feel that performance funding is simply a symbolic reform meant to convey that state policymakers are taking accountability demands seriously and "getting tough" on higher education, then it may not matter whether performance funding really does work. For more on the symbolic element of performance funding, see Moynihan (2008, pp. 11–12).

mance funding. Meanwhile, the other bodies of research deepen our awareness of how those and other obstacles operate. Policy design theory suggests that we must consider obstacles not just to the operation of financial incentives but also to state leaders' efforts to communicate their goals for performance funding and communicate how well institutions are meeting those goals. Furthermore, policy implementation and principal–agent theory suggest that we carefully examine the perspectives of both policy framers and local implementers. In other words, we must look for obstacles from both a top-down and a bottom-up perspective—that is, as arising on the one hand from inadequacies of communication, resource provision, and expertise and arising on the other hand from differences in understandings, goals, and interests within the higher education policy subsystem.

Although public colleges and universities experienced performance funding in different ways, our respondents were in broad agreement on the main factors that hindered their institutions from responding effectively to the state perfor-

Table 7.1   Summary of Reports of Obstacles to Performance Funding Effectiveness (Number of Individuals Reporting)

Obstacle	Number of individuals	Community colleges with reports (out of 9)	Universities with reports (out of 9)
Student-body composition	63	9	7
Inappropriate performance funding measures	61	9	8
Insufficient institutional capacity	42	8	6
Institutional resistance	38	8	7
Insufficient state funding of higher education	36	7	7
Insufficient knowledge of performance funding	30	8	5
Instability in funding, indicators, and measures	21	5	4
Insufficient state funding of performance funding	8	2	6
Decrease in enrollment	4	3	1
Other	12	3	6
Total number of reports	315		
Total unduplicated number of individuals reporting	163		

Note: The total number of unduplicated respondents is the number of respondents who mentioned one or more obstacles. It is lower than the total number of reports because some respondents mentioned more than one obstacle. The data for this table do not include the 1979 program in Tennessee and the 2013 revision of the program in Ohio.

mance funding programs. Respondents at universities and community colleges indicated that student-body composition, inappropriate performance funding measures, insufficient institutional capacity, institutional resistance, inadequate state funding of higher education, and insufficient knowledge of performance funding made it difficult for their respective institutions to respond effectively to the demands of the performance funding programs. The following sections elaborate on the most frequently mentioned obstacles (obstacles reported by 30 or more respondents), as summarized in table 7.1.

Student-Body Composition

University and community college respondents widely reported that features of their institution's student-body composition inhibited its ability to improve on the state performance funding indicators. Sixty-three respondents (over one-third of those responding to our obstacles question) cited student-body composition as an obstacle for their institution. This includes high numbers of students who are not prepared for college-level coursework, are not seeking degrees, are from low-income families or are struggling financially, or are only attending part-time (see table 7.2). In the discussion below, we focus on the top three obstacles related to student-body composition.

Table 7.2   Student-Body Composition as an Obstacle (Number of Individuals Reporting)

Obstacle	Community colleges	Universities	Total number of individuals	Community colleges with reports (out of 9)	Universiti with repoi (out of 9
Underprepared students	25	5	30	7	3
Non-degree-seeking students	17	1	18	8	1
Low-SES students	12	0	12	4	0
Fear of debt / financial burden	1	6	7	1	5
Part-time status	4	2	6	2	1
Resistance to higher education	2	0	2	2	0
Total number of reports	61	14	75	9	7
Total unduplicated number of individuals reporting	51	12	63		

Note: SES = socioeconomic status. The total number of unduplicated respondents reporting is the number of respondents who mentioned one or more obstacles related to student-body composition. It is lower than the total number of reports because some respondents mentioned more than one obstacle. The data for this table do not include the 1979 program in Tennessee and the 2013 revision of the program in Ohio.

INADEQUATE PREPARATION FOR COLLEGE

Across the institutions, we received frequent reports that many students were not academically prepared to do college-level coursework and that this interfered with the capacity of institutions to respond effectively to performance funding. This is because performance funding rewards colleges based on student progression and completion, but these are made difficult by having many underprepared students. An Ohio community college dean noted, "I think our student population comes in incredibly unprepared and without the foundational skills, without what would be considered college-level reading, writing, and comprehension. So quite honestly . . . they just don't have the skills—whether it be that they never learned how to study in high school, whether it be they got passed through high school—but they just don't know how to attack college and the level of work that's required in a college class." A senior administrator at a community college in Indiana echoed this concern: "There's huge numbers of students coming to us and sometimes scoring a 12 on the ACT, for example. It's almost impossible to remediate someone when they come to us as an adult and they're lacking skills to that level."

Although lack of student readiness for college was more often mentioned at community colleges, some university respondents were also concerned with student preparation. A Tennessee university senior administrator stated, "We're constrained in many ways by the products coming out of the high schools. . . . I mean, it's scary stuff, to think that we're somehow going to be able to take a student coming out of some of these high schools and do what we're supposed to do, and what we need to do."

Concern that serving high percentages of academically unprepared students hinders institutions' performance on state metrics is not unwarranted. Multiple studies find that the precollege academic preparation of students is a major predictor of college retention and graduation (Astin & Oseguera, 2005; Cabrera, Burkum, & La Nasa, 2005; Titus, 2004). Moreover, a study of the Texas performance funding program found that underprepared students—whether GED holders or those scoring more than one level down in placement tests for math proficiency—would bring institutions significantly less money from the state performance funding program than would students who are better prepared (McKinney & Hagedorn, 2015). Because of this, there is the danger, as we will discuss in chapter 8, that broad-access institutions may be tempted to reduce the number of less prepared students they enroll.

NON-DEGREE-SEEKING STUDENTS

Performance funding programs emphasize graduation. Yet, many of our respondents, particularly at community colleges, pointed out that a sizable number of their students do not plan to complete a certificate or degree. This perception is backed by existing research. Among two-year college entrants surveyed in their first year as part of the 2003–4 Beginning Postsecondary Students survey, 16% stated that they had no plans to secure a degree or certificate (Berkner & Choy, 2008, p. 7).

Our respondents pointed to various reasons why students might not be seeking a degree, including that they were experimenting with education and had not decided on a degree or that they wanted vocational training that did not require a certificate or degree. A senior community college administrator in Tennessee said, "Someone might decide that at their particular job, it would really help them if they took the beginning course of accounting. They might just take that one course; that's all they need. That's the difficulty in a community college, is assuming that everyone who comes here will get an associate's degree. . . . Another example is, we get students who are going to university, and they're home for the summer, and they just want to pick up one class. I just [find that] the funding formula totally misses the purpose of a community college."

At other times, the issue was that students wanted a baccalaureate degree but not an associate's degree. In this case, if the state performance funding program did not reward community colleges for the number of students who transfer to a four-year institution, whether or not they get an associate's degree, the college would not be fully rewarded for successfully preparing students for transfer. We found that this was largely the case in Indiana.* A community college faculty member from Indiana noted, "Some of our students will transfer to a four-year. We have a lot of those that are happening, because it's cheaper to come here to get your gen eds [general education courses] out of the way and then go to your four-year. I think they should take that into consideration, especially since . . . the formula is based on that, on completion."

---

* The state had a transfer incentive in place only for the 2007–9 and 2009–11 biennia and dropped it afterward (Indiana Commission for Higher Education, 2013a). Ohio and Tennessee rewarded community colleges for the numbers they transferred (see appendix A).

LOWER SOCIOECONOMIC STATUS AND ITS
FINANCIAL BURDENS

Regardless of whether the institution was a community college or four-year university, institutions noted that serving high percentages of students of low socioeconomic status (SES) made it difficult for them to do well on the formula. These concerns are realistic; there is evidence that low-income students are less likely to stay in college, transfer, and graduate (Astin & Oseguera, 2005; Cabrera, Burkum, & La Nasa, 2005; Dougherty & Kienzl, 2006; Titus, 2004). At the same time, it should be noted that all three states weight student outcomes for low-income students more highly than for more advantaged students (see appendix A).*

Low-income students may fare less well than higher-income students because they are less likely to be prepared to meet college academic standards. A senior administrator at an Indiana community college noted, "A lot of our Pell Grant students are first-generation students, or they're low-income students, or they're minority students. Some of them come in the door at a disadvantage, and they may need remediation, or they don't understand what the rigors of college are, or they've had bad experiences academically in the past that really has shaken their self-confidence. So, I see a lot of these students come in my door. They're frustrated. They're upset. They don't understand what it means to go to college."

In addition, low-income students are more likely to encounter financial barriers to college persistence (ACT, 2012; Astin & Oseguera, 2005; Bailey & Dynarski, 2011). Even with financial aid, many low-SES students still find it hard to cover the full costs of higher education, including tuition, transportation, books, and living expenses (Monaghan & Goldrick-Rab, 2016).† As a result, they more often have to work while enrolled, and this impedes their completion. A university senior administrator in Tennessee explained, "It may be harder to move a first-generation college student who is working three jobs through the program as effectively as someone . . . who's not a first-generation college student and who has the financial means to be able to attend college by working one part-time job or something."

---

* However, it is not clear whether this additional weighting is enough to overcome the disincentive colleges encounter from enrolling low-income and therefore often less prepared students. See chapters 8 and 9 for more on this.

† And if the financial aid was available in the form of loans, several respondents noted that low-income students were reluctant to take them out, for fear of accumulating debts they might not be able to pay off (authors' interviews; see also Heller, 2013; Scott-Clayton, 2012).

In sum, from an institutional perspective, serving many low-income students takes greater institutional effort, and in the end student outcomes may still be less good than those of institutions that have fewer low-income students. This presents institutions with the temptation—societally undesirable but institutionally attractive—of restricting their intake of less prepared and low-income students in order to increase their retention and graduation numbers. In the concluding chapter we discuss how states might design their performance funding programs so as to counteract this temptation.

Inappropriate Performance Funding Measures

The second most commonly reported general obstacle was that performance funding measures did not always align well with institutional missions, making it difficult for institutions to perform well on the state metrics. Sixty-one respondents (over one-third of those responding to our question) at nine of nine community colleges and eight of nine universities mentioned such an obstacle (see table 7.1).*

Some university respondents, particularly at the more selective universities in Indiana, were frustrated because they felt they had little room to improve and therefore could not achieve large gains. For these institutions, there was a ceiling effect on the amount of funds they could earn for improvement. A senior administrator in Indiana argued, "In setting the measures, it doesn't take into account or reward when a campus is doing very well. . . . [The University of Indiana at] Bloomington has one of the [highest], if not the highest, completion rates in the state. It's a very good place. They have good students who are full-time, and they are doing very well. Bloomington got exactly zero. . . . [The performance funding program] only rewards change in the positive direction. What if you achieve some positive things and stay there? It doesn't do anything there."

Other university respondents, particularly those at broad-access institutions, thought that the performance funding formula did not take into account the characteristics of their student bodies. These university respondents explained that their students were less academically prepared and that their institution's progress could not be fairly compared, without qualification, to that of more selective, high-capacity universities. For example, a faculty member at an Indiana university stated, "I think it's a one-size-fits-all model. And the problem with that

---

* In addition, there may be metrics that do not pose obstacles to institutions demonstrating their effectiveness but are nonetheless still inappropriate. We will return to this point in the concluding chapter.

is that each of the state institutions serves a different student population. So, you know, in our case, I think that the students that get missed are the nontraditional students. At our institution, they're the ones that may take five, six, or seven years to complete their degree, because they're working, or they don't have the financial aid to do the types of things they need to do to be a full-time student."

This concern that the performance funding formula did not sufficiently take into account the particular situation of broad-access institutions was particularly strong among our community college respondents. They often perceived that the performance funding formulas treated community college students the same as university students, even though their goals and other characteristics are frequently not the same as those of students at four-year institutions. For example, while a sizable number of students at community colleges do not intend to get a certificate or degree, this is true of a much smaller number of four-year university entrants. Among students entering higher education in AY 2003–4 and surveyed that year as part of the Beginning Postsecondary Students Longitudinal Study, 16% of two-year entrants but only 6% of four-year entrants stated that they did not intend to earn a certificate or degree (Berkner & Choy, 2008, p. 7; see also Hoachlander, Sikora, & Horn, 2003). From the perspective of our community college respondents, asking their students to secure the same outcomes as four-year college students was unrealistic. They noted that the state performance metrics, with their emphasis on graduation, did not provide for students who did not intend to get a degree but rather were interested only in taking certain courses or acquiring particular skills. A high-level community college administrator in Tennessee stated, "The students that come to community college may not all be intending to earn an associate's degree. They may be coming to upgrade some of their skills as incumbent workers. There may be some students that are coming back to retool in certain areas. So a completion agenda may not always be first and foremost for a community college student the same way it would be for a four-year university student."

Community college students also differ from four-year students for reasons other than graduation goals. These students may have life circumstances that distinguish them from the average four-year college student, and these differences may not be well captured by a state emphasis on on-time graduation. A senior administrator in Indiana observed,

The state [is] not understanding the mission of the community college, as compared to four-year universities. And they evaluate us on the same plane, or

they try to. For example, people in a community college have a different mission. They may be married, they may be working, and they may be laid off. . . .
It could be all of those things in life that can screw you up. Now, why is that
different than a four-year college? Because a four-year college has more of a
captive audience when they walk in the door. You have a group of freshmen
who are going to enter this year; they are all out of high school. . . . We should
not be judged the same.

State policy designers in Indiana, Ohio, and Tennessee were aware of the
importance of matching performance funding indicators and measures to institutional missions (Dougherty et al., 2014a). As such, the performance funding
metrics were rather different for universities and community colleges, particularly
in Ohio and Tennessee. For example, in both states, the performance indicators
for community colleges, but not those for universities, included completion of
developmental education and attainment of certificates. In addition, Tennessee
further differentiated its metrics by giving them different weights based on an
institution's Carnegie classification (Indiana Commission for Higher Education,
2013b; Ohio Board of Regents, 2015a, 2015b; Tennessee Higher Education Commission, 2012b, 2014a).

Moreover, state policy designers were aware that student-body composition
could affect how well colleges and universities would perform on the state
metrics for performance funding. To make up for this, all three states weighted
completions by less advantaged students more heavily than for other students.
Indiana has a low-income degree incentive (Indiana Commission on Higher Education, 2013a). Ohio weights course and degree completions by whether students
are at risk, defined in terms of varying combinations of family income, race/eth-
nicity, and age (Ohio Board of Regents, 2015a, 2015b). And Tennessee has extra
weighting for adult learners and low-income students on indicators for credit accumulation and degree production (Tennessee Higher Education Commission,
2012b, 2014a).

That said, the comments above from our respondents suggest that the states
need to do more to tailor performance funding indicators to the circumstances
of students entering community colleges and broad-access universities and communicate these nuances more effectively. The issue still remains of how well the
state performance funding programs take into account the large number of
students entering community colleges and broad-access public universities
who are less likely to progress and to graduate because they are less prepared

academically, less well-off financially, and less committed to securing a degree.* We will return to this question in the concluding chapter.

Insufficient Institutional Capacity

Research on policy design and implementation highlights the role that capacity building plays in successful policy implementation (see chapter 2). Despite this, the states have not done much to build up the institutional capacity of their institutions to respond to performance funding (see chapter 3). Hence, it is not surprising that 42 respondents (26% of those answering our obstacles question) stated that insufficient institutional capacity was a major obstacle to their institution being able to respond effectively to performance funding (see table 7.1). Table 7.3 lists the organizational-capacity obstacles reported to us.

The greatest capacity issue was inadequate capacity for institutional research (IR). Institutions often did not have sufficient personnel and the right analytic skills to collect, analyze, and use data to make changes that would improve their performance on the funding formula. In our study, 19 individuals at seven community colleges and five universities reported too little IR capability as an obstacle to effectively responding to performance funding.† A Tennessee community college dean noted, "Any time you talk about implementing any programs or additional assessment . . . anything of that nature . . . [it] requires resources. And our IR department is woefully understaffed." Similarly, in Indiana, a dean at a community college observed that it was very difficult to keep track of students who go on to four-year colleges, making it hard for community colleges to know whether they are succeeding in terms of advancing their students: "We've had trouble tracking students who go on to a four-year school. It's hard for us to get solid numbers."

Other forms of insufficient institutional capacity, including inadequate IT, a shortage of qualified staff and faculty, limited student services, small institu-

---

* This raises the point about the need to make performance funding metrics more appropriate to varying institutional missions. This point, which we will take up in the concluding chapter, has been forcefully raised by Tiffany Jones with particular reference to minority-serving institutions (Jones, 2014, 2015).

† Perhaps this capacity issue leads the list, in part, because we asked our respondents specifically whether their institutions had sufficient IR or IT capacity to support improvement. Yet previous research on performance funding has also identified insufficient IR capacity as a barrier to institutions' ability to respond effectively to performance funding (Dougherty & Reddy, 2013; see also Light, 2004).

Table 7.3   Insufficient Institutional Capacity as an Obstacle
(Number of Individuals Reporting)

Obstacle	Number of reports at community colleges	Number of reports at universities	Total number of reports	Community colleges with reports (out of 9)	Universities with reports (out of 9)
Inadequate IR capacity	11	8	19	7	5
Shortage of staff/faculty	5	2	7	3	2
Small institution	6	0	6	2	0
Limited student services	3	0	3	2	1
Inadequate IT capacity	2	1	3	1	1
Too much to respond to	2	1	3	1	2
Need more time to make changes	3	1	4	2	0
Other	1	2	3	3	1
Total number of reports	33	15	48	8	6
Total unduplicated number of individuals reporting	27	15	42		

Note: The total number of unduplicated respondents reporting is the number of respondents who mentioned one or more obstacles related to institutional capacity. It is lower than the total number of reports because some respondents mentioned more than one obstacle. The data for this table do not include the 1979 program in Tennessee and the 2013 revision of the program in Ohio.

tional size, and inability to perform additional tasks necessary to improve in the time allotted, also posed challenges for the institutions in our study. These various capacity issues affected all institutions to some extent, but the institutions that reported obstacles involving the size of their institution or shortage of qualified staff and faculty were primarily in rural locations, where recruiting strong and competitive faculty and staff proved difficult.

As seen in chapter 3, our states did too little to anticipate and mitigate institutional needs for greater capacity to respond to performance funding. The states did not carefully envision the organizational learning and other demands that colleges would face when responding to performance funding and determine what kinds of capacity-building assistance they would require. The states did make some effort to foster discussions among institutions about best practices in academic and student support policies. However, with the partial exception of Ohio, we found no evidence of dedicated state efforts to build up the IR and IT capacity of institutions. None of the three states provided funding or technical assistance to allow colleges to enlarge their IR and IT capacities and improve their understanding of how to use data analysis and organizational reflection to improve student outcomes. The vast majority of administrators and faculty we interviewed at 18 public colleges and universities in the three states rated the extent of the states' effort to build up institutional capacity as low or nonexistent (see chapter 3).

Insufficient State Funding of Higher Education

Thirty-six respondents (22% of those responding to our obstacles question) brought up insufficient state funding of higher education as an obstacle to improving on the state performance funding metrics. During the Great Recession and for several years after, state appropriations for higher education dropped sharply, which made it difficult for institutions to respond to demands for improved performance. In Indiana, the total operating appropriation for public higher education declined from $1.282 billion for the 2008–9 biennium to $1.215 billion for the 2012–13 biennium, a drop of 5% (Indiana Commission for Higher Education, 2013a). In Ohio, the state appropriation for the State Share of Instruction declined 10% between FY 2009 and FY 2013, from $1.953 billion to $1.751 billion (Ohio Board of Regents, 2010, 2013c). And in Tennessee, state appropriations dropped from $775 million in FY 2010 to $725 million in FY 2011 (a drop of 6%), and they did not recover until FY 2014 (Tennessee Higher Education Commission, 2014b, p. 82).

Respondents reported that budget cuts made it hard for institutions to fund new programs to support student improvement.* Community colleges, in particular, did not have adequate resources to improve their students' performance. For example, a community college senior administrator in Ohio told us that inadequate funding made it very difficult to strengthen programmatic offerings that are essential to the education of at-risk students: "The challenge is at community college, how do you get at-risk students to persist and complete? . . . That requires beefing up of some support services. . . . You need to do dev. ed. [developmental education] differently, not as a block before they enter the college courses. You need to do some modeling where they do it simultaneously with college courses. How do you get at-risk students to move through and persist and complete? That takes some funding. The current funding models do not allow for that."

Along similar lines, in Indiana, a senior-level administrator at a community college remarked, "We get no funding in Indiana for remediation. Yet, well over

---

* Even if state appropriations were not cut, institutional revenues per FTE student could drop if state appropriations do not keep pace with rapidly rising enrollments. This happened during the Great Recession (State Higher Education Executive Officers, 2013).

50 percent of our students take one or more remedial courses. You know, we get no additional funding to do that, at a cost to Ivy Tech of about $40 million a year, above and beyond what tuition and fees cover."

In fact, respondents reported that their colleges sometimes had to support new programs by cannibalizing other ones, as explained by a Tennessee administrator: "We have robbed Peter to pay Paul. We're doing all we can with what we have. We have definitely looked at where our resources were, and what might work better to increase student success, and areas where we might be able to do a little less to be able to put the money where we need to make the funding formula, to increase student success, not to just necessarily increase funding, but so we can reach our goals that we want to make."

Shriveling state funding also impaired university response to growing demands for better student outcomes. A senior administrator at an Indiana university said that the more at-risk students colleges serve, the more services they need to provide; however, with dwindling revenue streams, it becomes very challenging to do this: "We have a heavy teaching load, a heavy advising load, a heavy service load. . . . I think in terms of the implementation, our resource reality is a fundamental challenge in terms of doing some of the things that would help us to do even better under the performance funding formula. Again, I'll go back to that reality that when you have 30% of your student population that is first-generation, one in four students is 25 years old or older, you need certain special services. That takes money."

Institutional Resistance to Performance Funding

The research literature on organizational change and innovation finds that it is a difficult process, and the process of colleges adapting to performance funding is no exception. A major source of difficulty is institutional resistance. Thirty-eight respondents (23% of those answering our question) identified institutional resistance as an obstacle to institutions improving their performance on the state funding metrics (see table 7.4). The majority of resistance was attributed to faculty, but, as we discuss below, these reports need to be treated with some care.

In Ohio and to a small degree in Tennessee, a common perception was that faculty resisted performance funding because it threatened their professional autonomy. Faculty resistance was interpreted in varied ways by different respondents. Mid-level and senior administrators argued that it was mostly about faculty hideboundedness and resistance to change. One mid-level nonacademic administrator in Tennessee succinctly summarized this sentiment: "Obviously,

Table 7.4   Institutional Resistance as an Obstacle (Number of Individuals Reporting)

Obstacle	Number of reports at community colleges	Number of reports at universities	Total number of reports	Community colleges with reports (out of 9)	Universities with reports (out of 9)
Faculty resistance	12	11	23	7	5
General resistance	7	9	16	5	5
Resistance from senior administrators	0	1	1	0	1
Total number of reports	19	21	40	8	7
Total unduplicated number of individuals reporting at least one obstacle	18	20	38		

Note: The total number of unduplicated respondents reporting is the number of respondents who mentioned one or more obstacles related to institutional resistance. It is lower than the total number of reports because some respondents mentioned more than one obstacle. The data for this table do not include the 1979 program in Tennessee and the 2013 revision of the program in Ohio.

it's a change, so everybody is scared. Nobody likes change. It's the worst possible thing in the world." While this sentiment was more common among administrators, there were faculty members who agreed. A faculty member in Tennessee stated, "People don't like change. I mean, really, beyond that, it's our own selfishness, our own desire to maintain that strict control of our classrooms and what we do, and stay-out-of-my-way type of attitude. But, I mean, really, the holdback is getting people to buy in."

Another reason stated for faculty resistance was that—given the emphasis of performance funding programs on course and degree completion—teachers would have to spend more time advising students in order to get students to complete a degree or certificate on time, which would negatively impact faculty time for research, teaching, and other activities. A mid-level university administrator in Ohio noted, "I think faculty do [have some] resistance because it takes more time for the faculty. Faculty advise the students the last two or three years. . . . It does take away time from faculty."

However, other respondents had a less jaundiced view of faculty resistance. They suggested that faculty resisted more out of concerns about maintaining academic standards. A mid-level academic administrator in Tennessee argued that faculty feared that they would be forced to resort to grade inflation: "I'm closer to faculty than I am to other groups. And, again, the reason for their objections is because they're concerned that they're going to be expected to pass more students in order to raise the numbers." We heard much the same from a mid-level university administrator in Ohio: "I mean, so there goes your rigor, there goes your standard, and there goes your learning outcomes. So that is a concern—like 'Sure, I can get everybody to complete a course; I'll just give out grades.'" (For more on this concern about a weakening of academic standards, see chapter 8.)

Additionally, we heard about faculty and staff feeling underappreciated in their efforts to help students. A senior administrator at an Ohio community college observed, "I think the problem that you run into in higher education, [from] faculty members to administrative staff, is they see the work that's done on a daily basis, and I think the feeling you get from them is there's no recognition of that, that the more you see in the public, in the media, that higher education seems to be almost a fraudulent experience now—that, for some reason, there's the whole notion of, well, it's just a money sucker, and that's all there's any aspiration to. These are individuals who are professional educators."

This feeling of alienation is tied in part to a perception that the performance funding formula had been imposed top-down. For example, one mid-level Indiana academic administrator said, "Well, I do think the top-down thing is bad because it doesn't get buy-in from the stakeholders."

Performance funding advocates in Indiana, Ohio, and Tennessee were concerned that performance funding could encounter strong institutional resistance if it were accompanied by big shifts in funding or by the use of indicators that were perceived as unfair to institutions (Dougherty et al., 2014a; see also Lederman, 2009). In order to prevent large funding fluctuations, the states decided to phase in their new PF 2.0 programs gradually (Dougherty et al., 2014a; see also Fingerhut, 2012; Ohio Board of Regents, 2009a, 2009b). Policymakers in Tennessee opted to phase in performance funding over three years in order to give campuses an opportunity to see how the program would work before encountering the brunt of the new system (Tennessee Higher Education Commission, 2011b). Ohio included a "stop-loss" provision that limited how much funding colleges might lose from one year to the next during the first few years of its new performance funding program (Fingerhut, 2012; Ohio Board of Regents, 2009a, 2009b). Finally, Indiana's policymakers chose to increase the percentage of funding attached to the program gradually (Indiana Commission for Higher Education, 2011b; Stokes, 2011). Despite these efforts, it is clear that there is noticeable resistance to performance funding in our three states which policymakers may want to address.

Insufficient Knowledge of Performance Funding

The sheer complexity of the performance funding formulas was often viewed as a hindrance to effective institutional response to the funding policy. Thirty respondents (18% of those answering our question) identified this obstacle. A mid-level community college administrator in Ohio noted,

> I can honestly say that over those probably 10 years where I have been working in higher education in Ohio, the formula for funding higher education, in Ohio is so complex and difficult to understand that I think people just naturally migrate away from trying to explain to people. Business and finance officers understand how it works. There's some people in institutional research who might understand and some other people around the state, but it's just so difficult to understand all of the different models that go into determining how funding is allocated that I think it's a combination that people just don't want to have to because it is so complicated.

Similarly, a faculty member at a Tennessee university observed, "The formula is so complex that it's almost like you can keep the money from going out of one pocket, you can stop the hole there, and the hole happens in a different pocket. It's so complex that you can do very well on one measure and spend a lot of effort there and then, by doing that, not do well on another measure and wind up losing money."

The advocates and designers of performance funding were aware that insufficient knowledge could hinder its effectiveness (Dougherty et al., 2014a). Hence, state officials took pains to spread the word about the goals and desired methods of performance funding through meetings with local officials, reports, e-mails, and coverage in local news media. However, these information dissemination efforts were focused on senior college administrators and less often reached faculty and mid-level administrators (see chapter 3). As a result, we have evidence that those efforts failed to effectively reach many mid-level administrators and faculty. Even if they were *aware* of the performance funding program, they often did not *understand* it in any detail (see chapter 3). For example, a mid-level academic administrator at an Indiana community college stated, "The communication and actual details and purpose and all those things sometimes are not communicated as well as they should be. It leaves people to speculate or guess, and that's not good. I think they sent out email notices and a few mentions in meetings, but I do think we're lacking of having a real focused effort toward filling people in on what really needs to happen."

It could be argued that it is not important that faculty and mid-level administrators understand performance funding; it is enough that senior administrators do. However, this misses the fact that higher education institutions have a culture of shared governance in which faculty not only are the main suppliers of the essential professional services but also play a key role in the governance of the institution (Rhoades, 1998; Schmidtlein & Berdahl, 2011). Hence, their understanding and appreciation of performance funding are key to whether it will work as effectively as intended. Hence, in the concluding chapter, we suggest actions that states can take to improve the involvement and knowledge of faculty and staff in the design and implementation of performance funding.

Variations within Our Main Findings

In this section we investigate the variations to be found within the main patterns described above. We find substantial differences between states and types of institutions in the number and kind of obstacles reported.

DIFFERENCES BY STATE

For the most part, respondents in each of the states agreed on the biggest obstacles to improving on their performance. However, there were some interesting variations by state (see table 7.5). To begin, Tennessee had considerably fewer respondents mentioning obstacles (37) than did Indiana (65) and Ohio (61). Part of this may be due to the fact that Tennessee has had the longest history of performance funding, so more of the kinks may have been worked out and college respondents may have become more comfortable with performance funding. Also, our data suggest that Tennessee college administrators and faculty were more aware of and better understood the performance funding policy in their state than their counterparts in the other states, which would lessen reports of insufficient knowledge as an obstacle (see chapter 3). The perceived obstacles Tennessee respondents most often cited tended to focus on contextual or local challenges instead of challenges that are inherent to the policy design. Student-body composition is a good example of this.

In terms of specific obstacles, Ohio respondents more often mentioned obstacles related to insufficient knowledge and institutional resistance. What makes Ohio different from the other states? Two possible factors may be at work. From a top-down implementation perspective, the less complete communication from policy framers in Ohio versus Tennessee (see chapter 3) may have left local actors in Ohio more confused about or resistant to the policy design. And from the bottom-up perspective, there may have been more local resistance due to

Table 7.5   Reports of Obstacles by State (Number of Individuals Reporting)

Obstacles	IN	OH	TN	Total
Student composition	23	17	23	63
Inappropriate performance funding measures	31	20	10	61
Insufficient institutional capacity	8	18	16	42
Institutional resistance	7	18	13	38
Insufficient state funding of higher education	13	16	7	36
Insufficient knowledge of and responsibility for performance funding	6	17	7	30
Instability in funding, indicators, and measures	15	5	1	21
Insufficient state funding of performance funding	3	4	1	8
Decrease in enrollment	0	3	1	4
Other	5	6	1	12
Total number of reports	111	124	80	315
Total unduplicated number of individuals reporting at least one obstacle	65	61	37	163

Note: The total number of unduplicated respondents reporting is the number of respondents who mentioned one or more obstacles. It is lower than the total number of reports because some respondents mentioned more than one obstacle. The data for this table do not include the 1979 program in Tennessee and the 2013 revision of the program in Ohio.

divergent local institutional values because of Ohio's tradition of decentralized higher education governance (authors' interviews; Moden & Williford, 2002). However, we also attribute some of the heightened response from Ohio to the fact that our interviews occurred around the time that the 2009 formula was revised in 2013. Ohio's revised formula ties considerably higher percentages of community college funding to outcomes and likely made our community college interviewees more alert to and uncomfortable with performance funding than their counterparts in the other states.

In comparison to Tennessee and Ohio, Indiana had the fewest reports of resistance to the performance funding program. However, it did have the highest number of reports of obstacles related to inappropriate measures and to instability in funding, indicators, and measures. This is probably due to the fact that the state indicators in Indiana have changed repeatedly over the years (Indiana Commission for Higher Education, 2013a). A senior administrator at an Indiana university discussed how difficult it is to keep up with the changes in the performance indicators:* "It's very difficult from year to year to plan what our campus

* Recent research in public administration has pointed to the negative impact of funding instability on the effective functioning of public agencies (see Andersen & Mortensen, 2009).

budget will be or income from the state. They did change the criteria from fiscal year 2012–13 to 14–15. At one point, there was a dual credit for completion. So the campus really put an emphasis on dual credit for high school students . . . and then they changed the funding formula."

DIFFERENCES BY INSTITUTIONAL TYPE

Given the different missions and structures of community colleges and universities, it is no surprise that respondents at these two types of institutions report different amounts and types of obstacles. Respondents at community colleges more often reported obstacles (87 individuals) than did those at universities (76 individuals). Moreover, our respondents at community colleges more often perceived student-body composition, insufficient institutional capacity, and insufficient knowledge as hindrances to performance, while the university respondents focused more on inappropriate performance funding measures and instability in the metrics as hindrances (see table 7.6).

Table 7.6   Reports of Obstacles by Type of Institution
(Number of Individuals Reporting)

Obstacle	Community colleges	Universities	Total
Student composition	51	12	63
Inappropriate performance funding measures	24	37	61
Insufficient institutional capacity	27	15	42
Institutional resistance	18	20	38
Insufficient state funding of higher education	19	17	36
Insufficient knowledge of and responsibility for performance funding	19	11	30
Instability in funding, indicators, and measures	5	16	21
Insufficient state funding of performance funding	3	5	8
Decrease in enrollment	3	1	4
Other	3	9	12
Total number of reports	172	143	315
Total unduplicated number of individuals reporting at least one obstacle	87	76	163

Note: The total number of unduplicated respondents reporting is the number of respondents who mentioned one or more obstacles. It is lower than the total number of reports because some respondents mentioned more than one obstacle. The data for this table do not include the 1979 program in Tennessee and the 2013 revision of the program in Ohio.

The focus on student-body composition by our community college respondents is to be expected. Community colleges enroll more academically underprepared and economically disadvantaged students than do universities. Among students surveyed as part of the 2003–4 Beginning Postsecondary Students study, 43% of two-year college entrants had parents with a high school degree or less, compared with 23% of four-year college entrants. Moreover, among the two-year college entrants who had taken the SAT or ACT, 42% scored in the lowest quartile, compared with 13% of four-year college entrants (Berkner & Choy, 2008, pp. 10–11). It is the community colleges' mission to help these students, but open-door enrollment does make it harder for community colleges to post graduation numbers as high as those at universities.

Community colleges also appeared to struggle more with insufficient institutional capacity to respond to performance funding. In comparison to the universities, respondents at the community colleges indicated more often that they needed more resources to improve the ability of their IR offices to collect and analyze data. Additionally, they more often reported shortages of qualified staff and faculty.

Compared to their community college counterparts, university respondents more often stated that their institutions were hindered by inappropriate performance funding measures. But even this challenge varied according to how wealthy and well positioned the university was. Respondents at low-capacity four-year institutions more often mentioned that they were being unfairly expected to perform as well on graduation metrics as the more selective and higher-capacity universities in the state. Meanwhile, several respondents at the high-capacity and more selective campuses mentioned that their institutions were limited by a ceiling effect, where they had a hard time improving on their already high performance.

DIFFERENCES BY INSTITUTIONAL CAPACITY

In selecting institutions for our study, we picked colleges in the top, middle, and bottom third in their states in expected capacity to respond to the demands of the performance funding formula (see chapter 2 for the derivation of our measure). In table 7.7, we focus on the high- and low-capacity institutions.*

---

* We had two high-capacity institutions in each state: one that was research intensive and one that was not. In order to maintain an equal number of high- and low-capacity universities, we are including only the research-intensive universities in our count of reports from high-capacity institutions.

Table 7.7   Reports of Obstacles by Institutional Capacity
(Number of Individuals Reporting)

Obstacle	High-capacity institutions	Low-capacity institutions
Student composition	17	28
Inappropriate performance funding measures	20	28
Insufficient institutional capacity	16	16
Institutional resistance	5	17
Insufficient state funding of higher education	11	15
Insufficient knowledge of and responsibility for performance funding	8	12
Instability in funding, indicators, and measures	2	11
Insufficient state funding of performance funding	3	0
Decrease in enrollment	1	2
Other	4	5
Total number of reports	87	134
Total unduplicated number of individuals reporting at least one obstacle	45	70

Note: This table excludes medium-capacity institutions (see text for reasons). The total number of unduplicated respondents reporting is the number of respondents who mentioned one or more obstacles. It is lower than the total number of reports because some respondents mentioned more than one obstacle. The data for this table do not include the 1979 program in Tennessee and the 2013 revision of the program in Ohio.

Table 7.7 illustrates how reports about obstacles varied across low- and high-capacity colleges and universities. On the whole, low-capacity institutions much more often reported obstacles than did high-capacity ones: 70 respondents versus 45. Respondents at low-capacity colleges and universities were more likely than those at high-capacity colleges to report obstacles due to student-body composition, inappropriate performance funding measures, insufficient state funding of higher education, lack of knowledge about performance funding, and faculty and other resistance to performance funding.

However, this main tide of evidence includes some interesting cross currents. The overall pattern of low-capacity colleges and universities more often reporting obstacles is due to the lopsided tendency of respondents at low-capacity universities to report them. Respondents from low-capacity universities were much more likely to report obstacles than their colleagues at high-capacity universities. However, respondents at high- and low-capacity community colleges split evenly.

Summary and Conclusions

Although policy framers in Indiana, Ohio, and Tennessee intended for performance funding policies to change institutional behavior in order to improve student performance, there are several persistent obstacles that hinder high performance on the states' metrics. The most commonly perceived obstacles to improved student outcomes were student-body composition (in the cases of community colleges and broad-access public universities), inappropriate performance funding metrics, and insufficient institutional capacity.

The reason that student-body composition topped the list of respondents' concerns in our research was due to the fact that open-access institutions educate many students who face academic, social, and economic challenges. Students who attend community colleges and broad-access universities tend to be less prepared academically and less advantaged socioeconomically than students who attend more selective four-year institutions. These qualities make it harder for students to graduate and make it more difficult for their institution to meet the demands of the funding formula. Respondents at community colleges were particularly vocal about the difficulties they experienced trying to do well on the state metrics for retention and graduation.

These concerns of our community college respondents could be interpreted as somewhat self-serving. The great stress on student-body composition as an obstacle could verge on "blaming the victim" if it were to exempt institutions from having to examine how their policies and programs might be contributing to poor student outcomes for less advantaged students (Kezar et al., 2008; Witham & Bensimon, 2012; see also Ryan, 1976). On the other hand, it would be unfair to broad-access institutions to argue that they do not face obstacles that are greater than those faced by more selective, resource-rich institutions.

Many respondents also stated that they perceived the performance funding metrics to be poorly matched to their institutions' goals. This is due in part to the challenge of deriving and implementing a formula that affects a wide swath of institutions that range greatly in student-body composition and organizational mission. Respondents at community colleges often perceived the state metrics as unrealistically holding them to the same standards as four-year institutions. These respondents noted that many students at community colleges do not intend to get a degree, unlike students at four-year institutions, or will not do so in a timely fashion because they more often attend part-time. Hence, performance metrics for graduation, particularly on-time graduation, would be more difficult for community colleges to realize. The metrics did not provide for students who attended community colleges in order to take a number of courses or acquire certain skills but did not intend to get a degree or who would be attending part-time for an extended period of time. Meanwhile, respondents at high-capacity universities, particularly in Indiana, were frustrated because they felt that their institutions had little room to improve. They felt that there was a ceiling effect in that institutions that were already doing well had little room to make big gains in student outcomes. As we noted, state officials in Indiana, Ohio, and Tennessee were aware of these issues and made efforts to correct for them. However, there is some question about whether these corrections go far enough. We return to this question in the concluding chapter.

Finally, many of our respondents pointed to their institution's lack of sufficient organizational capacity as a major obstacle. Respondents at most community colleges and universities reported having too little IR capability. We also sometimes heard about inadequate IT capacity, shortages of qualified staff and faculty, limited student services, small institutional size, and inability to perform additional tasks necessary to improve in the time allotted. These findings highlight the importance of state support for building up institutional capacity, particularly the development of IR capacity. This is something to which the states have not given enough attention (see chapter 3), and we will take up what they can do in the concluding chapter.

Underlying these aggregate findings, we also found important differences by state and type of institutions. Our respondents in Tennessee reported substantially fewer obstacles overall than did those in the other two states. We attributed this to Tennessee's long experience with performance funding, its better communication of the goals and methods of performance funding, and the fact that our interviews came in the midst of dramatic changes in Ohio's funding formula, particularly for community colleges. Additionally, respondents at community colleges and at public universities weighed the importance of certain obstacles differently. Our community college respondents emphasized student-body composition and insufficient organizational capacity, while the university respondents stressed inappropriate performance funding measures. Finally, respondents' perceptions of obstacles also varied according to the expected capacity of an institution to respond to performance funding. Respondents at low-capacity colleges and universities more often than those at high-capacity colleges reported that student-body composition, inappropriate performance funding measures, insufficient state funding, lack of knowledge about performance funding, and faculty and other resistance to performance funding were important obstacles to responding effectively. The greater incidence of obstacles reported for low-capacity institutions clearly calls for greater attention by policymakers to addressing their particular needs.

The presence of these reported obstacles to institutions being able to respond effectively to performance funding pressures raises the specter that they may resort to illegitimate means to succeed (Dougherty & Reddy, 2013; Moynihan, 2008). Sociologist Robert Merton (1968, 1976) identified this conjunction of high societal pressure to succeed and structural constraints on being able to do so legitimately—a condition he termed "anomie," following the lead of Émile Durkheim—as a major source of deviance. Do we see the organizational equivalent in the case of higher education institutions exposed to strong pressure to perform well by performance funding programs but also facing major obstacles to doing so? That is the subject of our next chapter.

CHAPTER 8

Unintended Impacts of Performance Funding

O rganizational theory and research on policy implementation and performance management in government find that a policy often produces outcomes that are not intended by policymakers (Honig, 2006; Merton, 1968, 1976; Mica, Peisert, & Winczorek, 2012; Moynihan, 2008; Radin, 2006). In fact, our research finds that performance funding policies can produce sizable unintended, negative impacts. Moreover, our research shows that some of these unintended impacts have the potential to negatively affect the very students who are already the least likely to be successful in higher education. However, we should add that those outcomes—though unintended by policy designers—may actually be *intended* by institutional actors.* We will explore this disjunction below.

This chapter builds on existing scholarship about performance funding by focusing on impacts of performance funding not intended by policymakers. It provides a rich account of both observed and potential unintended impacts experienced and discussed at nine community colleges and nine four-year colleges in three states: Indiana, Ohio, and Tennessee.

In order to illuminate the unintended impacts of performance funding, we apply perspectives drawn from the research literature on performance funding implementation and impacts, performance management in government agencies, policy design theory, policy implementation theory, and principal–agent theory (see chapter 2). When we pull together these various empirical and theoretical strands, they suggest that we view the unintended impacts of performance funding in higher education as part of a more general pattern involving accountability systems for government agencies. The unintended impacts of performance

Hana Lahr and Lara Pheatt took the lead in writing the report on which this chapter draws (see Lahr et al., 2014).

* We wish to thank Dr. Tiffany Jones of the Southern Education Foundation for her helpful recommendation that we clarify what is unintended and intended in the impacts of performance funding.

funding may well resemble those of similar efforts to improve the performance of public agencies. Moreover, our review of the literature in chapter 2 suggests that we view these unintended impacts from both a top-down and a bottom-up implementation perspective—that is, that we take into account the perspectives and interests of both state policy framers and local institutional implementers. We cannot judge the impacts of performance funding from just the intents of the state policy framers or even of the senior college administrators responding to such a policy. We must also consider the perceptions and experiences of the faculty and mid-level administrators who are, in the end, implementing state policies.

In this chapter, we first present our main findings, discussing the most commonly mentioned unintended impacts across Indiana, Ohio, and Tennessee. Toward the end of the chapter, we examine how reports of unintended impacts vary by state, by type of institution (community college versus four-year institution), and by differences in colleges' estimated capacity to respond effectively to the demands of performance funding.

Our cross-state analyses reveal frequent reports of unintended impacts of performance funding across the three states (see table 8.1). The most commonly mentioned unintended impacts are restriction of admissions to community colleges and universities (67 interviewees), weakening of academic standards (55 interviewees), compliance costs (19 interviewees), lessening of institutional cooperation (10 interviewees), decrease in staff morale (10 interviewees), less emphasis on missions not rewarded by performance funding (8 interviewees), and decrease of faculty voice in academic governance (7 interviewees).* Our main unit of analysis is the number of unduplicated interviewees who discussed a given unintended impact. However, we also indicate the number of institutions at which interviewees discussed the unintended impacts. To count an institution, we required that at least two respondents mentioned that a particular unintended impact was occurring or could occur at that institution.

Because of the relatively recent adoption of several performance funding programs and their ongoing implementation, we have differentiated between observed unintended impacts and potential unintended impacts. We classified instances as "observed" when the interviewee discussed that an impact has

---

* Note that these totals reflect the unintended impacts reported only for PF 2.0 programs and therefore do not include reports of unintended impacts from Tennessee's PF 1.0 program adopted in 1979.

Table 8.1   Summary of Reports of Unintended Impacts in Three States
(Number of Individuals Reporting)

Impact	Community college interviewees	University interviewees	Community colleges with individuals reporting (out of 9)	Universities with individuals reporting (out of 9)	Total interviewees
Restriction of student admissions	23	44	5	5	67
Weakening of academic standards	28	27	8	5	55
Compliance costs	10	9	3	3	19
Lessening of institutional cooperation	3	7	1	2	10
Lower morale	6	4	2	0^a	10
Narrowing of institutional mission	4	4	1	1	8
Less faculty voice in academic governance	3	4	0^b	1	7
Other	10	9	n/a	n/a	19
Total number of reports	87	108			195
Total unduplicated individuals reporting[c]	66	76			142

Note: These totals do not include the Tennessee 1979 PF 1.0 program.

[a] Though four university interviewees mentioned lower morale, they were scattered across four institutions. Hence, we count no institutions as having reports, since our standard is that there must be at least two reports from a given institution.

[b] Although we had three reports of less faculty voice from our community college respondents, they were scattered across three different institutions.

[c] The total number of reports is higher than the total number of unduplicated respondents because many respondents mentioned more than one unintended impact.

occurred or concrete steps have been taken toward producing it (e.g., a college has already taken specific steps to change admission practices in ways that would restrict access for certain kinds of students). Unintended impacts are classified as "potential" if the respondent noted that there was the possibility of a certain impact occurring, but it has not yet occurred or no clear steps have yet been taken toward producing that impact.* The following discussion of the most frequently mentioned unintended impacts employs this distinction.

Restrictions of Student Admission

The most frequently reported unintended impact of performance funding across our colleges was restriction of admission of less prepared students. Sixty-seven of our respondents reported the actuality or potential of such restriction. At five community colleges and five universities, we had at least two respondents reporting this unintended impact.† Such a move to greater admissions selectivity clearly undermines the open-door mission of the community college (Brint & Karabel, 1989; Cohen, Brawer, & Kisker, 2014; Dougherty, 1994). And while increased selectivity might be regarded as welcome in the case of selective four-year colleges, it is problematic for the many public universities that are historically committed to expanding college access and that enroll many low-income and minority students (Jenkins & Rodriguez, 2013; Jones, 2014).

Table 8.2 shows how our respondents are distributed by whether the respondents indicated that the unintended impact had already occurred or was on its way ("observed") or whether it was a possible future impact ("potential"). Across our 18 institutions, there were 26 interviewees who discussed restricted admission practices that we classified as observed. There were another 41 interviewees who reported unintended impacts that we classified as potential restrictions of admissions, for a total of 67 interviewees.

With regard to community colleges, restricted admissions are of concern because of the fundamental mission of community colleges as open-access institutions: accepting all students—regardless of their ability and previous academic records—as long as they have completed a high school diploma or GED (Brint & Karabel, 1989; Cohen, Brawer, & Kisker, 2014; Dougherty, 1994). Yet, this open-door mission does not fit easily with the concerns of the college completion movement. Community colleges have long struggled with low persistence and

* Two of our researchers separately classified each unintended impact mentioned as observed or potential. Where their classifications diverged, they met to resolve the discrepancies. In the few cases when they could not resolve a discrepancy, the principal investigator cast the tie-breaking vote.

† As indicated in table 8.1, we counted an institution as reporting a certain unintended impact only when at least two respondents at that institution reported it. This did produce instances when we might have three or four reports but no institutions because those reports were scattered across as many institutions.

Table 8.2   Reports of Mechanisms by Which Institutions Could Restrict Admission (Number of Individuals Reporting)

Type of restriction mechanism	Indiana	Ohio	Tennessee	Total	Potential	Observed
General restrictions	8	13	1	22	21	1
Raising admission requirements	16	12	2	30	7	23
Selective student recruitment	3	11	0	14	10	4
Shift toward non-need-based financial aid	0	6	0	6	5	1
Other	3	3	0	6	5	1
Total number of reports	30	45	3	78	48	30
Total unduplicated individuals reporting	25	39	3	67	41	26

Note: The total number of unduplicated respondents is the number of respondents who mentioned one or more unintended impacts. It is lower than the total number of reports because some respondents mentioned more than one unintended impact. These totals do not include the Tennessee 1979 PF 1.0 program.

completion rates. A report by the National Center for Education Statistics showed that only 35% of students entering public two-year colleges in AY 2003–4 completed a credential—whether a certificate, associate's degree, or bachelor's degree—within six years of entering college (Radford et al., 2010, table 2). Given this low rate of completion, when states start to hold institutions accountable for the number of students who successfully complete a certain number of credits and who eventually graduate, community colleges are placed in a difficult position. Any institutional changes to improve student outcomes will often be expensive, time-consuming, and uncertain in effectiveness (Jenkins & Rodriguez, 2013). Unfortunately, for many colleges, the easier resolution of this dilemma may lie less in programmatic improvement than in cutting back the admission of students less likely to graduate, thus narrowing the historically open door. This move toward greater selectivity need not require an overall restriction in enrollments. It could involve keeping up enrollment numbers but changing how those enrollees are distributed by academic preparation. As we will see below, several of our respondents pointed to efforts to recruit more students from higher-performing high schools.

For universities, raising the admission requirements may not at first appear to be as problematic as it is for community colleges, given that the mission and ethos of many universities is to become more selective. However, there is also a strong tradition of mass-access, community-based universities committed to opening up college opportunities for underserved student groups (Jenkins &

Rodriguez, 2013). Yet even those institutions may also be tempted to become more selective, reducing the number of less prepared students they enroll.

Buttressing our analysis of the incidence of restrictions of admission of less prepared students is a recent multivariate study of the impact of performance funding in Indiana. Umbricht, Fernandez, and Ortagus (2015) examine the impact of Indiana's PF 1.0 and PF 2.0 programs on the average ACT scores of students at the 25th and 75th percentile for Indiana public four-year institutions during the years 2003–12. They estimated nine different models involving three different lag times and three different comparison groups. Differences between earlier and later ACT scores were calculated, allowing for no lag, a one-year lag, or a two-year lag between policy implementation and institutional response. Three comparison groups were used: 29 public four-year institutions in three states similar to Indiana (Kentucky, Missouri, and Wisconsin) but without performance funding in the years 2003–12; 21 private four-year institutions in Indiana, which were not subject to performance funding; and 55 public four-year institutions in six surrounding states also without performance funding (Iowa, Illinois, Kentucky, Missouri, Minnesota, and Wisconsin). A difference-in-differences analysis was used with year and institutional fixed effects and the following control variables: FTE enrollments for the entering class in each year, state appropriations for the public institutions, and state-level unemployment rate. The study found that—across all nine models—performance funding in Indiana led to highly significant increases in ACT scores at both the 25th and 75th percentile for Indiana public four-year colleges, indicating that the institutions were becoming more selective (Umbricht, Fernandez, & Ortagus, 2015).

In the remainder of this section, we discuss several of the mechanisms most commonly mentioned by our respondents by which institutions are actually or potentially restricting admission of less prepared students. Table 8.2 shows the number of mentions for each of these mechanisms.

GENERAL RESTRICTIONS

Our findings include 22 reports from individuals who discussed restrictions of student admission in response to performance funding, without specifying any particular mechanism. Nearly all of these reports were classified as potential impacts of performance funding. In only one case did the respondent discuss a restriction of admission which had already occurred. Furthermore, of these 22 mentions, 16 of them came from community college respondents, and these individuals spoke very broadly about the *possibility* of limiting access without mentioning any specific steps or actions to reduce admission. For example, a dean at an Ohio community college reported that the college could be more successful under the 2013 revision of the funding formula if it did not admit students more likely to struggle in college: "I guess if we weeded the students out that really don't have any plan of being a completer here, [that would help] with our success rates." Similarly, a senior administrator from an Indiana four-year institution said that because of the pressure from performance funding, the institution is less likely to offer admission to "weaker" students "because if they are weaker . . . there is a chance they will bring down your performance numbers."

However, in addition to these general mentions of admissions restriction, our interviewees also discussed specific mechanisms by which their institution is either currently restricting admissions or could in the future restrict the admission of less prepared students. They include raising admission requirements, decreasing the number of "conditional student admits," targeting student recruitment to certain areas, and redirecting institutional aid to better-prepared students. We discuss these below.

RAISING ADMISSION REQUIREMENTS

Across our institutions, there were 30 reports by our respondents of restricting access in response to performance funding by raising admission requirements. It is of note that these 30 reports all came from respondents located at four-year institutions; none came from community colleges. Twenty-three of these reports mentioned raising admission selectivity as an observed impact and seven as a potential impact. Respondents discussed raising admission requirements by requiring higher standardized test scores and grade point averages or by decreasing the number of conditionally admitted students accepted each year.

A mid-level nonacademic administrator at an Ohio university discussed how the university was raising the academic profile of the student body in order to improve the university's performance on the state metrics:

> Instead of a graduation rate of 80 percent, we really need to bump that up so that we have a higher graduation rate. And some of that is being achieved by [changing] the type of student that we bring in. If we increase the quality of the student coming in, we anticipate then that completion of courses will go up, and then your retention will go up, and then your graduation will go up. It's kind of like a little domino. So by raising our average ACT score of our incoming class by one point, the question is, "Can we anticipate then higher

course completions, higher number of degrees awarded?" . . . So yes, there's a deliberate approach being made by our enrollment management office.

This statement is echoed by others in a news article that appeared in the *Dayton Daily News* (Lambert, 2015). It quotes several Ohio university officials who state that performance funding demands have led their university to increase their admissions requirements. For example, a senior administrator at an Ohio university states, "Everybody is chasing the same finite carrot. [Higher admission requirements] protected our share of state funding" (quoted in Lambert, 2015).

In Tennessee, there were far fewer reports of restricting admission in response to performance funding. However, a mid-level nonacademic administrator at a Tennessee university did note that the institution has become more selective since 2010 (the year that the state's PF 2.0 program was adopted): "I think that, over the past few years, at least since 2010, we have started being a bit more selective in terms of the students that are admitted to [the university]. What we know is that our average student ACT score is now between 26 and 27, which is comparable to our peer and aspirational institutions."

Finally, a faculty member at an Indiana university discussed its transition from being a broad-access institution to one that is more selective about the students it admits and how this shift was influenced by performance funding: "When I was here in the '70s, late '70s, and into the '80s, we were an open-admission institution that was here to serve an underserved population. . . . We were designated last year, for the first time, as a selective institution. And I think that the performance funding has played a role in that because you are going to do much better with your retention and your completion rates if you raise your admission standards."

Several respondents at Indiana universities stated that their institutions have lowered or are considering lowering the number of conditionally admitted students accepted each year. Seven of these eight reports involved observed impacts. According to an interviewee at an Indiana university, conditionally admitted students are those who did not meet admission requirements but were given the opportunity to take a university-developed test; if they scored at a certain level, they were conditionally admitted to the institution. They had to take certain classes (including a freshman seminar) and meet regularly with an advisor. Students remained conditionally accepted until they got to 24 credits with a 2.0 grade point average and all passing grades. According to our data, the decline of this practice is directly related to the institutions' move toward becoming more selective in response to performance funding. A senior administrator at an Indiana university discussed this:

> There's no question, we revised [our] admissions policies. Now, we've actually increased our academic standard of progress and increased expectations. The combination of narrowing the chute in terms of admissions along with those increased academic standards of progress actually has led to a real buzz among the area high school counselors because it goes against what the narrative of what [this university] has traditionally been. I had one mother call me a couple of summers ago and said, "I told my son he could always get into [this university] and now you're not admitting him." So that phrase, "you could always go to [this university]," it's not happening. That's an unintended consequence that frankly for us, for our reputation and our positioning, I'm comfortable with navigating. I think it was a change that had to happen.

Despite the negative implications of restricting enrollment of less prepared and therefore often less advantaged students, the practice was strongly defended by many faculty members and senior administrators. For example, a university faculty member argued that, before this shift occurred, there were too many students admitted who were unprepared for college-level work:

> Well okay, in my honest opinion, tightening up the standard . . . how do I want to put this . . . the people that you talked to spun that as a negative. But here when you consider the fact that we were letting in a lot of students who probably shouldn't have been in college. . . . I don't mean that in a terrible way. I'm very egalitarian, but students probably should have gone and done remedial work at Ivy Tech [Indiana's multicampus community college] or something before they came here. And that has really tightened up. And I think that's a good thing.

This statement clearly suggests that for this faculty member—and for like-minded faculty and administrators—the restriction of admissions may not be an unintended impact of performance funding but rather one that is quite welcome and intended.

SELECTIVE STUDENT RECRUITMENT

Fourteen respondents discussed different ways that their institutions are practicing (four respondents) or could practice (ten respondents) selective recruitment practices. In order to maximize the likelihood that their students will graduate, these institutions are increasing or might increase their efforts to attract better-prepared students, including out-of-state and international students. At the same time, respondents discussed how their institutions might de-emphasize or are actually de-emphasizing recruitment of students from high schools with many less well prepared students.

A senior administrator from an Ohio community college explained that the focus on various metrics of student success might lead to a focus on recruiting students who are more likely to be successful, but noted that this practice would be in opposition to the community college's open-door mission: "One unintended consequence may be that if you're getting incentives on how many students persist and complete or transfer, aren't you going to try to recruit students who are smarter and who have better ability? So, then, what happens to the other students? Isn't our admission an open-door policy?"

Another senior administrator at an Ohio community college explained that during recruitment, each student requires substantial attention and effort. Therefore, by cutting back on this outreach and support, the college could reduce the number of students who are not college ready:

> In so-called recruiting practices, there's a lot of hand-holding that goes on with students in community colleges. I know in our own institution there's tremendous hand-holding with students. They have to be reminded of everything. They have to be reminded of a deadline. They have to be reminded of what paperwork and what tests they have to take. It's a tremendous amount of time and effort we place in just getting one student into class. So if that's the case, you could merely de-emphasize that portion of your services, and invariably a number of those students are going to fall by the wayside.

At an Indiana four-year institution, a senior administrator discussed how the performance funding formula could shape what types of students they recruit and how this change could lead to conflict with the institution's mission of access, even if there is no evidence of this happening yet: "It could be that some institutions might make decisions about their admissions and their enrollments that respond very closely to that. For example, exclude students of color from urban high schools, because they are a liability."

A senior administrator at an Ohio university discussed the tension that arises from being an institution in an urban community and trying to serve students in that community, even though they might not be as well prepared as other students and therefore may not be as likely to contribute to desired institutional outcomes as defined by performance funding:

> There's a recognition [as has been brought up in some discussions] of the fact . . . that the more we focus on suburban kids with high GPAs and high ACT scores, the less we're able to serve . . . an urban population that tends to be from poorer school districts. And even if they do have GPAs that appear to be good, their ACT scores reflect a lack of preparation. . . . I mean there's a tension between continuing to recruit a very diverse student population and being an urban-serving institution and being an institution that has high performing students who are successful in getting a degree.

As it happens, a news article in the *Dayton Daily News* (Lambert, 2015) reported that a number of Ohio universities are planning to increase their efforts to recruit students from suburban high schools. A senior administrator at an Ohio public university is quoted as stating, "We are telling our recruiters to expand the variety of schools they go to. If you're in Dayton, maybe not go to just Dayton Public, but also to Beavercreek and Centerville" (quoted in Lambert, 2015).

DIRECTING INSTITUTIONAL AID TO BETTER-PREPARED STUDENTS

We received six reports that institutions were considering restricting admissions by shifting the focus of the college's institutional aid program from providing assistance to needy students to attracting better-prepared students.* A senior administrator at an Ohio community college explained how performance funding could encourage the college to offer scholarships to higher-performing students who are more likely to complete:

> My theory is that we're going to be raising the bar for who we give some of our scholarships to . . . if it was my business I would be looking for ways to attract people that I thought were very likely to complete. And along with that, I would be looking for what are the tendencies or what are the attributes for those that tend to be non-completers. Now I think that raises some ethical questions because we are an open-access institution, and so we still need to offer that access, but I think we also need to tweak and, again, encourage more completions as opposed to just numbers of enrollment.

* Lambert (2015) reports a similar finding.

Although this unintended impact is still classified as "potential" given that the proposed changes have not yet gone into effect, the discussion surrounding redirecting aid has moved beyond being purely hypothetical. As another senior administrator at the same college noted, performance funding has motivated the college to work on developing new scholarships in order to focus recruiting efforts on students more likely to be successful at the institution:

> We have an institutional grant that we call the "[X] Scholarship." . . . Heretofore, any student who graduated from a local high school was able to come to [our college] with a guarantee that their tuition needs would be met either by Pell Grant or by that [X] Scholarship. And what we're finding is we need to tweak that to put more emphasis on those students who are serious about their education. I can't tell you what the recommendations are going to be because I didn't work closely with the committee. But I think, from what I understand, the recommendations are winding their way up to [senior college leadership]. . . . So I anticipate that there will be some recommendations aimed at completers as opposed to purely access.

At an Ohio university, respondents also discussed the possibility of a shift toward offering merit aid in order to attract higher-performing students. A faculty leader noted, "If we are incentivized to go to a much higher completion rate, that kind of favors the idea of handing out merit-based [financial aid]. Because let's just face it, I can graduate a valedictorian in three years no problem. That's pressing the easy button."

As this section has demonstrated, there are numerous paths that both four-year institutions and community colleges have taken or could take to restrict admission and enroll better-prepared students who are more likely to graduate on time. Whether institutions are raising or are considering raising their standardized test and grade point average requirements, targeting certain student populations for recruitment while de-emphasizing others, or offering merit aid, such practices would reshape who enrolls in public institutions of higher education. They would favor better-prepared and more advantaged students to the detriment of minority and low-income students and students who are not as well prepared by their secondary schools.

Indiana, Ohio, and Tennessee have tried to address the threat of institutions moving to de-emphasize admission of less prepared students by providing extra funding to institutions for graduating students who are deemed at risk or of special concern. Indiana provides greater weight for students lower in socioeconomic background and those graduating in STEM fields (Indiana Commission for Higher Education, 2013a, 2014). Ohio's performance funding program provides greater weight for completions by students who are Pell Grant eligible, are members of underrepresented minorities (Native American, African American, or Hispanic), are 25 years of age or older when they first enroll at a state institution of higher education, and receive STEM degrees (Ohio Board of Regents, 2015a, 2015b, 2015c).* Tennessee's formula weights more heavily outcomes for students who are Pell Grant eligible, over age 25, and (beginning in FY 2016–17) academically underprepared on indicators for credit accumulation and degree production (Tennessee Higher Education Commission, 2015a, 2015c, 2015d). As can be seen, socioeconomic status is taken into account in all three states. Older students and STEM graduates are considered in two states. However, only one of the states takes into account either race/ethnicity or academic underpreparation. We will return to this point in chapter 9.

These premiums for at-risk students can have a considerable impact on institutional allocations. In Tennessee, they can shift institutional allocations by as much as 12%, with an average of about 4% (authors' TN interviews). However, it is not clear whether the at-risk premiums are enough—particularly in Ohio and Indiana—to really deter colleges from becoming more selective and turning away less prepared (and less advantaged) students. As we have seen, we have frequent reports in those states—though not in Tennessee—that colleges and universities are restricting admissions now or might end up doing so in the future. Moreover, senior administrators at several colleges and universities reported to us that the premium provided for at-risk student completions had little impact on their institutions' actions. For example, a senior administrator at an Indiana university that had benefited from the premium for low-income students stated, "Yes, that pays off for us. How much does that influence us? . . . We're certainly not against it because it's been an advantage for us in recent years. The funds are not at any kind of level that's going to change our ability to allocate funds, and . . . it probably has a minimal influence of how we would prioritize degree completion for our students."

---

* Ohio initially did not provide this funding bonus for community colleges because simulations indicated that it seemingly would not affect community college revenues one way or the other (Ohio Board of Regents, 2011a). However, such a bonus appears in the state funding formula for community colleges for FY 2015 (Ohio Board of Regents, 2015a).

It is heartening to hear that institutions still remain committed to admitting and graduating at-risk students. Moreover, the fact that institutions remain highly dependent on tuition means that they still have an incentive to pursue high enrollments. Nonetheless, it is of concern that the premium provided for at-risk students does not seem to be strengthening the motivation to accept them as much as one might want. We will return to this topic in the final chapter to consider what additional steps might be in order.

Weakening of Academic Standards

The second most commonly mentioned unintended impact of performance funding was the weakening of academic standards. Across our community colleges and four-year institutions, 55 respondents reported this unintended impact, with at least two reports coming from eight of nine community colleges and five of nine universities (see table 8.1). Table 8.3 shows the total number of mentions of the weakening of academic standards by particular mechanism and whether the reports involved observed or potential instances.*

The majority of respondents indicated that the weakening of academic standards was a *potential* consequence of performance funding and has not yet come to fruition. Forty respondents indicated that performance funding has the potential to cause colleges to weaken their academic standards in various ways, while 15 respondents indicated that performance funding has actually led to the weakening of academic standards. Respondents noted several ways in which academic standards could be or have been weakened, particularly by lowering academic requirements in class and reducing degree requirements.

LOWERING ACADEMIC DEMANDS IN CLASS (GRADE INFLATION)

Pressure to lower academic demands in class and to practice grade inflation was reported by 32 respondents as either a potential or observed unintended impact of performance funding (see table 8.3). Twenty-eight interviewees mentioned potential impacts, and four mentioned actual ones. A senior campus administrator at an Indiana community college worried that the push for degree completions, which is the most heavily weighted metric within the Indiana performance-based funding formula, will encourage faculty and institutions to move students through to graduation without sufficient care for whether or not

---

* We note that the number of duplicated and unduplicated mentions was nearly the same. We received 57 reports from 55 respondents.

Table 8.3   Reports of Mechanisms by Which Institutions Could Weaken Academic Standards (Number of Individuals Reporting)

Mechanism	Indiana	Ohio	Tennessee	Total	Observed	Potential
Lowering academic demands in class (grade inflation)	8	14	10	32	4	28
Reducing degree requirements	5	3	3	11	8	3
Reducing time in developmental education	0	3	1	4	1	3
Grade forgiveness policies	0	3	0	3	2	1
Advising into easier courses	0	0	1	1	1	0
Other	0	5	1	6	0	6
Total number of reports	13	28	16	57	16	41
Total unduplicated individuals reporting	12	28	15	55	15	40

Note: The total number of unduplicated respondents is the number of respondents who mentioned one or more unintended impact. It is lower than the total number of reports because some respondents mentioned more than one unintended impact. These totals do not include the Tennessee 1979 PF 1.0 program.

academic standards are maintained: "It's putting faculty in a position of the easiest way out is to lower the standards and get people through. And so it's something that's of great concern I think." In Ohio, several administrators and faculty members at one community college expressed concern about potential grade inflation in response to the 2009 performance funding program. A faculty member stated, "You hear all the terrible things in other parts of the nation as well as our own [state] about grade inflation, and just all the bad things that can happen when you want to be able to produce numbers to get funded on."

This sense of pressure in Ohio is likely to have increased since our interviews, as the state moved to base 100% of state funding for community colleges in FY 2015 on performance indicators (Ohio Board of Regents, 2015a). Several respondents at Ohio community colleges expressed concern that this more intense performance funding formula could result in weakened academic standards. A senior-level administrator at a community college argued, "I think it's also going to be important to keep academic standards high, which is something that's very important to us here at [this college]. But we do hear that there are other colleges where they are planning to basically just abolish Fs and get people through that way and call them completions. . . . I don't know that any college is actually planning to just abolish Fs. But I think that what we hear is that there is an incentive built-in to potentially get into grade inflation, so the incentive is there."

In Tennessee, the watering down of academic demands in order to produce higher completion numbers was cited as a potential unintended impact of performance funding by one community college dean. The respondent acknowledged that the college's administration had not exerted such pressure—in fact, they had actively rejected doing so—but the respondent felt that the potential is there: "The push is to get students to graduate, or at least the message that we get is [that] students have to graduate. There's concern among faculty [that] that's going to become the overriding goal and they're going to be forced to water down the curriculum, which does not sit well with faculty on any level."

Within the universities, there was also widespread concern about grade inflation and pressure to lower academic expectations in order to maximize performance on the state indicators. In Indiana, one senior university administrator questioned whether the performance indicators were incentivizing institutions to improve quality or actually encouraging institutions to lower quality in order to increase completion numbers: "It's just kind of a theoretical question as to whether these are effective metrics. You know, somebody could probably reduce the academic quality on their campus and allow students to pass through their programs much easier. Receive a credential and improve their bottom line in terms of degree production."

Meanwhile, a faculty member at an Ohio university discussed feeling "pressure" not to fail students by inflating grades: "Well, in an effort to promote student success, there is a substantial pressure to minimize the failure rates of the students in some of these undergraduate courses. And of course that would translate into inflation of grades in order to make sure that the students are passing all of these courses and so forth. So I as a faculty member have a concern as to the watering down of our course materials as well as the quality of our majors, the programs." When asked a follow-up question about how this pressure is expressed, the same faculty member continued, "It's not a direct pressure. It's simply public discussion of which courses have high failure rates, low failure rates, and they are essentially promoting those courses that have low failure rates as being successful, [as] well as being those courses that promote student success. So it's implicit, but I think there is a general implicit pressure."

Finally, a faculty member from Tennessee also highlighted the pressure felt by faculty members to contribute to better student outcomes. As this individual explained, they see restricting admission as a nonoption because it would run counter to the goal of increasing the number of graduates, so they see the only other option as lowering academic demands:

Yeah. I know that sounds strange but the average faculty person, if you ask them how do you increase student outcomes, it's raise admission standards, which is directly in opposition to what the state wants, which is more graduates. They seem somewhat in opposition to each other. The other option that faculty see is [that] you must be just asking me to water down what I'm doing, which faculty are not going to accept. In Tennessee, there seems to be an emphasis on a percentage of our people to have degrees. There's somewhat of a disconnect between that goal and the goal of what the degrees should mean.

REDUCING DEGREE REQUIREMENTS

Across all three states, 11 individuals said that performance funding could lead or was leading institutions to reduce barriers to graduation and to focus on awarding credentials, typically by reducing the number of credits required to complete a degree. Of these 11 respondents, the majority—8 interviewees—discussed observed cases of reduced degree requirements; the remaining 3 individuals discussed the potential effect of performance funding. Several respondents noted that their respective institutions had recently changed degree requirements in order to ensure that students receive their degrees as soon as possible. While this may often be a good change, by removing unnecessary barriers to graduation, the focus on easing attainment of credentials can also negatively affect the quality of learning. A faculty dean at an Indiana university noted the danger of focusing on attaining credentials at the expense of learning: "[It] seems like we were encouraged to get students out the door with their degree, and at times that may mean truncating their education. We have students, as I mentioned earlier, who really want to continue and want to take their time and develop their own research and ideas and have a full and rich academic experience. We all have a little bit of pressure to get them to the classes they are supposed to take and get them out the door. As if it was some kind of ticket to a job rather than an education."

The concern about excessive easing of credentialing was also present at an Ohio university. A senior administrator discussed how maintaining degree quality is complicated when the focus is on increasing graduation numbers: "Part of the discussion that has been increasing of late, and we are clearly in this, is quality. Where does quality fit in here? . . . All of the discussion is about increasing numbers. And as you know from your viewpoint, the discussion of quality in higher education is kind of a 'third rail' because nobody knows quite how to measure that."

In Indiana community colleges, interviewees discussed the recent state initiative to ensure that once students obtain 60 credits they are awarded an associate's degree, regardless of whether or how many times they switched majors or concentrations. Moreover, the Indiana community college system has taken steps to remove courses from degree programs requiring more than 60 credits. Interviewees at the central office of the Indiana community college system were quite clear that this policy change was in direct response to performance funding pressure to increase the number of college graduates. As a senior-level administrator explained, "We've pounded on advisors that when they hit the 60 mark, they're done. We award the degree and they are out of here, right. Certainly they can stay with us longer and take more classes, but they are going to be degreed. We were keeping them here too long."

In all three states, state-level advocates anticipated that performance funding might result in a weakening of academic standards, with institutions reducing degree requirements and with faculty demanding less in class in order to keep up course and degree completions (Dougherty et al., 2014a). To combat the danger of weakening of academic standards, policymakers in Tennessee decided to rely on its existing PF 1.0 program, which would continue as a quality assurance adjunct to its new PF 2.0 funding formula (authors' interviews). It has various measures of quality of student learning. Ohio, meanwhile, decided that faculty professionalism would be its main counter to the danger of weakening of academic standards (Fingerhut, 2012).* We have no evidence that Indiana took particular steps to address the possibility of a weakening of academic standards, at least at the time that we conducted our interviews (authors' interviews).

Compliance Costs

Costs of complying with the demands of performance funding elicited mentions from 19 of our respondents (see table 8.4). Compliance costs include the expenses of building IR capacity, extra work resulting from the need to more closely track student progress, and less attention to instruction. Note that, with the exception of one respondent, these impacts were reported as having already taken effect.

---

* Ohio also has other means at its disposal to determine whether academic standards are weakening, including examining data to see whether there is evidence of unexplained spikes in completion or grades (authors' interviews).

Table 8.4   Reports of Compliance Costs (Number of Individuals Reporting)

Types	Indiana	Ohio	Tennessee	Total	Potential	Observed
Cost of improving IR capacity	1	1	2	4	0	4
Increased workload	2	0	3	5	0	5
Less attention to instruction	0	2	1	3	1	2
Cost of increasing learning support	0	0	1	1	0	1
Other	0	4	2	6	0	6
Total number of reports	3	7	9	19	1	18
Total unduplicated individuals reporting	3	7	9	19	1	18

Note: The total number of unduplicated respondents is the number of respondents who mentioned one or more unintended impact. It is the same as the number of reports because none of our respondents mentioned more than one form of weakening of academic standards. These totals do not include the Tennessee 1979 PF 1.0 program.

COST OF IMPROVING INSTITUTIONAL RESEARCH CAPACITY

Several respondents pointed out that performance funding increased their institution's need to expand its capacity to track student outcomes but that the college was not compensated for the expenses of building that capacity. In Ohio, a senior community college administrator noted, "They [the state] put into place initiatives and metrics that we have to follow [without] giving any funding to help us get there. Our funding is tied to this, but if you need additional research or things like that, [they should] give us a little money to help us get the information."

Meanwhile, in Indiana, a higher education administrator noted that, as a result of performance funding, the state community college system has had to increase staff levels in the IR office: "I think the compliance costs have been pretty burdensome on all of the institutions. I mean that's a whole new dataset that we have to collect and we only have six people in our [central office] IR department right now. So you know, just probably the 100 man-hours that we've had to spend just to do this, just to get the baseline data for them [the state higher education commission]."

In Tennessee, interviewees reported that the state's 2010 program has resulted in additional costs associated with tracking students and implementing new software to comply with the data requirement of the program. The performance funding program has resulted in a proliferation of new certificate programs, which students often complete in less than a year; therefore, an additional and uncompensated cost has resulted from the need to track, process, and award these credentials. A community college senior administrator said, "That's a lot of tracking for what are we really benefitting? I mean there's some money being spent to do that. And that bothers me a little bit that we're spending so much time tracking and trying to get the credit for something. Is that really benefitting anybody?"

INCREASED WORKLOAD

Five additional respondents discussed the increased workload that performance funding has required, including the need for more assessment. As an Indiana academic dean explained, the demands of performance funding have placed an additional assessment burden on faculty members, without any additional resources: "Well I would say the biggest unintended consequence is the burden of a lot of the work—especially assessment-type work, looking at outcomes—at least from the academic side, has been placed on faculty members, with little to no increase in resources to meet those new demands." A mid-level nonacademic administrator from Tennessee reiterated that compliance with performance funding has led to increased workload: "I think it may have increased the workload of some units . . . all of the different things that you may be tracking that you hadn't previously tracked. Or we're going to purchase this system and you're going to implement it. And so that requires so much work to implement a system while you're still doing your other job."

A good part of the compliance costs discussed above stem from the need of institutions to build up their capacity to engage in organizational learning. But as we saw in chapters 3, 4, and 7, our respondents indicate that their institutions have received little help from the states in meeting the costs of doing so. The states—with Ohio being a partial exception—did not carefully envision the organizational learning and other demands colleges would face in responding to performance funding (see chapters 3, 4, and 7). None of the three states provided funding and technical assistance to compensate colleges for the cost of enlarging their IR and IT capacities. In fact, the vast majority of administrators and faculty we interviewed at 18 public institutions in the three states rated the extent of the state effort to build up institutional capacity as low or nonexistent (see chapter 3). In the concluding chapter we suggest steps that could be taken to address this absence.

Reduced Institutional Cooperation

Ten respondents noted how performance funding has reduced or could reduce institutional cooperation and the free flow of best practices across institutional boundaries (see table 8.1). Of these ten respondents, seven described impacts that had already taken effect, while three described a potential effect of performance funding. As explained by an Indiana senior administrator, "Instead of thinking of a higher education system that should work to best serve the students, people are lately . . . worried about protecting their assets. . . . And I think it kind of pits 'them against us.' "

In Tennessee, according to a college administrator, a similar competition for funds is taking place, with colleges trying to outdo each other: "If I gain money that means that [another college] has to lose it because it's a zero sum game. That's been the discussion. . . . You know that joke about there's a bear that's chasing us and I don't have to run faster than the bear, all I have to do is run faster than you? . . . I don't really have to do that well; all I have to do is do better than you."

This sense of competition could lead easily to a feeling that it is against institutional interests to cooperate with other colleges and share best practices. Since funding is dependent not just on one's own college performance but also on the performance of the other colleges and universities in the state, college officials who find something that works may have little reason to tell their counterparts at other institutions. A Tennessee faculty member mentioned this potential, in recalling a conversation when a state higher educational official visited the college:

> And my question directly to him was, "Why would I ever share? If I come up with an idea to help my students succeed and be successful and graduate, which will mean more money in the funding formula for my school, why would I share that with other schools in my system?" Because then, you know we're all fighting for the same pie . . . we have the idea that might just level the playing field for us so we get our fair share. But other bigger schools who have already more funding, if they get our good idea that works, we give it to them, they have even more money to make it work even better, which means now they still get more of the pie.

Several administrators at an Indiana university pointed to a decrease in cooperation between institutions as a result of performance funding. For example, a mid-level university administrator noted, "Probably an unintended consequence is [that] it ends up creating animus between higher education institutions that should probably be partners. So that probably is an unintended consequence because now we're competing for funds. They're viewing it as a way of getting universities to compete, and that's a healthy thing. . . . I'm not against competition, but the competition's on the wrong dimensions."

Lower Faculty and Staff Morale

Ten respondents reported another unintended consequence of performance funding: a decline in faculty and staff morale (see table 8.1). All of these responses were observed. An Indiana academic administrator stated that faculty morale has suffered in the wake of an increased emphasis on poor student outcomes within community colleges: "It [performance funding] continually brings the poor results to the attention of our faculty. They've indicated to me that it's demoralizing. . . . They're underappreciated." A Tennessee faculty member described this feeling in more emphatic terms: "Completely demoralizing. Because we work very hard to enable our students to succeed, and our goal is our student success. . . . The implication from this type of funding is that we're not working hard enough, we're not willing to change, and we're not willing to improve. We're not willing to look at what we do and try and do better."

Less Faculty Voice in Academic Governance

Seven respondents from Ohio and Tennessee institutions perceived that performance funding has resulted in a decrease in faculty voice in academic governance. A faculty member at an Ohio university explained that performance funding had been used to criticize faculty:

> I mean I don't know that this has been the case at other universities, but at least at [this university] there's been a strong sense that this discourse has been used to sort of marginalize and excoriate faculty. I mean there's been a discourse not of "we need you as a partner to improve this" but [of] "in case you're noticing how underperforming you are in retaining students, so you need to do better." If your goal is to scold the faculty for not doing a good enough job, then you aren't going to actually be reaching out to communicate with them or give them tools.

One community college academic dean described a case in which the pressure to respond to performance funding demands had resulted in a process of curricular deliberation and change that weakened faculty's traditional voice:

> There was a committee . . . working on a redesign for the developmental [education] program. . . . We met every couple of weeks or so [on] very detailed

deliberations as to how we could improve our system, the structure of the program and everything. . . . And then what happened at one point . . . we came to the meeting and our coordinator simply told us that the vice president had decided on what needed to be done with developmental [education] and that's what we were going to do. And that was it. And the changes were made. And it was very drastic. . . . So it was a circumventing of the process that we had in place for developing change, and she was anxious to improve the success rates right away I think, and she thought that this would do it. In her better judgment she felt that this system would work really well.

Although there were few mentions of marginalizing faculty as an unintended impact, it is still important. In discussing the possibilities of restricted admission and weakening of academic standards, several faculty respondents claimed that they would strongly resist any such attempts. However, this faculty opposition is less likely to be effective if faculty voice in academic governance is reduced.

Narrowing of Institutional Mission

Eight of our respondents noted that performance funding had led or could lead to a narrowing of mission, where important missions are dropped or de-emphasized because they are not addressed by performance funding metrics. An Ohio community college dean observed that the funding formula's focus on completion and job readiness could negatively impact colleges' attention to general education courses. As this individual explains, the benefits of the liberal arts are not easily quantifiable, yet these courses contribute to a student's "ways of knowing" and ability to think creatively:

How do I, for example, not allow the Gen Ed area to become too formulized where we're measuring like, "Did you get another ten students to finish?" when you really can't measure what the Gen Ed areas do until you're five or ten years out from when they have had something. And I fear that with some of the pressures we're getting on the funding side of the house for performance, that we're not looking at a lifetime of working; we're looking at did they get into that job. I think of this a lot when I put myself through college . . . it was really the thinking processes that I developed, ways of knowing the world through the wonderful menu of courses I took that has allowed me to adapt to change and evolve through all the jobs and cultures and countries and things I've lived in. And I'm really worried that we could narrow a person's future.

Variations within Our Main Findings

This section analyzes how reports of unintended impacts vary along several dimensions. First, we find notable differences in reports of unintended impacts by state, with many more reports in Ohio than in Tennessee or Indiana. Next, we compare the number of reported unintended impacts by type of institution (two-year versus four-year) and organizational capacity of institution.

DIFFERENCES BY STATE

The total number of reported unintended impacts varies across our three states, with Ohio respondents reporting more than their Indiana and Tennessee counterparts (see table 8.5). Note that these totals include all mentions of unintended impacts, not just those highlighted in this report. Across both community colleges and four-year institutions, there were 58 (unduplicated) individuals reporting unintended impacts in Ohio, 46 in Indiana, and 38 in Tennessee.

The higher number of reports in Ohio may in part be due to the fact that the performance funding formula was revised during our interviews there. Therefore, the program may have weighed more heavily on the minds of Ohio faculty and administrators, particularly at community colleges, where the revisions were particularly major. A possible explanation for why Tennessee has the lowest number of reports is that it has had the longest history with performance fund-

Table 8.5   Reports of Unintended Impacts by State (Number of Individuals Reporting)

Impact	Indiana	Ohio	Tennessee	Total	Observed	Potential
Restriction of student admissions	25	39	3	67	26	41
Weakening of academic standards	12	28	15	55	15	40
Compliance costs	3	7	9	19	18	1
Lessening institutional cooperation	4	0	6	10	7	3
Low morale	4	1	5	10	10	0
Narrowing of institutional mission	1	6	1	8	3	5
Less faculty voice in academic governance	0	5	2	7	6	1
Other	8	2	9	19	13	6
Total number of reports	57	88	50	195	98	97
Total unduplicated individuals reporting	46	58	38	142		

Note: The total number of reports is higher than the total number of unduplicated respondents who mentioned any unintended impact, as it includes individuals who reported more than one unintended impact. The Tennessee reports reflect only the 2010 PF 2.0 program.

ing of the three states. This may have provided the state with more time to work out the kinks in performance funding and for institutions to become more used to it. In Indiana, meanwhile, the percentage of state funding awarded through performance funding (6%) is low compared to that in Tennessee and Ohio, which may account for the lower number of reported unintended impacts in Indiana versus Ohio.

DIFFERENCES BY INSTITUTION TYPE

Table 8.6 compares the number of reports of unintended impacts by community colleges and four-year institutions, including the number of reports that were coded as potential and observed.

Overall, there were fairly similar numbers of individuals from the community colleges and four-year institutions mentioning unintended impacts. However, notable differences emerged when comparing the reports of specific impacts and the number of potential and observed impacts. We had 44 university respondents reporting restricted admissions (26 were observed impacts, and 18 were poten-

Table 8.6   Reports of Unintended Impacts by Type of Institution (Number of Individuals Reporting)

Impact	Community college			University			Total
	Observed	Potential	Total	Observed	Potential	Total	
Restriction of student admissions	0	23	23	26	18	44	67
Weakening of academic standards	4	24	28	11	16	27	55
Compliance costs	9	1	10	9	0	9	19
Lessening institutional cooperation	0	3	3	7	0	7	10
Lower morale	6	0	6	4	0	4	10
Narrowing of institutional mission	1	3	4	2	2	4	8
Less faculty voice in academic governance	2	1	3	4	0	4	7
Other	5	5	10	8	1	9	19
Total number of reports	27	60	87	71	37	108	195
Total unduplicated individuals reporting			66			76	142

Note: The total number of reports is higher than the total number of unduplicated respondents who mentioned any unintended impact, as it includes individuals who reported more than one unintended impact. The Tennessee reports reflect only the 2010 PF 2.0 program.

tial impacts), but at the community colleges we had only 23 respondents mentioning restricted admission (all potential). This could simply reflect greater resistance to admission restriction at community colleges because of the open-door ethos. However, we wonder whether the university respondents may have been more likely to discuss admission restriction and to point to steps that had been taken to effectuate it because it is less taboo to discuss restricting access at a four-year institution than it is at an open-access community college.

The bulk of reports of unintended impacts at community colleges were coded as "potential" impacts. That is, they were impacts that were discussed as a possibility but had not yet occurred or the institution had not yet taken steps to implement. In contrast, at the four-year institutions, the bulk of the reports were coded as "observed." This difference has several possible explanations. First, it is possible that because our interviews at community colleges occurred between 12 and 18 months before our interviews at the universities, and because the performance funding programs were still developing, particularly in Ohio, the impacts were farther away from being potentially realized at the community colleges than at the universities. Second, returning to restriction of student admission, universities perhaps were more likely to report that this impact had already taken place because they do not feel as constrained by a historical mission as open-access institutions, as is the case with community colleges.

DIFFERENCES BY INSTITUTIONAL CAPACITY

Table 8.7 presents a breakdown of reports of most frequently mentioned unintended impacts by estimated college capacity to respond to performance funding (see chapter 2 for the derivation of this measure). Our findings reveal that the number of reports of unintended impacts was somewhat higher at low-capacity colleges (61 individuals) than high-capacity colleges (50 individuals).* This fits what we would expect: low-capacity institutions would tend to be less able to respond effectively to performance funding demands. As we saw in chapter 7, respondents at low-capacity institutions more often reported obstacles than did their counterparts at high-capacity institutions: 70 individuals versus 45 (see chapter 7). This greater incidence of obstacles might make it more likely that these institutions would consider or actually carry out practices not intended by policymakers in order to appear to successfully respond to performance funding.

---

* As discussed in chapter 2, we focus only on high- and low-capacity colleges because we had fewer medium-capacity colleges in our sample.

Table 8.7 Reports of Unintended Impacts by Institutional Capacity
(Number of Individuals Reporting)

Impact	High-capacity colleges			Low-capacity colleges		
	Potential	Observed	Total	Potential	Observed	Total
Restricted student admissions	12	7	19	22	5	27
Weakening of academic standards	13	4	17	18	6	24
Compliance costs	0	5	5	0	5	5
Lower morale	0	2	2	0	5	5
Decrease in faculty voice	0	0	0	0	5	5
Lessening of institutional cooperation	2	1	3	1	1	2
Narrowing of institutional mission	2	2	4	1	0	1
Other unintended impacts	2	5	7	2	3	5
Total number of reports	31	26	57	44	30	74
Total unduplicated individuals reporting	27	23	50	35	26	61

Note: The table excludes medium-capacity institutions (see text for reasons). The total number of reports is higher than the total number of unduplicated respondents who mentioned any unintended impact, as it includes individuals who reported more than one unintended impact. The Tennessee reports reflect only the 2010 PF 2.0 program.

Despite the difference in total number of reports of unintended impacts, there was little difference by institutional capacity in the distribution of reports across categories of unintended impacts. For example, 33% of our reports from high-capacity institutions (19 out of 57) involved restriction of student admissions, while the comparable figure for low-capacity institutions was 36% (27 out of 74). However, an analysis we conducted of Integrated Postsecondary Education Data System data on freshmen test scores shows an interesting difference among universities differing in capacity. We traced how the test scores of entering freshmen changed between 2009 and 2013.* For the low-capacity state universities in our sample, the SAT Verbal, SAT Math, and ACT Composite I scores of students at the 25th percentile rose by 3%, 3.5%, and 3.7%, respectively.† However, for the three high-capacity, research-intensive universities in our sample, the comparable figures were 0.7%, 1.0%, and 2.3%. (A similar pattern held for students in the 75th percentile.) Granted, the rising test scores at the low-capacity

* We were unable to conduct a similar analysis for community colleges because they largely do not ask for or collect SAT or ACT scores.
† For our third low-capacity institution, we had data only for the ACT Composite I. The average changes for the SAT Verbal and SAT Math pertain to only two of the institutions.

universities could be due to such factors as better-prepared students being priced out of the higher-capacity, typically more expensive universities. But it could also indicate a stronger push by the lower-capacity universities to attract better-prepared students who are more likely to graduate and bring more performance-based funding to those universities. High-capacity institutions would have less incentive to do so because they already attract better-prepared students.

Summary and Conclusions

The sociological and organizational literature tells us that when institutions cannot use legitimate methods, they may resort to illegitimate means to realize socially expected goals (see Merton, 1968, 1976; Mica, Peisert, & Winczorek, 2012). In the case of performance funding, our findings show that the use of outcomes-based metrics can have unintended impacts in that higher education institutions respond to performance demands in ways not intended by policymakers.

In our analysis of nine community colleges and nine universities in three states, the most commonly reported unintended impacts are restrictions in admissions to college and weakening of academic standards, with unreimbursed costs of compliance with performance funding demands, weakening of institutional cooperation, lower morale, and narrowing of institutional missions garnering fewer mentions. These negative unintended impacts are similar to those that have been reported by Dougherty & Reddy (2013) in their review of the literature on performance funding in higher education and by studies of performance management in government (Grizzle, 2002; Heinrich & Marschke, 2010; Moynihan, 2008, 2010; Rothstein, 2008b).

Admission of students who are less prepared academically and therefore less likely to finish college can be restricted by such means as higher admission requirements, selective recruitment, and focusing institutional financial aid on better-prepared students. Colleges can restrict admission of less prepared students by requiring higher standardized test scores and grade point averages or by decreasing the number of conditionally admitted students accepted each year. Selective recruitment can occur by de-emphasizing outreach efforts to high schools with many students who are not well prepared academically. Admissions can also be affected by shifting the focus of the college's own financial aid funds from assisting needy students to attracting better-prepared students through so-called merit aid.

This restriction of access for less prepared students is particularly of concern because of the association between academic preparation and social class and race/ethnicity (Astin & Oseguera, 2005; Cabrera & La Nasa, 2001). There is evidence that when state performance funding programs lead to restrictions in admission of less prepared students, this is associated, in turn, with drops in the enrollment of minority and, perhaps, low-income students. In their study of the impact of performance funding on Indiana public four-year institutions (see above), Umbricht, Fernandez, and Ortagus (2015) found that it was associated with drops in the enrollment of minority students in all nine models they estimated, with two of those models yielding statistically significant results. Moreover, while performance funding was associated with *increases* in the enrollment of federally aided (presumably lower-income) students in four models (two of them statistically significant), it was also associated with drops—although not statistically significant—in five models (Umbricht, Fernandez, & Ortagus, 2015).

Academic standards can be weakened by reducing academic demands in class (grade inflation) or reducing degree requirements. Calling attention to low course or degree completion rates can lead faculty to decrease their academic demands (and therefore to grade more easily) in order to produce higher rates of course completion. Degree requirements can be weakened by reducing the number of credits required to complete a degree and by recommending that students take easier courses.

We should underscore that many of our reports of unintended impacts involved *potential* impacts—that is, forecasts of what might happen, particularly if performance funding demands get more intense. These reports of potential impacts could be testimony more to our respondents' fears than to their understanding of processes actually unfolding. Still, it should be noted that half of the impacts mentioned were ones that we classified as *observed* in that they were reports not of possible impacts but of ones that respondents described as having occurred or where active steps were being taken to produce them. Furthermore, we have to keep in mind that our interviews occurred before Tennessee and, especially, Ohio had fully phased in their performance funding programs. Hence, we have to wonder how many of the potential impacts mentioned might in time become actual. Finally, even if we still conclude that the potential unintended impacts will mostly remain only potential, they still testify to a widespread disquiet about performance funding among higher education administrators and faculty which needs to be sensitively addressed by the advocates of performance funding.

Within this general pattern we also found some important variations by state, type of college, and organizational capacity of institutions. We received many more reports of unintended impacts in Ohio than in Indiana and, especially, Tennessee. An important contributor may have been that our Ohio respondents more often reported obstacles than did their counterparts in Indiana and, especially, Tennessee. In addition, the fact that performance funding in Ohio was revised during the time we were conducting our interviews there may have weighed heavily on the minds of Ohio faculty and administrators, contributing to more often reporting unintended impacts. With regard to type of college, we had few differences in reports from our community college versus our university respondents, except for the fact that the latter were substantially more likely to report actual or potential restrictions in admissions. This seems to testify to the continued impact of community colleges' traditional commitment to the ideal of maintaining open-door admissions. Finally, our data reveal that respondents at low-capacity colleges and universities more often reported unintended impacts. This fits our finding that such colleges reported more obstacles to meeting performance demands than did high-capacity colleges (see chapter 7). However, there was little difference by college capacity in the distribution of reports across different kinds of unintended impacts.

The policy implementation literature and principal–agent theory (reviewed in chapter 2) provide a lens through which we can understand how unintended outcomes can arise from performance funding policies. The top-down perspective in the policy implementation and organizational change literatures suggests that unintended impacts may arise from the obstacles that local implementers face in meeting the goals of higher-level policy designers. The obstacles that our respondents frequently cited as interfering with their institution's ability to respond to performance funding included enrolling many students who are not well prepared for college, lack of institutional capacity for IR, and performance indicators that do not fit well with institutional missions, particularly for community college (see chapter 7).

Confronted by these obstacles, institutional actors may be tempted to resort to actions that are potentially harmful but allow them to meet the demands placed on their organizations. If states demand higher levels of degree completion but disregard the need of colleges for more resources to cope with higher performance demands (see the discussion on capacity building in chapter 3), then institutions may move toward becoming more restrictive in the admission of less prepared (and less advantaged) students who are less likely to graduate. Similarly, if state officials and college senior administrators demand higher course completion rates but disregard the need to provide colleges with assistance in increasing rates through legitimate means, administrators and faculty may feel pushed to increase completion by reducing academic standards and giving out fewer failing grades.

This is not to say that institutions resort to tactics that produce impacts unintended by policymakers only because the institutions feel no alternative. On occasion, those societally unintended impacts may be *intended* by institutions. As we have seen, some administrators and faculty, particularly at less selective universities, welcome the opportunity to have their institutions become more selective, by excluding less prepared students, because greater selectivity is associated with higher institutional prestige. We also have to keep in mind that a number of state policymakers may have also welcomed the possibility that performance funding might lead institutions to become more selective.

Because restricting admissions of less prepared students and reducing academic quality are institutionally tempting but societally undesirable approaches for colleges to improve their performance on state metrics, states need to take decided steps to reduce this temptation. As we noted above, our three states did make efforts to combat the appearance of unintended impacts. However, it is clear that more needs to be done. We take up this point in our concluding chapter.

CHAPTER 9

Summary and Conclusions

This book has addressed six questions: What policy instruments have states used as part of their performance funding (PF) programs in order to influence the behavior of institutions? What deliberative processes have colleges and universities used to determine how to respond to performance funding? What institutional responses to performance funding have we seen from colleges and universities? How have performance funding programs affected student outcomes? Have institutions encountered obstacles in trying to effectively respond to the demands of performance funding? And finally, has performance funding produced outcomes unintended by policymakers?

To answer these research questions, we analyzed the performance funding experiences of three leading states (Indiana, Ohio, and Tennessee) and 18 universities and community colleges within them. We picked these three states because they are leaders in performance funding—particularly PF 2.0—but otherwise differ substantially in the histories of their performance funding programs and in their political and socioeconomic structures. Within each state we examined the experiences of three community colleges and three public universities that differed in their expected capacity to respond effectively to performance funding. To shed light on the experiences of these institutions and on key features of the state performance funding programs, we interviewed 261 institutional administrators and faculty, state officials, and state-level political actors. We also drew on documentary sources such as academic research studies, public agency reports, newspaper articles, and state and institutional websites.

In this chapter, we reflect on our findings and draw their implications for policy and research. We conclude with some observations about the future of performance funding.

Key Findings

Chapters 3–8 each end with detailed summaries, so there is no need to repeat their findings in the same detail here. In this section, we highlight the most noteworthy findings. In particular, we wish to call attention to the inadequate state effort to build up the organizational capacity of institutions to respond to performance funding, the frequency with which college personnel report insufficient organizational capacity as an obstacle to responding effectively to performance funding, and the ways in which that lack of capacity hinders institutions from improving student outcomes and pushes them toward unintended impacts.

POLICY INSTRUMENTS

Our interviews with campus personnel yielded substantial evidence that performance funding programs in Indiana, Ohio, and Tennessee do influence higher education institutions to change their policies and practices by providing financial incentives, communicating state priorities, and communicating institutional performance on state metrics. Our campus respondents testified to the sizable impact of all three policy instruments, particularly the financial incentives, on campus-level efforts to improve student outcomes. However, we found little evidence that the states vigorously built up institutional capacity to respond effectively to performance funding as a principal policy instrument. Although our state-level respondents did note capacity-building efforts, our institutional respondents overwhelmingly rated the state efforts as quite minimal. This is of great import because—as we found in chapters 4 and 7—insufficient institutional capacity emerged as an important obstacle to organizational deliberation on performance funding and to effective institutional response to performance funding.

ORGANIZATIONAL LEARNING

We distinguish among three types of structures our 18 institutions used to deliberate on how to improve student outcomes: general administrative structures, such as designated positions in charge of improving student outcomes; special-purpose deliberative structures, such as strategic planning and accreditation self-study committees; and informal deliberative structures outside of any particular formal structure. Each of the 18 institutions typically used all three kinds of deliberative processes. However, there was a strong tendency for community colleges to rely more heavily on special-purpose structures than did universities. We attribute this to the greater involvement of community colleges in initiatives to improve student outcomes, such as Achieving the Dream and Completion by Design, which ask for the creation of special-purpose deliberative structures such as steering committees. Institutional respondents cited many factors that, by their presence or absence, contributed to aiding or hindering the deliberative processes used to address performance funding demands: organizational commitment and leadership, communication and collaboration, time and opportunity to implement changes, and timely and relevant data. We wish to call attention to the importance of timely and relevant data, which depend, in turn, on organizational capacity for IR.

INSTITUTIONAL CHANGES

The most common changes campuses made following the adoption of performance funding involved revamping developmental education programs and altering advising and counseling services. Changes in these programs and services were described as clearly helping to improve institutional outcomes on performance funding metrics. At the same time, performance funding is but one of several concurrent external influences that seek to improve institutional outcomes in higher education. States have encouraged or even legislatively mandated institutional changes involving developmental education, course articulation and transfer, and advising. Institutions are also influenced by accreditors, foundations, and other nonprofit associations that fund or otherwise advocate for similar reforms. Consequently, it is difficult to disentangle the unique influence of performance funding from the influence of other external factors on institutions' decisions to make particular campus-level changes. Performance funding clearly made a major contribution to the institutional changes discussed, but we must still address the question of whether these changes ultimately resulted in significant improvements in student outcomes.

STUDENT OUTCOMES

Multivariate statistical analyses allow researchers to compare the higher educational performance of states with performance funding to that of states without, while also controlling for a host of other factors affecting student outcomes: shifts in enrollments, variations in the state of the economy, changes in tuition and student aid, the impact of other state policies to improve student outcomes, and so forth. When these factors are in good part accounted for in careful multivariate analyses of graduation numbers or retention rates, the research we reviewed largely fails to find a significant positive impact of performance funding in higher education. However, there is some evidence of delayed effects on four-year college graduation, impacts on short-term community college certificates, and, in some states, impacts on community college associate's degrees. These findings certainly suggest the need for more research on performance funding before we can definitively conclude that it either works or does not. (We comment below on what forms that new research should take.) Meanwhile, the lack of evidence clearly tying performance funding to better student outcomes raises the question of whether that lack of impact stems from obstacles institutions encounter in responding effectively to performance funding.

OBSTACLES TO RESPONDING TO PERFORMANCE FUNDING

Policy framers in Indiana, Ohio, and Tennessee intended for performance funding policies to change institutional behavior in order to improve student performance, but our respondents reported several persistent obstacles that have hindered their ability to respond effectively to performance funding. These obstacles are similar to those reported by research on performance management in government (see chapter 2). The most commonly perceived obstacles to improving student outcomes were the following: the college readiness of incoming students (open-access institutions educate many students who face academic, social, and economic challenges to graduating), performance funding metrics that are poorly matched to differences in institutional missions and student-body composition, and insufficient institutional capacity, particularly for IR. This last obstacle is rooted in part in inadequate state efforts to build up the capacities of institutions to respond to performance funding. The presence of these various reported obstacles to effective institutional responses to performance funding raises the specter that college actors may resort to illegitimate means to succeed. If colleges face both strong pressure to perform well on state outcomes metrics and major obstacles to doing so by legitimate means, will they be tempted to resort to illegitimate means to succeed, thus producing impacts unintended by state policymakers (see Merton, 1968, 1976)?

UNINTENDED IMPACTS

In our analysis of 18 public institutions in three states, the most commonly reported unintended impacts are restrictions in admission of underprepared students to college and the weakening of academic standards, with unreimbursed costs of compliance with performance funding demands, weakening of institutional cooperation, lower morale, and narrowing of institutional missions garnering fewer mentions. These negative unintended impacts are similar to those that have been reported in the literature on performance management in government (see chapter 2). But even if not unanticipated, these unintended impacts are still disturbing. Weakening of academic standards and restricting the admission of less prepared students are disturbing practices, particularly if pursued by institutions historically committed to broad access to higher education. Such practices undermine basic aspects of the mission of higher education, particularly of institutions such as community colleges and broad-access public universities historically committed to broadening access to higher education. Because of this, we devote considerable attention later in this chapter to ways state policymakers might best guard against these unintended impacts and the organizational obstacles that contribute to them. An important thread in these policy prescriptions is a recognition that while certain societally negative impacts might be unintended by policymakers, they may be intended by institutional actors.

DIFFERENCES WITHIN THESE MAIN PATTERNS

As we expected, our three states of Indiana, Ohio, and Tennessee exhibited important differences in the implementation and outcomes of performance funding. The most striking pattern involved Tennessee. Compared to their counterparts in Indiana and Ohio, our Tennessee respondents more often reported that the policy instruments associated with performance funding were energetically pursued and had a sizable impact. The one exception was capacity building, where there was little discernible difference among the states. Moreover, our Tennessee respondents reported fewer obstacles and unintended impacts than did their Indiana and Ohio counterparts. These patterns may testify to the fact not only that Tennessee's performance funding program has put more state funding in play than is the case in Indiana and Ohio but also that Tennessee has worked with performance funding far longer and has had more opportunity to "work out the kinks." In our policy recommendations below, we will analyze the lessons to be drawn from Tennessee's long experience with performance funding.

We consistently found differences by type of institution in each of the areas we examined, stretching from policy instrument implementation to unintended impacts. Many of these differences were not surprising. For example, we would expect community colleges to more often respond to performance funding demands by revamping developmental education, while public universities more often reported such responses as improving STEM education and residence life. However, two differences are worth underscoring. Our community college respondents reported more obstacles to responding to performance funding, with student-body composition differences contributing most to this difference. This raises the question of what can be done to help community colleges better address the obstacles they encounter. On the other hand, our community college respondents less often reported restrictions of admissions as an unintended impact (particularly as an observed impact) than did their university counterparts. This may testify to the continued influence of the community college ideal of open-door admissions. The question then remains whether we need to bolster the egalitarian ethos of public universities that historically have been committed to encouraging wide access to higher education but are being drawn away from their egalitarian commitment by the pressures of performance funding.

On the whole, high- and low-capacity institutions differed less strikingly than did community colleges and universities in their reports on the implementation and impacts of performance funding. However, it is noteworthy that our respondents at low-capacity institutions were considerably more likely to report obstacles and unintended impacts than were their counterparts at high-capacity colleges, including more often reporting actual or potential efforts to weaken academic standards and restrict admissions. Given these patterns, what do we need to do to help low-capacity institutions address performance funding demands in less deleterious ways?

Implications for Policy

Many states are currently considering performance funding. Below, we offer our thoughts for policymakers in need of guidance on how to guard against potential obstacles and unintended impacts produced by performance funding programs.

REDUCING UNINTENDED NEGATIVE IMPACTS

We focus on the two main unintended impacts of performance funding: weakening of academic standards and reducing admission of less prepared students. In addressing these unintended impacts, we need to remain aware that although they may be unintended by state policymakers, they may actually be intended by many institutional actors (see chapter 2).

Protecting Academic Standards. As we saw in chapter 8, we had many reports that institutions in our three states have resorted or might resort to weakening academic standards in order to respond to performance funding. This matches reports from other states reviewed in previous research (Dougherty & Reddy, 2013). For the most part, our three states have not directly dealt with this threat. They have mostly relied on institutional and faculty commitment to preserve academic standards (Dougherty et al., 2014a). This is indeed a crucial bulwark, but it is not enough, as indicated by the large number of reports we received from our institutional respondents concerning observed or potential weakening of academic standards. What should therefore be done?

States and colleges can carefully monitor degree requirements and course grade distributions to determine whether they change substantially after the advent of performance funding (Dougherty & Reddy, 2013; Snyder, 2015). Moreover, states and colleges can conduct anonymous surveys of faculty to see whether they report substantial pressure to weaken academic requirements in order to keep up rates of course completion, retention, and graduation (Dougherty & Reddy, 2013). Finally, states can conduct learning assessments to determine whether student academic performance has dropped, possibly indicating a weakening of academic standards (Dougherty & Reddy, 2013). Tennessee has retained its original PF 1.0 program to act as a quality measure flanking the PF 2.0 program it established in 2010, and this PF 1.0 program includes various measures of student learning, such as student performance on major field and general education examinations (Bogue & Johnson, 2010; Dougherty & Natow, 2015, chap. 4; Tennessee Higher Education Commission, 2010).* Similarly, Missouri's performance funding program includes measures of quality of student learning: assessments of general education, assessments in the major field, and passage rates on professional/occupation licensure tests (Jones, 2013; Missouri Department of Higher Education, 2014).

Any measures of student learning should be very carefully developed and implemented. The development of student learning measures should involve faculty in order to increase the probability of utilizing measures that are seen as legitimate and instructionally valid.† Otherwise, a state performance funding system may encounter the widespread criticism directed at the general learning examinations that were mandated by the Tennessee PF 1.0 program (Dougherty & Reddy, 2013).

---

* The Tennessee PF 1.0 program also has included three other sets of measures: evaluation of instructional programs (based on surveys of current students, recent alumni, or employers), evaluation of academic programs (by peer review teams of scholars from institutions outside the state and/or practicing professionals in a field), and program accreditation (proportion of eligible programs in the institution's inventory that are accredited) (Bogue & Johnson, 2010; Dougherty & Natow, 2015, chap. 5).

† For promising approaches to academic assessment which involve faculty in a central way, see Gold et al. (2011) and Smith (2015).

Besides monitoring whether academic standards are weakening, it is also important to build in protections. One of the most important is ensuring that there is no direct tie between course completion rates and decisions on rehiring, promoting, and tenuring faculty. Otherwise, faculty may experience strong institutional pressure to reduce course requirements and engage in grade inflation (see Claeys-Kulik & Estermann, 2015, p. 48).

Countering Disincentives to Enrolling Less Prepared and Less Advantaged Students. As we also reported in chapter 8, we received many reports of observed or potential efforts by institutions to restrict their enrollment of less prepared students, who also tend to be minorities and less advantaged socioeconomically. Hence, it is crucial that states take steps to reduce this temptation to restrict enrollments by instead providing incentives for institutions to serve underprepared students (Dougherty & Reddy, 2013; Snyder, 2015).

State policy designers in Indiana, Ohio, and Tennessee were aware that colleges and universities with high numbers of less prepared and less advantaged students would have a more difficult time retaining and graduating their students than institutions with better-prepared and more advantaged student bodies, and that this would tempt the former institutions to avoid such students (Dougherty et al., 2014a). Hence, state policy designers added provisions to their performance funding programs to incentivize institutions to take in at-risk students (see chapter 8 and appendix A). Indiana has indicators specifically related to the graduation of low-income students (Indiana Commission for Higher Education, 2013a, 2014). Ohio weights course and degree completions for the university main and regional campuses by whether students are at risk, defined in terms of varying combinations of family income, race/ethnicity, and age. The state plans to do the same for community colleges by FY 2015–16 (Ohio Board of Regents, 2015a, 2015b, 2015c). Tennessee has extra weighting for low-income students, adult learners, and (beginning in FY 2016–17) academically underprepared students on indicators for credit accumulation and degree production (Tennessee Higher Education Commission, 2014a, 2015a, 2015c, 2015d). Other states have pursued this path as well. An analysis of the performance funding programs in 25 states found that 13 had some means of prioritizing underrepresented students (Snyder, 2015). For states that have not yet provided premiums for graduating at-risk students, we would recommend that they include metrics for, at the very least, low-income, racial-minority, adult, and academically underprepared students.

These premiums can have a considerable impact on institutional allocations. In Tennessee, they can shift institutional allocations by as much as 12%, with an average of about 4%, above what institutions would get without the premiums for credit accumulation and graduation of at-risk students (authors' interviews). And in Indiana, a senior administrator at a university observed, "Our share or position in the performance funding has been at least in the positive, and part of that is gradually we're doing better with overall completion rates, but also with something like three quarters of our students having high levels of need when we graduate them. Yes, that pays off for us."

Still, senior administrators at several other institutions—particularly community colleges in Indiana and Ohio—largely dismissed the usefulness of the premium for at-risk students. These actors instead called for more help from the state government to meet the needs of at-risk students. For example, on the subject of giving greater weighting for disadvantaged students on the graduation indicator, a senior administrator at an Indiana community college stated, "Well, I think it helps some. I think that it could help more. I mean, again, these are, a lot of these are first-generation college students. If we had additional funding, I think that there are some ways that we could help them more."

At the very least, this argues that the premium for at-risk students should probably be made substantially greater. It is instructive that Tennessee has greatly raised its premiums for at-risk students (termed "focus populations") beginning in FY 2017. In the case of universities, there are two at-risk student categories receiving a premium: low-income and adult students. For the community colleges, there is an additional category: academically underprepared students.* Students who fall into one of the at-risk categories will be weighted an additional 80%. Those falling into two categories will be weighted an additional 100%. And students meeting all three categories (only possible at community colleges) will be weighted an additional 120% (Tennessee Higher Education Commission, 2015e).

A second means by which states can counteract the temptation to engage in "cream skimming" through restricted admissions is to make reducing social class and racial/ethnic gaps in college outcomes a goal of performance funding (HCM Strategists, 2015). One way to do this is to incorporate race and social class gap metrics in the performance funding program (Jones, 2015; Shulock, 2011). For example, the performance funding program for the institutions in the

---

* These are students who meet one of three criteria: they are identified as requiring remediation, they score an 18 or below on the ACT Composite, or they score either an 18 or below on the ACT Reading or Mathematics component or a 17 or below on the ACT Writing component (Tennessee Higher Education Commission, 2015e).

Pennsylvania State System for Higher Education includes metrics for closing achievement gaps for Pell Grant recipients and for underrepresented minorities (Cavanaugh & Garland, 2012; Jones, 2013). However, such "closing the gap" metrics should be carefully designed, taking into account ways that they might possibly disadvantage minority-serving institutions by pushing them to reduce their proportion of students of color (Jones, 2015).

Third, states can also reduce the temptation to engage in restrictive admissions by allowing performance targets to vary across colleges according to their student characteristics, by comparing colleges to peer colleges, or (as is done by the Student Achievement Initiative in Washington) by comparing a college's performance now to its performance in the past (Bailey, 2011; Institute for Higher Education Policy, 2006; Jenkins & Shulock, 2013; Reindl & Reyna, 2011; Shulock, 2011; Shulock & Jenkins, 2011). Regression analysis can be used to develop input-adjusted metrics that take into account differences in student-body composition (Miller, 2014).* Finally, states can bolster colleges taking in many underprepared students by including metrics for intermediate achievements such as completing developmental education, passing key gatekeeping courses, and accumulating certain numbers of credits. These indicators will register progress by underprepared students, even if they do not in the end graduate from a college. This "momentum points" approach was pioneered by the state of Washington and adopted as well by Ohio and Tennessee (Dougherty & Natow, 2015; Jenkins & Shulock, 2013; Jones, 2014; Shulock & Jenkins, 2011).

These efforts to reduce the incidence of unintended outcomes would become even more effective if states address the obstacles that institutions encounter in being able to respond effectively to performance funding. We now turn to how those obstacles can be reduced.

REDUCING OBSTACLES TO EFFECTIVELY RESPONDING
TO PERFORMANCE FUNDING

It is clear that the states have tried to anticipate and prevent these obstacles, but the frequency with which they are reported indicates that more needs to be done. In particular, performance funding programs need to do more to address

---

* Such a procedure needs to be carefully done. Without due care, input-based adjustment carries the danger of enshrining already-existing selective admissions practices on the part of colleges (Bailey, 1988) or insufficiently pushing colleges that enroll many underprepared students (Miller, 2014).

these three main obstacles to effective institutional response: differences in student-body composition, inappropriate performance metrics, and insufficient capacity for organizational learning.

Addressing Differences in Student-Body Composition. It will certainly help mass-access institutions if they are better rewarded for enrolling and graduating less prepared students who are less likely to graduate. But this still leaves the question of what can be done to improve their capacity to graduate such students. According to many senior administrators and faculty, colleges and universities need more funding for financial aid and student services in order to improve their capacity to help their less prepared and low-income students succeed (see chapter 7). In addition, states need to create initiatives—drawing on national research and policy experience—to help institutions determine the best ways to improve the education of less advantaged students. Perhaps the most important efforts lie in improving developmental education and in laying out clear student pathways into and through higher education. Tennessee has been particularly noteworthy for its efforts on both counts (Bailey, Jaggars, & Jenkins, 2015; Boatman, 2012; Complete College Tennessee Act, 2010; Hodara, 2013).

Better Fitting Performance Metrics to Institutional Missions. As discussed in chapter 7, performance funding metrics that do not align well with institutional missions and student-body characteristics are a major obstacle to effective institutional response to performance funding. As such, policymakers need to better differentiate performance metrics by institutional missions and student-body characteristics (Dougherty & Reddy, 2013; Jones, 2012; Snyder, 2015).

Policymakers in Indiana, Ohio, and Tennessee have attempted to address the problem posed by inappropriate indicators and measures by (to varying degrees) differentiating the indicators for different kinds of institutions. For example, states have devised different metrics for two-year versus four-year institutions. And in the case of Tennessee, the metrics have been weighted differently according to institutional mission (Snyder, 2015; Tennessee Higher Education Commission, 2012a, 2012b). In addition, a number of states, such as Missouri and Pennsylvania, have allowed colleges to identify a number of indicators specific to their institution (Cavanaugh & Garland, 2012; Missouri Department of Higher Education, 2014).

Nevertheless, these efforts can and should go further. In the case of retention and completion, graduation measures for community colleges should be broken down by whether or not students intend to get a degree, a predisposition that could be determined by whether students demonstrate certain behaviors (Bailey, 2011; Claggett, 2011; Committee on Measures of Student Success, 2011; Offenstein & Shulock, 2010). For example, student intention to get a degree could be determined by whether students take more than six credits in the first year and enroll within the first two years in a course such as college-level math or English, a combination that is usually exhibited only by degree-seeking students (Offenstein & Shulock, 2010).

In addition, community college graduation measures should be coupled with transfer measures. Given how many students transfer from a community college to a four-year college without first getting a community college degree, performance funding programs should include indicators of successful transfer and pair them with measures of graduation (Claggett, 2011; Committee on Measures of Student Success, 2011; Jobs for the Future, 2008).* As it is, the Committee on Measures of Student Success, appointed by Secretary of Education Arne Duncan, recommended in 2011 that, in the case of community colleges, completion be defined to include not just graduation but also transfer to a four-year college, even without a community college degree.

Another key consideration in producing cohort graduation rates that fairly represent community college outputs is extending the time frame for tracking outcomes for students. Many community college students do not complete a degree or demonstrate other successful outcomes within the three years mandated by the federal Graduation Rate Survey because they attend part-time or have to begin by taking noncredit remedial courses. When students are tracked through six years after entry instead of three, completion rates rise sharply (Calcagno et al., 2008; Horn, 2010; Jobs for the Future, 2008; Offenstein & Shulock, 2010).† However, it is worth keeping in mind that increasing the follow-up period between when students enter college and when their performance is measured will mean that colleges will be getting performance data less quickly, making it

---

* In order to account for all transfer students, researchers recommend that—rather than relying just on reports from in-state public four-year colleges and universities—state metrics draw on data from the National Student Clearinghouse to capture students who transfer out of state (Bailey, 2011; Offenstein & Shulock, 2010). In addition, to the degree that colleges are rewarded for students who begin at the college but graduate elsewhere, it also will be important to count students who go out of state to graduate.

† At the same time, it is not certain that longer follow-ups will produce a radically different picture of which institutions are doing better and which are doing worse. It may be that the colleges with the best outcomes when students are followed up three years later will also be at the head of the pack when the follow-up is after six years (Calcagno et al., 2008).

harder to respond rapidly to emerging conditions and perhaps weakening the performance funding incentive.

The difficulties faced by some colleges—particularly those in rural areas—in meeting demands for job placement in well-paying jobs can be addressed by performance funding metrics that acknowledge local labor market contexts. Corrections for geographical and temporal differences in labor market conditions should be built explicitly into job and wage placement measures.

Addressing Missing Indicators. Beyond improving existing indicators, states should consider adding performance indicators that are often missing in state performance funding programs. We have mentioned two already: indicators specific to retention, progression, and completion of low-income and racial-minority students, and indicators measuring changes in racial and social class gaps in student progress and completion. Another indicator to consider is one for successful graduation of transfer students from four-year institutions (Institute for Higher Education Policy, 2006). Given the increasing importance of transfer to baccalaureate attainment, it becomes increasingly important to make sure that students are able not only to transfer but also to graduate after transfer (Bailey, Jaggars, & Jenkins, 2015; Dougherty, 1994; Handel & Williams, 2012). To be effective, such a transfer success indicator should be applied to both community colleges and universities in order to ensure that the former better prepare and advise transfers and the latter better remove obstacles to credit accrual and graduation after transfer (see Bailey, Jaggars, & Jenkins, 2015).

Improving Institutional Capacity for Organizational Learning. As we saw in chapters 4 and 7, a major obstacle that institutions encounter in responding to performance funding pressures is insufficient capacity to analyze data on their performance, determine the causes of and solutions to performance gaps, and implement solutions. Moreover, as we saw in chapter 3, states have not done enough to address gaps in institutions' capacity. To be sure, states have tried to help institutions accommodate themselves to performance funding by phasing it in gradually, either by holding institutions harmless in the first few years or limiting how much state funding they could lose (Altstadt, Fingerhut, & Kazis, 2012; Dougherty et al., 2014a; Jones, 2013; Shulock & Jenkins, 2011; Snyder, 2015; see also appendix A in this book). However, much more needs to be done in order for institutions to really develop the capacity to effectively engage in the processes required to address campus shortcomings. Otherwise, low-capacity institutions might be subject to a negative cycle where low capacity generates low performance, which in turn leads to reduced state funding.

With regard to analyzing data on their performance, institutions need funds and technical assistance to acquire new data management systems, expand the number of institutional researchers, and train faculty members and institutional research (IR) staff to analyze performance data. The data collection systems employed by many colleges were designed to gather information on inputs, and they often cannot support the kind of data capture and reporting needed to produce the fine-grained data colleges really need to understand how to improve student outcomes (Allen & Kazis, 2007; Kerrigan, 2014; Morest & Jenkins, 2007; Rutschow et al., 2011). Moreover, colleges need help developing IR offices that have enough personnel skilled in data analysis and that are oriented to serving the data needs of various constituencies at a college (Allen & Kazis, 2007; Jones, 2014, 2015; Morest & Jenkins, 2007; Rutschow et al., 2011). Finally, colleges need funds to train faculty and administrators in how to analyze and even produce data on student outcomes at their colleges (Allen & Kazis, 2007; Kerrigan, 2015; Rutschow et al., 2011).

With regard to determining causes of and solutions to performance gaps, resource-poor colleges need financial and technical assistance in developing their capacity to devise solutions to performance problems. This entails providing technical assistance and creating opportunities for colleges to create communities of practice with colleges facing similar challenges (Dowd & Tong, 2007; Jenkins & Shulock, 2013; Ness, Deupree, & Gándara, 2015; Shulock & Jenkins, 2011). Moreover, many colleges need assistance in developing regular communication channels within the institution which allow for organized discussions about how to improve student success (Kerrigan, 2015; see also Moynihan, 2008). Following the work on organizational learning by Chris Argyris and Donald Schön (1996), it is important that these communication channels allow colleges not only to find solutions to gaps between their espoused values and their actual performance (single-loop learning) but also to examine how the college's very values, beliefs, and structures contribute to poor student outcomes (double-loop learning). Colleges must be encouraged to examine how their theories of learning and student performance—particularly ones that lodge the problems primarily in students, rather than in the structures and processes of educational institutions themselves—contribute to poor student performance (Kezar et al., 2008; Witham & Bensimon, 2012; see also Argyris & Schön, 1996). This kind of deep inquiry may require extensive financial and technical assistance from states to build the organizational structures and culture that allow for such deliberation.

Addressing the Needs of Low-Capacity Institutions. State efforts to build up institutional capacity should focus particularly on the needs of low-capacity institutions. As noted above, these institutions tend to report more obstacles and unintended impacts than high-capacity institutions. A good part of the solution may lie in better financial support for these institutions because they tend to be less well supported than more advantaged institutions (Dowd & Shieh, 2013). Better funding may allow such institutions to build up capacity to respond better to the pressures of performance funding.

However, funding is not enough. It is also important that such institutions be well represented when performance funding metrics are designed. Such representation will make it more likely that performance funding metrics are chosen and policy instruments used that reflect the particular missions and organizational constraints of low-capacity institutions, particularly community colleges.

THE IMPORTANCE OF EXTENSIVE INSTITUTIONAL CONSULTATION AND PERIODIC REVIEW

A prerequisite for many of the actions recommended above is extensive state consultation with public higher education institutions across all types of missions (HCM Strategists, 2015; Hearn, 2015; Jones, 2013; Jones, 2015; Kadlec & Shelton, 2014; Shulock & Jenkins, 2011; Snyder, 2015; see also Claeys-Kulik & Estermann, 2015).* College administrators and faculty can help identify performance indicators and measures and funding practices that may produce deceptive results or perverse impacts (Blankenberger & Phillips, 2014; Jones, 2014; Snyder, 2015). They can also help identify what kinds of assistance colleges need in order to engage in effective deliberation and action leading to the ultimate student outcomes state officials seek (Jenkins, 2011; Shulock & Jenkins, 2011). If nothing else, extensive consultation can be a means of securing institutional buy-in which helps protect performance funding from being eliminated in periods of fiscal stress when institutional political support is important (Dougherty & Natow, 2015). Moreover, because of the strength of the culture of academic self-governance, change within academia tends to come more easily when it is internally generated or enlists strong support from faculty and mid-level administrators (Bailey, Jaggars, & Jenkins, 2015, chap. 5; Schmidtlein & Berdahl, 2011; Stensaker, 2003).

---

* See Coburn (2003), Coburn & Stein (2006), and Spillane, Reiser, & Gomez (2006) on the importance of faculty buy-in in the case of performance accountability regimes in K–12 schooling.

This process of consultation should be cognizant of the diversity of higher education (Institute for Higher Education Policy, 2006; Jones, 2015; see also Claeys-Kulik & Estermann, 2015). The institutions consulted should include community colleges as well as universities, broad-access as well as highly selective institutions, minority-serving as well as predominantly white institutions, and technical as well as comprehensive institutions. This breadth of consultation heightens the probability that performance funding programs will recognize the complexity of higher education and avoid performance metrics that poorly capture institutional success and policy instruments that inadequately reach institutions.

Consultation with institutions about performance funding should also be ongoing, occurring throughout the life of the program and not just at the beginning. However thoroughly vetted beforehand, some performance metrics will prove to be hard to implement or have perverse consequences. Moreover, new state needs or institutional circumstances may arise that require new or modified metrics. Institutions will be key sources of information on these points, and their perspectives are best garnered through processes of periodic and systematic review (Bogue & Johnson, 2010; Jones, 2013; Snyder, 2015).

Tennessee provides a particularly fruitful guide on how to do periodic evaluation. From the beginning it has subjected its performance funding programs to a five-year review cycle. These periodic reviews involve extensive and formalized consultation between the Tennessee Higher Education Commission, the Tennessee Board of Regents, and the University of Tennessee (Bogue, 2002; Bogue & Johnson, 2010; Stinson, 2003; Tennessee Higher Education Commission, 2015a, 2015b). A statutory Formula Review Committee meets yearly and reviews reports and presentations from institutional representatives. Its members are as follows: the executive director of the Tennessee Higher Education Commission, the chancellor of the Tennessee Board of Regents, the president of the University of Tennessee, the state controller, the commissioner of the Department of Finance and Administration, the chairs of the House and Senate education committees and ways and means committees, and the budget analysis directors for the House and Senate (Tennessee Higher Education Commission, 2015b). One improvement on the Tennessee consultation process would be to include vigorous faculty representation not just on lower-level committees but also on the topmost Formula Review Committee, perhaps by having one or more designated positions for representatives of faculty senates or unions from a diverse set of colleges.

Implications for Research

Our three states and 18 institutions have provided us with varied perspectives on the implementation and impacts of performance funding, with particular attention to PF 2.0. To a considerable extent our research findings converge with previous research on the impacts of performance funding in higher education (Dougherty & Reddy, 2013) and performance management in government (see Heinrich & Marschke, 2010; Moynihan, 2008, 2010; Rothstein, 2008b). At the same time, our research has led us to findings not discussed in the extant research on performance funding, particularly the existence of important differences by type of program, state, college type, and estimated college capacity in the implementation and impacts of performance funding. These findings should be followed up in the following ways.

Clearly, we need more multivariate studies of the impact of performance funding. We lack enough studies of PF 2.0 programs, particularly ones that have been operating for a number of years, are fully phased in, and involve a very large share of state funding for higher education, as in Tennessee and Ohio. This multivariate research should examine the impact not only of whether a state has performance funding but also of the features of that program, for example, how long it has been in place, what proportion of total institutional funding it affects, which particular performance metrics and weights drive funding allocations, and what other state programs affecting student outcomes (such as initiatives to revamp developmental education or improve transfer pathways) are operating alongside performance funding and jointly affecting student outcomes (see Shaw, 2015). In doing this, researchers should keep in mind that features of a state's performance funding program can vary greatly over time, as performance metrics are revised, added or dropped, or changed in weight (see Dougherty & Natow, 2015). Finally, these new multivariate studies should examine the impacts of performance funding not just on student outcomes but also on intermediate institutional processes that may produce improvements in student outcomes, for example, institutional changes in academic policies and programs, student services policies and programs, and institutional research.

With regard to state differences, it would be instructive to investigate the implementation and impacts of PF 2.0 in states that have had little prior history with performance funding, unlike Ohio and Tennessee. Do such states approach the implementation of performance funding differently than states with a longer history of it? Do such states encounter obstacles and unintended impacts that differ in either nature or intensity from those reported in our three states? In addition, it would be interesting to study the implementation of performance funding in states that narrowly focus on financial incentives to drive performance funding, making little effort to use other policy instruments or to flank performance funding with curricular and instructional initiatives in such areas as developmental education. Compared to the more broad-gauged approach of our three states, do narrowly focused programs differ in the kinds of changes institutions make, the impacts on student outcomes, and the kinds and severity of obstacles and unintended impacts encountered?

With regard to institutional differences, it is important to further investigate dimensions of institutional differences that may affect the implementation and impacts of performance funding. We certainly need more studies that examine how the implementation and impacts of performance funding differ for two-year versus four-year colleges and high-capacity versus low-capacity institutions. Too much research on performance funding has been focused on just public four-year institutions. But there are other institutional differences that merit attention as well. For example, there is evidence that performance funding has considerably different impacts on minority-serving institutions than on predominantly white institutions (Jones, 2014, 2015; Jones, Jones, & Saumby, 2015). This is a very important topic that needs further research.

Concluding Thoughts

Performance funding tends to provoke polarized responses, with some making strong claims for how it is highly effective and serves the public interest in higher education (Complete College America, 2013) and others arguing that it is ineffective and may greatly harm higher education (Fichtenbaum, 2013). This polarization resembles the great divergence of perspectives on the prospects and impacts for performance management in government and public and social accountability more generally (see Hood, 1991; Neave, 1998; Power, 1994; Radin, 2006). This polarization of perspectives hampers our ability to truly understand whether and how we should use performance funding. We argue instead that performance funding should be approached more cautiously, using empirical data to guide our responses.*

---

* This polarization of research and debate has certainly occurred in the case of K–12 education, most notably with respect to charter schools. For an instructive analysis of how this polarization came about and how it can be tempered, see Henig (2008).

The relative absence of findings that performance funding does produce significant improvements in student outcomes should not lead us to dismiss it as yet. The multivariate studies of PF 2.0 which we reviewed in chapter 6, however well done, are still too few in number to yield definitive conclusions. Only a few studies have examined PF 2.0 programs that embed performance indicators in the base state funding formula and involve large shares of state appropriations for higher education, and none of these studies as yet have followed up those programs after they were fully phased in and had been in operation for several years. We need more studies, particularly ones that follow up the intriguing finding that performance funding may have delayed effects. If these additional studies still do not find any impact of performance funding on student outcomes, we have to take very seriously the possibility that potential effects are being undercut or even nullified by the obstacles that we documented in chapter 7.

Even if performance funding does prove to foster improved student outcomes, the fact still remains that it has substantial unintended impacts that need to be addressed. If higher retention and graduation numbers are purchased at the cost of restricting the admission of less prepared and less advantaged students or of lowering academic standards, this could well vitiate the benefits of performance funding. We need to move to vigorously counter these unintended impacts. If those unintended impacts are not kept in check, they will constitute strong arguments against performance funding. We must also keep in mind that unintended impacts that are now relatively weak—such as weakening faculty morale and reducing faculty voice in academic governance (see chapter 8)—may intensify as performance funding intensifies. If so, might performance funding greatly undercut faculty morale, as No Child Left Behind has done for K–12 teachers (Byrd-Blake et al., 2010; Finnigan & Gross, 2007)?

Regardless of the above, we need to keep in mind that the future of performance funding will not depend just on evidence of its effectiveness and of its ability to avoid major negative side effects. As with any other public program, it is subject to the vicissitudes of the political and economic environment, where fiscal crisis, changing governmental priorities, and loss of political champions can imperil even seemingly well-entrenched public programs (Dougherty & Natow, 2015). Still, evidence on the implementation and impacts (intended and unintended) of performance funding should play an important role in decisions over whether to adopt or retain performance funding in the future.

Appendix A: *The Nature and History of Performance Funding in Indiana, Ohio, and Tennessee*

The performance funding (PF) programs in Indiana, Ohio, and Tennessee all involve embedding PF indicators in the base state funding for higher education. However, the three states differ considerably in the amount of state funding based on performance indicators and in the precise way they embed the indicators. Tennessee and Ohio use a formula to determine state funding for higher education operations, with about four-fifths of the funding of those operating appropriations based on performance indicators. In Indiana, PF involves a much smaller amount (6% of state operational funding), and that funding involves both bonus funding and withheld funding that is paid back based on performance. For a detailed history of those programs, see Dougherty & Natow (2015). We will confine ourselves here to a simple chronology and description of the programs.

Indiana

Indiana first adopted PF in 2007 in the form of a bonus on top of the base state funding for higher education (HCM Strategists, 2011). However, this program was quickly replaced in 2009 by a new program in which 5% of each institution's base allocation would be withheld and then all or some of it would be awarded based on performance on certain metrics (Dougherty & Natow, 2015; SPEC Associates, 2012b). In the 2011–13 biennium, this 5% withholding amounted to roughly $61 million (Indiana Commission for Higher Education, 2011a, 2013a, p. 8). In 2013, the state general assembly decided to hold PF at 6% for both FY 2014 and FY 2015 but changed the allocation method. The 6% devoted to PF was split between 3.8% in "new money" and 2.2% from withholding funds from institutional appropriations. The portion withheld is put into a funding pool, and institutions can then earn back some or all of that withheld funding depending on how well they perform during the year and how well other institutions perform (authors' IN interviews).

The PF indicators are designed to measure change over time, based on comparing two three-year averages of institutional performance. For each metric, the PF formula takes average performance across three years and compares it to the three-year average for the preceding three years (e.g., for determining funding withheld in 2012, average number of completions each year between 2009 and 2011 compared to average number of degree completions each year between 2006 and 2008). If an institution's performance does not improve, the funding formula simply counts their improvement as "zero." An institution's allocation through the PF formula is based on how well its performance compares with all other comparable institutions. For the 2013–15 biennium, it is possible for the overall effect of PF to be a loss if an institution (1) wins only a small portion of the new money bonus and (2) is not able to earn back all of the 2.2% that is withheld to help fund the PF formula. Moreover, an institution is not funded for its performance if its overall rate of completion drops between the two three-year averages (even if the overall number of completions increased). In total, a school's eventual state appropriation includes base funding (which can fluctuate year to year based on enrollment), new money that is earned on the basis of the performance indicators, and the portion of the funds withheld the year before which the institution was able to win back based on its performance in the previous three years.

The PF indicators Indiana has used have changed each biennium. However, certain indicators have persisted (Indiana Commission for Higher Education, 2013a, 2014):

- Change in number of degrees awarded (2009–11, 2011–13, 2013–15, 2015–17 biennia).
- Change in number (or rate) of resident, undergraduate, first-time, full-time students graduating on time (2009–11, 2011–13, 2013–15, 2015–17 biennia).
- Change in degree completion by low-income students (2009–11, 2011–13, 2013–15, 2015–17 biennia).
- Change in number of successfully completed credit hours (2009–11, 2011–13 biennia).

Over the years, these four indicators have accounted for 70%–84% of the PF allocation. The commission added four new metrics in the 2013–15 biennium: a productivity metric defined by each institution, "high-impact" (STEM) degree completion, a remediation success incentive, and a student persistence incentive (Indiana Commission for Higher Education, 2014).

The state provides greater weight for certain kinds of students: those lower in socioeconomic background and those graduating in STEM fields (Indiana Commission for Higher Education, 2013a, 2014).

Ohio

Ohio established two PF programs in the 1990s and then replaced them with a new program established in 2009 (Dougherty & Natow, 2015).

In 1995, Ohio adopted the Performance Challenge. It rewarded colleges on the basis of nine different "service expectations," but only one focused on outcomes versus process variables, such as amount of vocational education programming.* This single outcome-oriented service expectation rewarded community colleges, technical colleges, and branch campuses based on the number of students who transferred or relocated after

---

* The other eight service expectations under the Performance Challenge involved additional state support for providing broad job training, offering effective developmental education, providing noncredit continuing education opportunities, fostering business partnerships, developing high school linkages, providing accessible learning environment and effective instructional delivery strategies, keeping tuition and fees low, and creating high community involvement (Burke & Serban, 1998, pp. 40–41; Dunlop-Loach, 2000, app. B; Moden & Williford, 2002, pp. 173–77).

completing at least 15 quarter hours or 10 semester hours of coursework and on the number of transfer or relocated students who completed baccalaureate degrees (Dunlop-Loach, 2000, app. B; Ohio Board of Regents, 1996). The Performance Challenge was abandoned in 2000 (Moden & Williford, 2002, pp. 174, 176).

In 1997, Ohio established the Success Challenge via a funding proviso in the budget bill for the 1997–99 biennium (HB 215, passed in 1997). Until it ended in FY 2010, the Success Challenge provided a bonus to universities based on the number of students who earned a baccalaureate degree. Two-thirds was based on numbers of in-state at-risk students graduating in any year; one-third was based on numbers of any in-state students who earned a baccalaureate degree "in a timely manner" (generally in four years, but extended for majors that required more than four years). The metric was the number who graduated, and not the graduation rate (percentage graduating), within four years (Moden & Williford, 2002, pp. 173–78). The Success Challenge began small, with $2 million in FY 1997–98, but funding rose rapidly in subsequent years, peaking at $53.7 million in FY 2008–9 (Petrick, 2012, p. 277). The money was unrestricted: it could be included in the institutions' overall budget and used in any way the institution so elected (O'Neal, 2007, pp. 49, 179–89). Success Challenge appropriations ceased after FY 2009.

In 2009, Ohio passed a budget bill embedding performance indicators in the state's formula for funding higher education operations (the State Share of Instruction). For the public universities, 80% of state operational funding would now be based on course and degree completions, with the remainder being set aside for doctoral and medical education. The degree completion share rose from 15% in FY 2011–12 to 50% in FY 2013–14 (Alstadt, Fingerhut, & Kazis, 2012; Ohio Board of Regents, 2011b, 2012b, 2013b, 2014, 2015b). Meanwhile, the proportion based on course completions dropped from 65% in FY 2012 to 30% in FY 2014. (The remaining 20% represents the portion set aside for doctoral and medical education.) For the 24 regional campuses of the state universities, funding initially was based solely on course completions (Ohio Board of Regents, 2011c, 2013b). However, in FY 2015, both the regional and main campuses were subject to the same funding formula (Ohio Board of Regents, 2014, 2015b). The course and degree completions for the university main and regional campuses are weighted by the cost of programs and whether students are at risk. This was defined initially in terms of being eligible for state need-based aid (Ohio Board of Regents, 2011c, 2013b; Petrick, 2010, 2012). However, by FY 2015, four different factors were being used: low income (Estimated Family Contribution is less than $2,190), older (over age 22 when began college), minority background, and academically at risk (scored less than a 17 on the ACT English or Mathematics component or took developmental education in college) (Ohio Board of Regents, 2015b).

For community colleges, the proportion of the state formula allocated on the basis of performance indicators started at 5% in FY 2011, jumped to 50% in FY 2014, and reached 100% in FY 2015 (Ohio Association of Community Colleges, 2013; Ohio Board of Regents, 2011a, 2012a, 2013a, 2015a). For FY 2011 through FY 2013, the performance indicators took the form of "Success Points": (1) number of students completing developmental English and math and subsequently enrolling in a college-level course in those subjects;

(2) number attaining certain credit thresholds in a given year; (3) number who earn at least an associate's degree, from that institution, in a given year; and (4) number who transfer (that is, enroll for the first time at a university having completed at least a certain number of semester credit hours of college-level coursework at a community college). Degree completions are weighted by program costs. In FY 2014, course completions drove 25% of the state funding formula for community colleges, along with 25% for the Success Points, and the enrollment-based share dropped to 50% (Ohio Board of Regents, 2013a). For FY 2015, course completions drove 50% of the Student Share of Instruction formula, Success Points (based on number of students completing developmental education or reaching certain credit thresholds) accounted for another 25%, and various degree completion metrics (numbers completing associate's degrees or long-term certificates or transferring to four-year institutions) accounted for the remaining 25%. Enrollments ceased to be part of the formula. Course completions and degree completions by "access" students—low socioeconomic status (Pell Grant eligible), older (over 25 when they entered college), and minority background—are weighted more heavily (Ohio Board of Regents, 2015a).

At the beginning, the universities and community colleges were cushioned against losses by a "stop-loss" provision ensuring that they get at least a certain proportion of their state funding. For FY 2010 the stop loss was 99% for the universities (the community colleges were still not subject to the new formula). For FY 2011, the stop-loss figure was 98% for universities and for community colleges. For FY 2012, the figures were 82.5% for universities and 88% for community colleges (these figures reflected the end of federal stimulus funding). For FY 2013, the stop-loss figure was 96% for both kinds of institutions (Ohio Board of Regents, 2009a, p. 6; Ohio Board of Regents, 2011a, p. 6; Ohio Board of Regents, 2011b, p. 11). The stop loss was ended for universities in FY 2014 and community colleges in FY 2015 (Ohio Association of Community Colleges, 2013; Ohio Board of Regents, 2013a, 2013b, 2015b). However, the state formula for universities retained a "bridge" allocation, which is very similar to a stop loss, for FY 2014, and the same appears to have been done for community colleges in FY 2015 (Ohio Board of Regents, 2015c).

The state's PF program provides greater weight for completions by students who are low income (Pell Grant eligible), are members of underrepresented minorities (Native American, African American, or Hispanic), are 25 years of age or older when they first enroll at a state institution of higher education, and receive STEM degrees (Ohio Board of Regents, 2014, 2015a, 2015b, 2015c).

Tennessee

Tennessee has established two PF programs: a PF 1.0 bonus program that was adopted in 1979 and still operates today, and a PF 2.0 outcomes-based formula funding program that was adopted in 2010 (Dougherty & Natow, 2015). The older program is intended to serve as a "quality assurance" bulwark for the new program (authors' TN interviews).

The Tennessee Higher Education Commission adopted PF for the state's public two- and four-year higher education institutions in 1979 (Dougherty & Natow, 2015). Funds were first allocated to institutions using PF in FY 1980–81. Under that system, higher education institutions could earn a bonus of 2% over and above their annual state appropriations for achieving certain goals based on five performance indicators: program accreditation (proportion of eligible programs in the institution's inventory which are accredited), student major field performance (student performance as assessed by major field examinations), student general education performance, evaluation of instructional programs (based on surveys of current students, recent alumni, or employers), and evaluation of academic programs (by peer review teams of scholars from institutions outside the state and/or practicing professionals in a field) (Banta, 1986, pp. 123–28; Bogue & Johnson, 2010). Tennessee added eight PF indicators and dropped four between 1979–1980 and 2009–2010. In addition, the percentage of additional funding that institutions could earn based on performance rose from 2% to 5.45% of the base state appropriation (Bogue & Johnson, 2010; Dougherty & Natow, 2015).

In 2010, the Tennessee legislature passed the Complete College Tennessee Act, part of which provided for a dramatic redesign of the basic higher education funding formula in which performance indicators were now embedded in that formula (Dougherty & Natow, 2015). During the first year of the new system's operation in FY 2011–12, university funding was based on the following indicators: numbers of students reaching 24, 48, and 72 hours of credit; research and service expenditures; number of degrees awarded (bachelor's and associate's, master's and education specialist, and doctoral and law degrees); number of degrees per FTE student; number of transfers out with at least 12 credit hours; and six-year graduation rate (Tennessee Higher Education Commission, 2011b, p. 1). Community colleges were funded based on somewhat different criteria: number of students reaching 12, 24, and 36 hours of credit; workforce training contact hours; number of dual-enrollment students; number of associate's degrees and certificates granted; number of awards per FTE enrollments; job placements; number of transfers out with 12 credit hours; and remedial and developmental success. In addition, an institution was eligible for a 40% premium for credit and degree completion for low-income and adult students. To protect institutions, the new program was gradually phased in over a three-year period, with the phase-in stopping at the end of FY 2014 (Dougherty & Natow, 2015; Tennessee Higher Education Commission, 2011b, 2012a, 2012b; Wright, 2015).

For the 2015–20 period, the state funding formula will change in various ways. For universities, the transfer-out metric has been dropped and the credit hour thresholds have been raised to 30, 60, and 90 hours. For community colleges, the short-term certificate metric has been changed and the remedial and development success metric has been dropped. The latter has been balanced by adding a new category of at-risk students who receive extra weight in the formula: academically underprepared students at community colleges.* Most importantly, the state has sharply increased the extra weight given for at-risk students, which originally was set at 40%. Beginning in FY 2017, students who fall into one of the at-risk categories will be weighted an additional 80%.

---

* These are students who meet one of three criteria: (1) they are identified as requiring remediation, (2) they score an 18 or below on the ACT Composite, or (3) they score either an 18 or below on the ACT Reading or Mathematics component or a 17 or below on the ACT Writing component (Tennessee Higher Education Commission, 2015e).

Those falling into two categories will be weighted an additional 100%. And students meeting all three categories (only possible at community colleges) will be weighted an additional 120% (Tennessee Higher Education Commission, 2015e).*

The Tennessee formula and allocation process are quite complex. Each indicator is weighted, but each institution has different weights assigned to each indicator by the Tennessee Higher Education Commission based on a variety of factors, including, but not limited to, the institution's preferences and Carnegie classification. Three-year rolling averages are first scaled, then multiplied by institution-specific weights, and finally totaled for institutional weighted outcome totals. These totals include extra weighting on indicators for credit accumulation and degree production for adult learners, low-income students, and (beginning in FY 2017) academically underprepared students at community colleges (Tennessee Higher Education Commission, 2011a, 2012a, 2012b, 2015e). Fixed costs and equipment costs are added to create a formula subtotal. At this point, the institution's PF allocation is calculated by multiplying the institution's percentage on the program indicators by 5.45% of the institution's subtotal. This is added to the subtotal to give the institution's total. The formula then assumes a 55/45 subsidy/fee policy, so the total is then multiplied by 55%, and there is finally a budget recommendation by the Tennessee Higher Education Commission.† For the 2014–15 appropriation, the legislature funded only 62.8% of the Tennessee Higher Education Commission's recommendation (Tennessee Higher Education Commission, 2014a). It is not expected that the program will produce big year-to-year variations in funding for two reasons: (1) the metrics are not ones that should change much from year to year, and (2) they are calculated in terms of three-year moving averages (authors' TN interviews; Tennessee Higher Education Commission, 2011a, 2012a, 2012b). In fact, the year-to-year shifts have typically fallen within the ±4% range. However, a number of institutions have consistently increased their funding and others have consistently dropped, so that a widening cumulative gap has occurred, and this has caused increased grumbling by several institutions. A number have called for adding metrics, such as enrollments, that will help stabilize their revenues (authors' TN interviews). The expansion of the state's program for free community college tuition has also led to a huge expansion in enrollments, which has stressed community college budgets and led to more criticism of the PF program's impacts on institutional funding (authors' TN interviews).

* Some additional changes include dropping the deduction of out-of-state student tuition and the salary multiplier used in the formula. Also, the metric for degrees/awards per full-time enrollment will change so that it only includes degree-seeking students (Tennessee Higher Education Commission, 2015e).

† Through FY 2016, the formula also involved a salary multiplier and a deduction for tuition collected from out-of-state students (Tennessee Higher Education Commission, 2015e).

Appendix B: *Interview Protocol for State Officials*

A. BACKGROUND

1. Explanation of study and procedures for maintaining confidentiality. Secure statement of consent to taping. *Explain sequence of questions*: goals for PF, how it was intended to work, how it has worked in practice, obstacles and unintended impacts, and thoughts about changes.

2. What is the exact title of your current position? How long have you been in it? What was your previous position, and how long were you in it? (Keep this short.)

B. POLICY DESIGN

Here we would like to ask you about the *intended goals* for the PF program and *how it was supposed to work*. We'll save for later how it actually has worked in practice.

Intended Goals of PF

1. What were the *goals* of the XX PF program in the minds of its advocates when it was *first enacted*?
   Prompts [to get at goals they might not mention otherwise]:
   • to increase the efficiency of higher education
   • to preserve funding for higher education in bad fiscal times

2. Did supporters of PF differ on which goal was most important?

Espoused Theory of Action: We would like to ask you about how the XX PF program was *intended to work* at the time it was first established.

3. How did PF advocates expect it to produce better institutional performance? What were the *mechanisms*?
   • Prompt: Besides financial incentives, were there other ways PF was supposed to get institutions to change?

4. What, if any, particular *changes in college policies or practices* was PF expected to stimulate? Did PF advocates spell out these expected changes?

5. Did PF advocates expect it to encounter any particular *obstacles or unintended impacts*? Were any preemptive countermeasures laid out in the enacting legislation, etc.?

C. IMPLEMENTATION: THEORIES OF ACTION IN USE

Here we would like to ask you how the XX PF program has worked in practice. [Start with mechanisms the interviewee discussed under espoused theory of action.]

Policy Instruments and Their Immediate Impacts

1. *Financial incentives*

1a. How big an impact has the state PF program had on colleges' funding? Has it caused any big year-to-year fluctuations in institutional revenues? How big have those gotten?

1b. How does the state determine the PF funding allocations for individual institutions? What is the role of XX [the implementing agency], the legislature, and the governor's office?

2. *Increasing institutional awareness of state PF goals and intended methods:*

2a. How widely diffused through colleges is there awareness of the state's PF goals and intended methods (espoused theory of action)? Are faculty and mid-level administrators as aware as top-level administrators? If not, what is the reason? *Note: To be asked only of officials of state higher education coordinating board.*

2b. Has the *state* tried to communicate to colleges its PF goals and intended methods? How so?

2c. Have the *colleges* tried to communicate the state's PF goals and intended methods to faculty and mid-level administrators? How so? Did the state provide suggestions?

3. *Increasing institutional awareness of their performance: Note: Questions 3a–e to be asked only of officials of state higher education coordinating board.*

3a. What PF data are collected by the state itself? Of the remaining data, how are they collected by the colleges? How do they report them to the state?

3b. How widely diffused through colleges is there awareness of how well the college is doing on the PF indicators, especially with respect to other colleges? Are faculty and mid-level administrators as aware as top-level administrators? If not, what is the reason?

3c. Has the *state* tried to communicate to colleges how well they're doing on PF indicators? How so?

3d. How publicly has the state compared the performance of different colleges on the PF indicators?

3e. Have the *colleges* tried to communicate to faculty and mid-level administrators how well the college is doing on the PF indicators? How so?

4. *Increasing institutional capacity:*
    Has the state PF program tried to enlarge colleges' *capacity* to improve their performance on PF indicators? Could you give me some examples? Prompts:
    *   Improving IT systems
    *   Improving IR capacity

- Training faculty and staff in data analysis methods
- Arranging meetings of local college officials

Institutional Changes: Academic and Student Support Policies, Program, and Practices

5. How have the colleges changed their policies, programs, and practices in order to improve its performance on the state PF indicators? Prompts:
   - Data gathering and analysis practices
   - Academic policies and practices
   - Student support policies and practices

Ultimate Student Outcomes

6. What impacts, if any, has the state PF program had on student outcomes? What evidence is there for these PF impacts?

7. What has been the main policy *mechanism* by which PF has affected student outcomes? Why do you say this? Prompts:
   - Financial incentives
   - Increasing institutional awareness of state PF goals and intended methods
   - Increasing institutional awareness of their performance
   - Increasing institutional capacity (IT, IR, etc.)

8. What specific changes in *colleges' policies and practices* have had the biggest impact on student outcomes? What evidence is there for this? Prompts:
   - Data gathering and analysis practices
   - Academic policies and practices
   - Student support policies and practices

9. Have these especially noteworthy policy mechanisms or changes in college policies and practices differed by type of college?

10. Have these especially noteworthy policy mechanisms or changes in college policies and practices been different for this PF program versus the state's (earlier or later) PF program?

D. OBSTACLES AND HOW ADDRESSED

1. What, if any, have been the main *obstacles* to the effectiveness of the state's PF program? Prompts:
   - Inappropriate measures
   - Instability of PF funding, indicators, or measures
   - Insufficient funding for PF
   - Uneven knowledge within college of PF and of college's own performance
   - Insufficient institutional capacity (IR, IT, etc.)
   - Resistance to PF within college (ask where the resistance has been greatest)

2. What steps, if any, have state officials and college officials taken to address these obstacles? When were these steps taken and at whose behest? How successful have these steps been, and what is the evidence for this?

3. What further steps *do you think* could be taken to reduce the obstacles and improve the effectiveness of the state PF program? Why do you think that?

E. UNINTENDED IMPACTS AND HOW ADDRESSED

1. What, if any, have been the main *unintended impacts* of PF? Prompts:
   - Compliance costs
   - Less emphasis on missions not rewarded by PF program
   - Weakening of academic standards
   - Lower admission of less prepared students
   - Lesser faculty voice in academic governance

2. What steps, if any, have state officials and college officials taken to address the unintended negative impacts? When were these steps taken and at whose behest? How successful have these steps been and what is the evidence for this?

3. What further steps *do you think* could be taken to reduce the unintended impacts of the state PF program? Why do you think that?

F. WRAPPING UP

1. Is there an important aspect of the XX PF program which we did not talk about?

2. People we should talk to? [Ask for any names or contact information we need.]

Appendix C: *Interview Protocol for University Administrators and Faculty**

A. BACKGROUND

1. *Explanation of study:*
   a. *Secure statement of consent to taping.*
   b. *Describe the state's PF program (older and newer), including the PF metrics for this institution.*
   c. *Explain sequence of questions: how PF has worked in practice, impacts on student outcomes, obstacles, and unintended impacts.*

2. What is the exact title of your current position? How long have you been in it? What was your previous position, and how long were you in it? (Keep this short.)

B. POLICY DESIGN: ESPOUSED THEORY

Here we would like to ask you about the *intended goals* for the PF program and *how it was supposed to work*. We'll save for later how it actually has worked in practice. [Ask only of president.]

1. What were the *goals* of the XX PF program in the minds of its advocates when it was *first enacted*?
   Prompts [to get at goals they might not mention otherwise]:
   • to increase the efficiency of higher education
   • to increase the effectiveness of higher education
   • to preserve funding for higher education in bad fiscal times

2. How did PF advocates expect it to produce better institutional performance? What were the *mechanisms*? Prompts:
   • Besides financial incentives, were there other ways PF was supposed to get colleges to change?
   • Did the advocates consider information provision or capacity building as a way PF would work?

3. What, if any, particular *changes in college policies or practices* was PF expected to stimulate? Did PF advocates spell out these expected changes?

---

* This is essentially the same as the protocol for community college administrators and faculty, with a few questions added.

4. Did PF advocates expect it to encounter any particular *obstacles or unintended impacts*? What were they? Were any preemptive countermeasures laid out in the enacting legislation, etc.?

C. IMPLEMENTATION: THEORIES OF ACTION IN USE

Here we would like to ask you how the XX PF program has *worked in practice*. [Lay out the four policy instruments.]

Policy Instruments and Their Immediate Impacts

1. *Financial incentives*:

1a. Has the PF program caused any big year-to-year changes in institutional revenues? How big have those gotten? How do you know that these changes are due to the PF program?

1b. Let's speak about the impact these funding changes had *on your college's efforts to improve student outcomes*. How would you rate the impact of these funding changes on a scale of 1 (no impact) to 5 (a lot of impact)? What is the basis of your rating?

2. *Increasing institutional awareness of state PF goals and methods*:

2a. Let's talk about how effectively the *state* has communicated to your college about the PF program's goals and methods (e.g., the goals of PF, how it works).

    1. Who has the state communicated with at the college, and how has it done this? (Prompt for methods.)

    2. How would you rate the state's effectiveness in communicating to the college on a scale of 1 (no effectiveness) to 5 (a lot of effectiveness)? What is the basis of your rating?

2b. Let's talk about how effectively *your college's leaders* have communicated to the rest of the college about the PF program's goals and methods.

    1. Who have the college's leaders communicated with at the college, and how have they done this? (Prompt for methods.)

    2. On a scale of 1 to 5, how effectively have *your college's leaders* communicated to the rest of the college about the PF program's goals and methods? What is the basis of your rating?

2c. Let's speak about *your awareness* of the state PF program's goals and methods. How would you rate your awareness on a scale of 1 (no awareness) to 5 (a lot of awareness)? What is the basis of your rating?

2d. What about awareness across the college about the state PF program's goals and methods? How would you rate the *campus's average awareness* on a scale of 1 (no awareness) to 5 (a lot of awareness)? What is the basis of your rating?

2e. Are faculty and mid-level administrators as aware as top-level administrators? Why is this?

2f. Let's speak about the *impact* your college's *awareness* of the state program's goals and methods—quite apart from any financial impacts of PF—has had on the col-

lege's efforts to improve student outcomes. How would you rate the impact of *just awareness of the state program* on a scale of 1 (no impact) to 5 (a lot of impact)? What is the basis of your rating?

3. *Increasing institutional awareness of their performance on state PF metrics:*

3a. Let's talk about how effectively the *state* has communicated to your college about how the college is doing on the state PF metrics (e.g., graduation numbers).

   1. Who has the state communicated with at the college about the college's performance on the state PF metrics, and how has it done this? (Prompt for methods.)

   2. How would you rate the state's effectiveness in communicating to the college on a scale of 1 (no effectiveness) to 5 (a lot of effectiveness)? What is the basis of your rating?

3b. Let's talk about how effectively *your college's leaders* have communicated to the rest of the college about how well the college is doing on the state PF metrics.

   1. Who have the college's leaders communicated with at the college about the college's performance on the state PF metrics, and how have they done this? (Prompt for methods.)

   2. On a scale of 1 to 5, how effectively have *your college's leaders* communicated to the rest of the college about the PF program's goals and methods? What is the basis of your rating?

3c. Let's speak about *your awareness* of how well your college is performing on the state PF metrics. How would you rate your awareness on a scale of 1 (no awareness) to 5 (a lot of awareness)? What is the basis of your rating?

3d. What about awareness across the college about the college's performance? How would you rate the *campus's average awareness* on a scale of 1 (no awareness) to 5 (a lot of awareness)? What is the basis of your rating?

3e. Are faculty and mid-level administrators as aware as top-level administrators? Why is this?

3f. Let's speak about the impact your college's awareness of its performance on the state performance indicators—quite apart from any financial impacts of PF— has had on the *college's efforts to improve student outcomes.* How would you rate that impact of *just awareness of the college's performance* on a scale of 1 (no impact) to 5 (a lot of impact)? What is the basis of your rating?

4. *Building up college capacity:*

4a. *As part of the PF program,* has the college received any assistance from the state to build up its capacity to improve student outcomes? [Go to 4b and 4c if they don't know how to answer.]

4b. Has the state made an effort to help colleges build up their IR capacity?

4c. Has the state supported any discussions or activities on PF best practices?

4d. Let's talk about what *impact* any state assistance to build up college capacity to improve student outcomes—quite apart from any financial impacts of PF—has had on your *college's efforts to improve those student outcomes*. How would you rate the impact of *just state capacity building* on a scale of 1 (no impact) to 5 (a lot of impact)? What is the basis of your rating?

4e. Quite apart from *any* state assistance, has your college made efforts to improve its IR capacity? What changes did it make and why?

4f. Does the IR office ask faculty and administrators what performance data they would like to see?

4g. Has the college made efforts to improve the capacity of faculty and staff to analyze data on your college's performance on PF indicators? How so?

Institutional Changes: Academic and Student Support Policies, Program, and Practices

5. What specific steps is your college taking to improve student outcomes?

6. *Thinking about the state's PF program*, has your college changed any *academic* policies, programs, and practices in order to improve its performance on the state PF indicators? How have these changes affected student outcomes? Prompts:
   - Alterations to academic *department* organization and staffing (e.g., adding or closing programs)
   - Alterations to academic *curricula and graduation requirements* (e.g., new course sequences, new graduation requirements)
   - Alterations to *course content and instruction technique* (e.g., changing pedagogy)

7. *Thinking about the state's PF program*, has your college changed any *student support policies*, programs, and practices in order to improve its performance on the state PF indicators? How have these changes affected student outcomes? Prompts:
   - Registration and graduation procedures
   - Financial aid
   - Retention programs for first-year students
   - Counseling/advising
   - Tutoring and other supplemental instruction
   - Job placement services

8. Which of these changes in your college's *academic or student service policies and practices* have had the biggest impact on student outcomes? How did this occur? What evidence is there for this?

9. To what extent would these changes in academic and student support policies have happened regardless of PF, as a result of other pressures (accreditation, Achieving the Dream, etc.)? On a scale of 1 (no influence) to 5 (a lot of influence), what influence did the PF program have on these changes?

Institutional Changes: Organizational Learning

10. Please take me through how your college *decided on one of the important changes above* in academic or student service policies and practices. [If the interviewee

can't come up with one, suggest one.] How did your college go about deciding and making that change? Prompts:

- Who was involved in deliberating and deciding on the change?
- How was it decided that a change was necessary?
- How was it decided that the change made was the right one to make?
- Was there any controversy over the change?

11. Does your college have any formal or informal *process for deliberating on its performance on the state PF indicators and how to improve it?* How does it work? Prompts:
    - Who is involved? How often do they meet?
    - How is it determined where the problems are with the college's student outcomes?
    - How is it determined what the solutions are to those problems?

12. How well has this process for deliberation worked?

13. Are there things that have made this deliberative process work *less* effectively than it could?
    - Prompt: How receptive have senior administrators been to input from faculty, mid-level administrators, or students on how to improve student outcomes? Can you give some examples?

14. Are there things that have helped this deliberative process work *more* effectively?

15. Has the college tried to create a *climate* that encourages bottom-up efforts to improve its performance on PF indicators?

16. Has your college's deliberative process ever led it to *question the state's goals* for PF?

17. Has your college's deliberative process ever led it to *question the college's own goals or fundamental ideas* (e.g., its basic understanding of how teaching and learning work or what explains poor student outcomes)?

Ultimate Student Outcomes

18. How much have your college's student outcomes—such as graduation numbers and [add another PF outcome]—improved since the state's PF programs began? What is the basis of your judgment?

19. Let's speak about the extent to which the state PF program is responsible for these improvements. How would you rate the *impact* of the state PF program on a scale of 1 (no impact) to 5 (a lot of impact)? What is the basis of your rating?

20. Are there other factors besides the state PF program that have affected student performance on the state PF metrics?

D. OBSTACLES AND HOW ADDRESSED

1. How have faculty and administrators reacted to the state PF program?

2. What, if any, have been the main *obstacles* to your college's ability to respond effectively to the state's PF program? *Note: ask general question and then follow up with questions asking italicized prompts:*
   - *Inappropriate measures*
   - Instability of PF funding, indicators, or measures

- Insufficient funding for PF
- *Insufficient institutional capacity (IR, IT, etc.)*
- *Faculty lack of knowledge about PF and college's own performance*
- *Resistance to PF within college* (ask where the resistance has been greatest)

3. What steps, if any, has the *state* taken to address these obstacles? How successful have these steps been, and what is the evidence for this?

4. What steps, if any, has *your college* taken to address these obstacles? How successful have these steps been, and what is the evidence for this?

5. What further steps *do you think* could be taken to improve the effectiveness of the state PF program? Why do you think that?

E. UNINTENDED IMPACTS AND HOW ADDRESSED

1. What, if any, have been the main *unintended impacts* of PF on your college? [Note: if the interviewee is reluctant, ask about other colleges.] *Note: ask general question and then follow up with questions asking italicized prompts:*
    - Compliance costs
    - *Less emphasis on missions not rewarded by PF program*
    - *Weakening of academic standards*
    - *Lower admission of less prepared students*
    - *Lesser faculty voice in academic governance*

2. What steps, if any, has the *state* taken to address these unintended impacts? How successful have these steps been, and what is the evidence for this?

3. What steps, if any, has *your college* taken to address these unintended impacts? How successful have these steps been, and what is the evidence for this?

4. What further steps *do you think* could be taken to reduce the unintended impacts of the state PF program? Why do you think that?

F. IMPACT OF THE COLLEGE'S CHARACTERISTICS ON ITS PERFORMANCE

1. Compare your college to other community colleges. Are there any ways in which your college's *distinctive characteristics*—whether its student-body composition, financial resources, IR capacity, or organizational culture—have made it *easier or harder* to perform well on the state performance indicators?

2. If [take a characteristic from F1] weren't the case, how do you think your college would behave differently?

G. WRAPPING UP

1. Are there any changes you would make in the PF program which we haven't talked about above?

2. Is there an important aspect of the state's PF program which we did not talk about?

3. People we should talk to? [Ask for any names or contact information we need.]

References

Achieving the Dream. (2015a). *State policy teams*. Silver Spring, MD: Author. Retrieved from http://achievingthedream.org/our-network/state-policy-teams.

Achieving the Dream. (2015b). *About us*. Silver Spring, MD: Author. Retrieved from http://achievingthedream.org/about-us.

ACT. (2012). *The condition of college & career readiness 2012: Low-income students*. Iowa City, IA: Author. Retrieved from http://www.act.org/newsroom/data/2012/states/pdf/LowIncomeStudents.pdf.

Addison, H. J. (2009). *Is administrative capacity a useful concept? Review of the application, meaning, and observation of administrative capacity in political science literature*. London: London School of Economics. Retrieved from http://personal.lse.ac.uk/addisonh/Papers/AC_Concept.pdf.

Alexander, F. K., & Ehrenberg, R. G. (Eds.). (2003). *Maximizing revenue in higher education: Universities, public policy, and revenue production*. New Directions for Institutional Research, 119 (Fall). San Francisco: Jossey-Bass.

Allen, L., & Kazis, R. (2007). *Building a culture of evidence in community colleges: Lessons from exemplary institutions*. Boston: Jobs for the Future.

Altstadt, D., Fingerhut, E., & Kazis, R. (2012). *Tying funding to community college outcomes: Models, tools, and recommendations for states*. Boston: Jobs for the Future.

Andersen, S. I., & Mortensen, P. (2009). Policy stability and organizational performance: Is there a relationship? *Journal of Public Administration Research and Theory, 20*(1), 1–22.

Anderson, J. (2011). *Public policymaking* (7th ed). Boston: Wadsworth.

Argyris, C., & Schön, D. A. (1996). *Organizational learning II: Theory, methods, and practice*. Reading, MA: Addison-Wesley.

Astin, A. W., & Oseguera, L. (2005). Precollege and institutional influences on degree attainment. In A. Seidman (Ed.), *College student retention: Formula for student success* (pp. 245–76). Westport, CT: Praeger.

Bailey, M. J., & Dynarski, S. M. (2011). *Gains and gaps: Changing inequality in U.S. college entry and completion*. NBER Working Paper No. 17633. Cambridge, MA: National Bureau of Economic Research.

Bailey, T. (1988). Market forces and private sector processes in government policy: The Job Training Partnership Act. *Journal of Policy Analysis and Management, 7*(2), 300–315.

Bailey, T. (2009). Challenge and opportunity: Rethinking the role and function of developmental education in community college. *New Directions for Community Colleges, 145* (Spring), 11–30.

Bailey, T. (2011). *Developing input adjusted metrics for community college performance.* Unpublished paper prepared for Context for Success Conference, HCM Strategists LLC, Washington, DC, December 9, 2011.

Bailey, T., Jaggars, S., & Jenkins, D. (2015). *Redesigning America's community colleges.* Cambridge, MA: Harvard University Press.

Baldwin, C., Bensimon, E. M., Dowd, A. C., & Kleiman, L. (2011). Measuring student success. *New Directions for Community Colleges, 153* (Spring), 75–88.

Banta, T. W. (Ed.). (1986). *Performance funding in higher education: A critical analysis of Tennessee's experience.* Boulder, CO: National Center for Higher Education Management Systems.

Barnetson, B., & Cutright, M. (2000). Performance indicators as conceptual technologies. *Higher Education, 40*(3), 277–92.

Barnett, C. (n.d.). *Rethinking organizational learning theories: A review and synthesis of the primary literature.* Unpublished manuscript, University of New Hampshire, Whittemore School of Business and Economics, Durham, NH.

Belfield, C. (2012). *Washington State Student Achievement Initiative: Achievement points analysis for academic years 2007–2011.* New York: Columbia University, Teachers College, Community College Research Center.

Bensimon, E. M. (2005). Closing the achievement gap in higher education: An organizational learning perspective. *New Directions for Higher Education, 131* (Fall), 99–111.

Bensimon, E. M., Dowd, A. C., Longanecker, D., & Witham, K. (2012). We have goals. Now what? *Change: The Magazine of Higher Learning, 44*(6), 15–25.

Berkner, L., & Choy, S. (2008). *Descriptive summary of 2003–04 beginning postsecondary students: Three years later* (NCES 2008-174). Washington, DC: National Center for Education Statistics. Retrieved from http://nces.ed.gov/pubs2008/2008174.pdf.

Bess, J. L., & Dee, J. R. (2008). *Understanding college and university organization.* 2 vols. Sterling, VA: Stylus.

Blankenberger, B., & Phillips, A. (2014). Performance funding in Illinois higher education: The roles of politics, budget environment, and individual actors in the process. *Educational Policy, 1–32.* DOI: 10.1177/0895904814556748.

Boatman, A. (2012). *Evaluating institutional efforts to streamline postsecondary remediation: The causal effects of the Tennessee Developmental Course Redesign Initiative on early student academic success.* NCPR Working Paper. Retrieved from NCPR website: http://www.postsecondaryresearch.org/i/a/document/22651_BoatmanTNFINAL.pdf.

Bogue, E. G. (2002). Twenty years of performance funding in Tennessee: A case study of policy intent and effectiveness. In J. C. Burke (Ed.), *Funding public colleges and universities: Popularity, problems, and prospects* (pp. 85–105). Albany: State University of New York Press.

Bogue, E. G., & Johnson, B. D. (2010). Performance incentives and public college accountability in the United States: A quarter century policy audit. *Higher Education Management and Policy, 22*(2), 1–22.

Bowen, H. R. (1980). *The costs of higher education: How much do colleges and universities spend per student and how much should they spend?* San Francisco: Jossey-Bass.

Brinkerhoff, D. W. (2010). Capacity and capacity development: Coping with complexity. *Public Administration and Development, 30*(1), 2–10.

Brint, S., & Karabel, J. (1989). *The diverted dream.* New York: Oxford University Press.

Büchel, B., & Raub, S. (2001). Media choice and organizational learning. In M. Dierkes, A. Berthoin Antal, J. Child, & I. Nonaka (Eds.), *Handbook of organizational learning and knowledge* (pp. 518–34). Oxford: Oxford University Press.

Burke, J. C. (Ed.) (2002). *Funding public colleges and universities: Popularity, problems, and prospects.* Albany: State University of New York Press.

Burke, J. C. (Ed.) (2005). *Achieving accountability in higher education: Balancing public, academic, and market demands.* San Francisco: Jossey-Bass.

Burke, J. C., & Serban, A. (1998). State synopses of performance funding. *New Directions for Institutional Research, 97* (Spring), 25–48.

Byrd-Blake, M., Afolayan, M. O., Hunt, J. W., Fabunmi, M., Pryor, B. W., & Leander, R. (2010). Morale of teachers in high poverty schools: A post-NCLB mixed methods analysis. *Education and Urban Society, 42*(4), 450–72.

Cabrera, A., Burkum, K., & La Nasa, S. (2005). Pathways to a four-year degree: Determinants of transfer and degree completion. In A. Seidman (Ed.), *College student retention: A formula for student success* (pp. 155–214). Westport, CT: Praeger.

Cabrera, A., & La Nasa, S. (2001). On the path to college. *Research in Higher Education, 42*(2), 119–49.

Calcagno, J. C., Bailey, T., Jenkins, D., Kienzl, G., & Leinbach, T. (2008). Community college success: What institutional characteristics make a difference? *Economics of Education Review, 27*(6), 632–45.

Callahan, R. (1962). *Education and the cult of efficiency.* Chicago: University of Chicago Press.

Carey, K., & Aldeman, C. (2008). *Ready to assemble: A model state higher education accountability system.* Washington, DC: Education Sector.

Cavanaugh, J. C., & Garland, P. (2012). Performance funding in Pennsylvania. *Change: The Magazine of Higher Learning, 44*(3), 34–39.

Center for Higher Education Policy Studies (CHEPS) and the University of London. (2010). *Progress in higher education reform across Europe.* 3 vols. Enschede, The Netherlands: University of Twente.

Claeys-Kulik, A-L., & Estermann, T. (2015). *Define thematic report: Performance-based funding of universities in Europe.* Brussels: European University Association. Retrieved from http://www.eua.be/Libraries/publications-homepage-list/define-thematic-report _-pbf_final-version.

Claggett, C. A. (2011, Oct. 10). Completion rates in context. *Inside Higher Ed.*

Clark, K. (2012, Mar. 26). New legislation caps undergraduate programs at 120 hours. *Indiana Daily Student.* Retrieved from IDSnews.com.

Coburn, C. E. (2003). Rethinking scale: Moving beyond numbers to deep and lasting change. *Educational Researcher, 32*(6), 3–12.

Coburn, C. E., & Stein, M. K. (2006). Communities of practice theory and the role of teacher professional community in policy implementation. In M. Honig (Ed.), *New directions in education policy implementation* (pp. 25–46). Albany: State University of New York Press.

Cohen, A. M., Brawer, F. B., & Kisker, C. B. (2014). *The American community college* (6th ed.). San Francisco: Jossey-Bass.

Cohen, J. M. (1995). Capacity building in the public sector: A focused framework for analysis and action. *International Review of Administrative Sciences, 61*(3), 407–22.

Colyvas, J. A. (2012). Performance metrics as formal structures and through the lens of social mechanisms: When do they work and how do they work? *American Journal of Education, 118* (special issue), 167–97.

Committee on Measures of Student Success. (2011, Dec.). *A report to Secretary of Education Arne Duncan.* Washington, DC: US Department of Education. http://www2.ed .gov/about/bdscomm/list/cmss-committee-report-final.pdf.

Complete College America. (2013). *The game changers: Are states implementing the best reforms to get more college graduates?* Washington, DC: Author.

Complete College Tennessee Act. 2010. Tenn. Stat. (2010).

Cragg, M. (1997). Performance incentives in the public sector: Evidence from the Job Training Partnership Act. *Journal of Law, Economics, and Organization, 13*(1), 147–68.

Davies, L. (2014). *State "shared responsibility" policies for improved outcomes: Lessons learned.* Washington, DC: HCM Strategists.

de Boer, H., Jongbloed, B., Benneworth, P., Cremonini, L., Kolster, R., Kottmann, A., Lemmens-Krug, K., & Vossensteyn, H. (2015). *Performance-based funding and performance agreements in fourteen higher education systems.* Enschede, The Netherlands: University of Twente, Center for Higher Education Policy Studies. Retrieved from http:// www.rijksoverheid.nl/documenten-en-publicaties/rapporten/2015/03/01/performance -based-funding-and-performance-agreements-in-fourteen-higher-education-systems .html.

de Boer, H., Jongbloed, B., Benneworth, P., Westerheijden, D., & File, J. (2012). *Engaging in the modernisation agenda for European higher education.* Enschede, The Netherlands: University of Twente, Center for Higher Education Policy Studies.

DeBruijn, H. (2002). *Managing performance in the public sector.* London: Routledge.

Dee, T., & Jacob, B. (2011). The impact of No Child Left Behind on student achievement. *Journal of Policy Analysis and Management, 30*(3), 418–46.

Deming, D. J., Cohodes, S., Jennings, J., Jencks, C. S. (2013). *School accountability, postsecondary attainment, and earnings.* NBER Working Paper No. 19444.

Developmental Education Initiative. (2015). *Overview.* New York: MDRC. http://www .mdrc.org/project/developmental-education-initiative#overview.

DiMaggio, P. J., & Powell, W. W. (1991). The iron cage revisited: Institutional isomorphism and collective rationality in organizational fields. In W. W. Powell & P. J. DiMaggio (Eds.), *The new institutionalism in organizational analysis* (pp. 63–82). Chicago: University of Chicago Press.

Dougherty, K. J. (1994). *The contradictory college: The conflicting origins, impacts, and futures of the community colleges.* Albany: State University of New York Press.

Dougherty, K. J., Jones, S. M., Lahr, H., Natow, R. S., Pheatt, L., & Reddy, V. (2014a). *Envisioning performance funding impacts: The espoused theories of action for state higher education performance funding in three states.* Retrieved from http://ccrc.tc.columbia .edu/publications/envisioning-performance-funding-impacts.html.

Dougherty, K. J., Jones, S. M., Lahr, H., Natow, R. S., Pheatt, L., & Reddy, V. (2014b). Performance funding for higher education: Forms, origins, impacts, and futures. *The ANNALS of the American Academy of Political and Social Science, 655*(1), 163–84.

Dougherty, K. J., & Kienzl, G. (2006). It's not enough to get through the open door: Inequalities by social background in transfer from community colleges to four-year colleges. *Teachers College Record, 108*(3), 452–87.

Dougherty, K. J., & Natow, R. S. (2015). *The politics of performance funding for higher education: Origins, discontinuations, and transformations.* Baltimore: Johns Hopkins University Press.

Dougherty, K. J., & Reddy, V. (2013). *Performance funding for higher education: What are the mechanisms? What are the impacts?* (ASHE Higher Education Report). San Francisco: Jossey-Bass.

Dowd, A. C., & Bensimon, E. M. (2015) *Engaging the "race question": Accountability and equity in U.S. higher education.* New York: Teachers College Press.

Dowd, A. C., & Shieh, L. T. (2013). Community college financing: Equity, efficiency, and accountability. *NEA 2013 Almanac of Higher Education* (pp. 38–65). Washington, DC: National Education Association.

Dowd, A. C., & Tong, V. P. (2007). Accountability, assessment, and the scholarship of "best practice." In J. C. Smart (Ed.), *Higher education: Handbook of theory and research* (vol. 22, pp. 57–120). Dordrecht, Netherlands: Springer.

Dunlop-Loach, B. J. (2000). *Ohio's two-year campus response to performance funding: A grounded theory approach* (doctoral dissertation). Available from ProQuest Dissertations and Theses: Full Text (Publication No. AAT 9980368).

Education Commission of the States. (2015). *State profiles—postsecondary governance structures database.* Denver, CO: Author. Retrieved from http://ecs.force.com/mbdata/mbpsmap.

Elster, J. (1989). *Nuts and bolts for the social sciences.* Oxford: Oxford University Press.

Erikson, R. S., Wright, G. C., & McIver, J. P. (2006). Public opinion in the states: A quarter century of change and stability. In J. E. Cohen (Ed.), *Public opinion in state politics* (pp. 229–53). Stanford, CA: Stanford University Press.

Espeland, W. N., & Stevens, M. L. (2008). A sociology of quantification. *European Journal of Sociology, 49*(3), 401–36.

Etzioni, A. (1961). *Comparative analysis of complex organizations.* New York: Free Press.

European Community / Eurydice Network (2008). *Higher education governance in Europe: Policies, structures, funding and academic staff.* Brussels, Belgium: Author.

Ewell, P. T. (1999). Linking performance measures to resource allocation: Exploring unmapped terrain. *Quality in Higher Education, 5*(3), 191–209.

Ferguson, M. (2013). Governors and the executive branch. In V. Gray, R. L. Hanson, & T. Kousser (Eds.), *Politics in the American states* (10th ed., pp. 208–50). Washington, DC: CQ Press.

Fichtenbaum, R. (2013). *Statement on the president's proposal for performance based funding.* Washington, DC: American Association of University Professors. Retrieved from http://www.aaup.org/news/statement-president%E2%80%99s-proposal-performance-based-funding.

Fingerhut, E. (2012). Ohio's new performance-based funding system. In D. Altstadt, E. Fingerhut, & R. Kazis (Eds.), *Tying funding to community college outcomes: Models, tools, & recommendations for states* (pp. 5–16). Boston: Jobs for the Future.

Finnigan, K., & Gross, B. (2007). Do accountability policy sanctions influence teacher motivation? Lessons from Chicago's low-performing schools. *American Educational Research Journal, 44*(3), 594–630.

Forsythe, D. W. (Ed.). (2001). *Quicker, better, cheaper? Managing performance in American government.* Albany, NY: Rockefeller Institute Press.

Frølich, N., Schmidt, E. K., & Rosa, M. J. (2010). Funding systems for higher education and their impacts on institutional strategies and academia: A comparative perspective. *International Journal of Educational Management, 24*(1), 7–21.

Fryar, A. H. (2011). *The disparate impacts of accountability—searching for causal mechanisms.* Paper presented at the Public Management Research Conference, Syracuse, NY.

Fuhrman, S. H., & Elmore, R. (Eds.). (2004). *Redesigning accountability systems for education.* New York: Teachers College Press.

Gold, L., Rhoades, G., Smith, M., & Kuh, G. (2011). *What faculty unions say about student learning outcomes assessment.* Champaign, IL: National Institute for Learning Outcomes Assessment.

Golden, M. M. (2000). *What motivates bureaucrats? Politics and administration during the Reagan years.* New York: Columbia University Press.

Gray, V., Hanson, R., & Kousser, T. (Eds.). (2013). *Politics in the American states: A comparative analysis* (10th ed.). Washington, DC: CQ Press.

Grizzle, G. A. (2002). Performance measurement and dysfunction: The dark side of quantifying work. *Public Performance and Management Review, 25*(4), 363–69.

Hamm, K. E., & Moncrief, G. F. (2013). Legislative politics in the states. In V. Gray, R. L. Hanson, & T. Kousser (Eds.), *Politics in the American states* (10th ed., pp. 163–207). Washington, DC: CQ Press.

Handel, S. J., & Williams, R. A. (2012). *The promise of the transfer pathway.* New York: College Board.

Harcleroad, F. F., & Eaton, J. S. (2011). The hidden hand: External constituencies and their impact. In P. A. Altbach, P. J. Gumport, & R. O. Berdahl (Eds.), *American higher education in the twenty-first century* (3rd ed., pp. 195–224). Baltimore: Johns Hopkins University Press.

Harnisch, T. L. (2011). *Performance-based funding: A re-emerging strategy in public higher education financing.* Higher Education Policy Brief. Washington, DC: American Association of State Colleges and Universities.

HCM Strategists. (2011). *Performance funding in Indiana: An analysis of lessons from the research and other state models.* Washington, DC: Author. Retrieved from http://hcmstrategists.com/wp-content/themes/hcmstrategists/docs/Indiana_Report_12.pdf.

HCM Strategists. Strategy Labs. (2015). *Addressing equity gaps in state goals for postsecondary educational attainment.* Washington, DC: Author.

Hearn, J. C. (2015). *Outcomes-based state funding in historical and comparative context.* Washington, DC: HCM Strategists.

Heckman, J. J., Heinrich, C. J., Courty, P., Marschke, G., & Smith, J. (2011). *The performance of performance standards.* Kalamazoo, MI: W. E. Upjohn Institute.

Heckman, J. J., Heinrich, C. J., & Smith, J. (2011). Do short-run performance measures predict long-run impacts? In J. J. Heckman et al. (Eds.), *The performance of performance standards* (pp. 273–304). Kalamazoo, MI: W. E. Upjohn Institute.

Hedstrom, P., & Swedberg, R. (1998). *Social mechanisms: An analytic approach to social theory.* New York: Cambridge University Press.

Heinrich, C. J., & Marschke, G. (2010). Incentives and their dynamics in public sector performance management systems. *Journal of Policy Analysis and Management,* 29(1), 183–208.

Heller, D. A. (2013). The role of finances in postsecondary access and success. In L. Perna & A. Jones (Eds.), *The state of college access and choice* (pp. 96–114). New York: Routledge.

Henig, J. R. (2008). *Spin cycle: How research gets used in policy debates—the case of charter schools.* New York: Russell Sage.

Hicks, D. (2012). Performance-based university research funding systems. *Research Policy,* 41(2), 251–61.

Hillman, N. W., Fryar, A. F., Tandberg, D. A., & Crespin-Trujillo, V. (2015, Nov. 18). *Evaluating the efficacy of performance funding in three states: Tennessee, Ohio, and Indiana.* Presentation to the 2015 annual meeting of the Association for the Study of Higher Education. Madison: University of Wisconsin, Madison.

Hillman, N. W., Tandberg, D. A., & Fryar, A. H. (2015). Evaluating the impacts of "new" performance funding in higher education. *Educational Evaluation and Policy Analysis.* DOI: 10.3102/0162373714560224.

Hillman, N. W, Tandberg, D. A., & Gross, J. P. K. (2014). Performance funding in higher education: Do financial incentives impact college completions? *Journal of Higher Education,* 85(6), 826–57.

Hoachlander, G., Sikora, A. C., & Horn, L. (2003). Community college students: Goals, academic preparation, and outcomes. *Education Statistics Quarterly,* 5(2), 121–28.

Hodara, M. (2013). *Improving students' college math readiness: A review of the evidence on postsecondary interventions and reforms.* CAPSEE Working Paper. New York: Columbia University, Teachers College, Center for Analysis of Postsecondary Education and Employment.

Holbrook, T. M., & La Raja, R. J. (2013). Parties and elections. In V. Gray, R. L. Hanson, & T. Kousser (Eds.), *Politics in the American states* (10th ed., pp. 63–104). Washington, DC: CQ Press.

Honig, M. (2006). Complexity and policy implementation: Challenges and opportunities for the field. In M. Honig (Ed.), *New directions in education policy implementation: Confronting complexity* (pp. 1–23). Albany: State University of New York Press.

Hood, C. (1991). A public management for all seasons? *Public Administration,* 69(1), 3–19.

Horn, L. (2010, Dec.). *Tracking students to 200 percent of normal time: Effect on institutional graduation rates.* Issue Brief 2011-221. Washington, DC: US Department of Education. Retrieved from http://nces.ed.gov/pubs2011/2011221.pdf.

Hughes, K. L., & Scott-Clayton, J. (2011). Assessing developmental assessment in community colleges. *Community College Review,* 39(4), 327–51.

Hurtado, D. (2015). *Effects of performance-based funding on Ohio's community colleges and on horizontal fiscal equity* (doctoral dissertation). Available from ProQuest Dissertations and Theses Global #1702955887.

Indiana Commission for Higher Education. (2007). *Reaching higher: Strategic directions for higher education in Indiana*. Indianapolis: Author. Retrieved from http://www.in .gov/che/files/Strategic_Directions_final_as_approved_06-08-2007_w_technical _corrections.pdf.

Indiana Commission for Higher Education. (2011a). *2011–13 CHE higher education budget recommendation* (PowerPoint presentation). Indianapolis: Author.

Indiana Commission for Higher Education. (2011b). *Frequently asked questions about higher education performance funding*. Retrieved from http://www.in.gov/legislative/senate _democrats/files/budgetdocs/BudgetHearing032411/CHE/CHEfaqsaboutperfor mancefunding.pdf.

Indiana Commission for Higher Education. (2013a). *History of performance funding*. Indianapolis: Author. Retrieved from http://www.in.gov/che/files/PBOF_White_Paper_2 -22-13_A.pdf.

Indiana Commission for Higher Education. (2013b). *Degree map guidance for Indiana's public colleges and universities*. Indianapolis: Author.

Indiana Commission for Higher Education. (2014). *Evolution of CHE performance formula metrics*. Indianapolis: Author. Retrieved from http://www.in.gov/che/files/PFF _Evolution_Update.pdf.

Indiana State Senate. (2013). *Senate Bill no. 182*. Retrieved from http://www.in.gov /legislative/bills/2013/SB/SB0182.1.html.

Institute for Higher Education Policy. (2006). *Making accountability work: Community colleges and statewide higher education accountability systems*. Washington, DC: Author.

Ivy Tech Community College. (2014). *The co-requisite initiative: An initial assessment of its impact at Ivy Tech Community College—Central Indiana region*. Indianapolis: Author. Retrieved from https://s3.amazonaws.com/jngi_pub/gce14/Co-Requisite+Initiative .pdf.

James, K. (2015). *Quality assurance in other sectors: Lessons for higher education reformers*. Nashville: National Center for Performance Incentives.

Jenkins, D. (2011). *Redesigning community colleges for completion: Lessons from research on high-performance organizations*. CCRC Working Paper No. 24, Assessment of Evidence Series. New York: Columbia University, Teachers College, Community College Research Center.

Jenkins, D., & Rodriguez, O. (2013). Access and success with less: Improving productivity in broad-access postsecondary institutions. *The Future of Children, 23*(1), 187–209.

Jenkins, D., & Shulock, N. (2013). *Metrics, dollars, and systems change: Learning from Washington's Student Achievement Initiative to design effective postsecondary performance funding policies*. New York: Columbia University, Teachers College, Community College Research Center.

Jobs for the Future. (2008) *Test drive: Six states pilot better ways to measure and compare community college student performance*. Boston: Author.

Johnson, N., & Yanagiura, T. (2015). *Early results of outcomes-based funding in Tennessee*. Washington, DC: HCM Strategists.

Johnstone, D. B. (2011). Financing higher education: Who should pay? In P. A. Altbach, P. J. Gumport, & R. O. Berdahl (Eds.), *American higher education in the twenty-first century* (3rd ed., pp. 315–40). Baltimore: Johns Hopkins University Press.

Jones, D. P. (2012). *Performance funding: From idea to action.* Washington, DC: Complete College America. Retrieved from http://dl.dropbox.com/u/28697036/Performance%20 Funding%20Think%20This.pdf.

Jones, D. P. (2013). *Outcomes-based funding: The wave of implementation.* Washington, DC: Complete College America. Retrieved from http://www.completecollege.org/pdfs /Outcomes-Based-Funding-Report-Final.pdf.

Jones, S. M., Dougherty, K. J., Lahr, H., Natow, R. B., Pheatt, L., & Reddy, V. (2015). *Organizational learning by colleges responding to performance funding: Deliberative structures and their challenges.* New York: Columbia University, Teachers College, Community College Research Center.

Jones, T. (2014). *Performance funding at MSIs: Considerations and possible measures for public minority-serving institutions.* Atlanta: Southern Education Fund.

Jones, T. (2015). A historical mission in the accountability era: A public HBCU and state performance funding. *Educational Policy*, 1–43. DOI: 10.1177/0895904815586852.

Jones, T., Jones, S., & Saumby, S. G. (2015). *New funding, same results: Examining performance- and outcomes-based funding inequities.* Presentation to the Association for the Study of Higher Education. Atlanta: Southern Education Fund.

Kadlec, A., & Shelton, S. (2014). *Outcomes-based funding and stakeholder engagement.* Washington, DC: HCM Strategists.

Kasl, E., Marsick, V. J., & Dechant, K. (1997). Teams as learners: A research-based model of team learning. *Journal of Applied Behavioral Science, 33*(2), 227–46.

Kelchen, R., & Stedrak, Luke J. (2015). *Does performance-based funding affect colleges' financial priorities?* Unpublished manuscript, Seton Hall University, South Orange, NJ.

Kerrigan, M. R. (2010). *Data-driven decision making in community colleges: New technical requirements for institutional organizations* (EdD dissertation). Columbia University, Teachers College, New York.

Kerrigan, M. R. (2014). A framework for understanding community colleges' organizational capacity for data use: A convergent parallel mixed methods study. *Journal of Mixed Methods Research, 8*(4), 341–62.

Kerrigan, M. R. (2015). Social capital in data-driven community college reform. *Community College Journal of Research and Practice, 39*(7), 603–18.

Kezar, A. (2005). What campuses need to know about organizational learning and the learning organization. *New Directions for Higher Education, 131* (Fall), 7–22.

Kezar, A., Glenn, W. J., Lester, J., & Nakamoto, J. (2008). Examining organizational contextual features that affect implementation of equity initiatives. *Journal of Higher Education, 79*(2), 125–59.

Kivisto, J., & Kohtamäki, V. (2015). *Impacts of performance-based funding on higher education institutions: A literature review.* European Association of Institutional Research 37th Annual Forum in Krems, Austria, August 30 to September 2, 2015. Retrieved from http://eairaww.websites.xs4all.nl/forum/krems/PDF/1710.pdf.

Lahr, H., Pheatt, L., Dougherty, K. J., Jones, S. M., Natow, R. S., & Reddy, V. (2014). *Unintended impacts of performance funding on community colleges and universities in three states.* CCRC Working Paper No. 78. New York: Columbia University, Teachers College, Community College Research Center.

Lake, T., Kvam, C., & Gold, M. (2005). *Literature review: Using quality information for health care decisions and quality improvement.* Cambridge, MA: Mathematica Policy Research.

Lambert, L. (2015, Aug. 22). State funding pushes up college standards: Ohio's new funding formula puts a premium on "college-ready" high school graduates. *Dayton Daily News.*

Lane, J. E. (2007). Spider web of oversight: Latent and manifest regulatory controls in higher education. *Journal of Higher Education, 78*(6), 1–30.

Lane, J. E., & Kivisto, J. A. (2008). Interests, information, and incentives in higher education: Principal-agent theory and its potential applications to the study of higher education governance. In J. C. Smart (Ed.), *Higher education: Handbook of theory and research* (pp. 141–79). New York: Springer.

Larocca, R., & Carr, D. (2012). *Higher education performance funding: Identifying impacts of formula characteristics on graduation and retention rates.* Paper presented to the Western Social Science Association Annual Conference. Oakland, MI: Oakland University.

Lavertu, S., & Moynihan, D. P. (2012). Agency political ideology and reform implementation: Performance management in the Bush administration. *Journal of Public Administration Research and Theory, 23*(3), 521–49.

Lederman, D. (2009, Dec. 28). Performance (de-)funding. *Inside Higher Education.* Retrieved from https://www.insidehighered.com.

Leisyte, L. (2012). *Trends in higher education and research funding in Europe.* Enschede, The Netherlands: University of Twente, Center for Higher Education Policy Studies.

Light, P. C. (2004). *Sustaining nonprofit performance: The case for capacity building and the evidence to support it.* Washington, DC: Brookings Institution Press.

Lingenfelter, P. E. (2008). The financing of public colleges and universities in the United States. In H. F. Ladd & E. B. Fiske (Eds.), *Handbook of research in education finance and policy* (pp. 651–70). New York: Routledge.

Lipshitz, R., Popper, M., & Friedman, V. J. (2002). A multifacet model of organization learning. *Journal of Applied Behavioral Science, 38*(1), 78–98.

Loeb, S., & McEwan, P. (2006). An economic approach to education policy implementation. In M. Honig (Ed.), *New directions in education policy implementation* (pp. 169–86). Albany: State University of New York Press.

Longanecker, D. (2012a). *Performance funding 2.0: From ideas to action.* Boulder, CO: Western Interstate Commission for Higher Education. Retrieved from http://www.wiche.edu/info/lac/2012/longanecker.pdf.

Longanecker, D. (2012b). *State efforts to assure affordability in the new normal.* Testimony before the US Senate Committee on Health, Education, Labor, and Pensions. Boulder, CO: Western Interstate Commission for Higher Education. Retrieved from http://www.wiche.edu/PPT/LonganeckerTestimonyBeforeCongress9-13-2012.pdf.

Lubbers, T. (2011). *Results matter: Performance pay and higher education.* Indianapolis: Indiana Commission for Higher Education. Retrieved from http://www.in.gov/che/files/101228_OPINION_-_Results_Matter_%28Performance_Pay_and_Higher_Education%29.pdf.

Lumina Foundation. (2009). *Four steps to finishing first: An agenda for increasing college productivity to create a better-educated society.* Indianapolis: Lumina Foundation. Retrieved from http://www.luminafoundation.org/publications/Four_Steps_to_Finishing_First_in_Higher_Education.pdf.

Lumina Foundation. (2015). *Addressing equity gaps in state goals for postsecondary education attainment.* Los Angeles: Center for Urban Education, University of Southern California.

Manna, P. (2006). *School is in: Federalism and the national education agenda.* Washington, DC: Georgetown University Press.

Marsh, J. A., Springer, M. G., McCaffrey, D. F., Yuan, K., Epstein, S., Koppich, J., Kalra, N., DiMartino, C., & Peng, A. (2011). *A big apple for educators: New York City's experiment with schoolwide performance bonuses.* Santa Monica, CA: RAND Corp.

Massy, W. F. (2011). Managerial and political strategies for handling accountability. In B. Stensaker & L. Harvey (Eds.), *Accountability in higher* education (pp. 221–44). New York: Routledge.

Matland, R. (1995). Synthesizing the implementation literature: The ambiguity-conflict model of implementation. *Journal of Public Administration Research and Theory, 5*(2), 145–74.

Mazmanian, D., & Sabatier, P. (1989). *Implementation and public policy* (rev. ed.). Latham, MD: University Press of America.

McCubbins, M. D., Noll, R. G., & Weingast, B. R. (1987). Administrative procedures as instruments of political control. *Journal of Law, Economics, and Organization, 3*(2), 243–77.

McDonnell, L. M., & Elmore, R. F. (1987). Getting the job done: Alternative policy instruments. *Educational Evaluation and Policy Analysis, 9*(2), 133–52.

McGuinness, A. C., Jr. (2003). *Models of postsecondary education coordination and governance in the states.* StateNote Report. Denver, CO: Education Commission of the States.

McGuinness, A. C., Jr. (2011). The states and higher education. In P. A. Altbach, P. J. Gumport, & R. O. Berdahl (Eds.), *American higher education in the twenty-first century* (3rd ed., pp. 139–69). Baltimore: Johns Hopkins University Press.

McKeown-Moak, M. P. (2013). The "new" performance funding in higher education. *Educational Considerations, 40*(2), 3–12.

McKinney, L., & Hagedorn, L. S. (2015). *Performance-based funding for community colleges in Texas: Are colleges disadvantaged by serving the most disadvantaged students?* Bryan, TX: Greater Texas Foundation. Retrieved from http://greatertexasfoundation.org/wp-content/uploads/2015/03/McKinney-Full-White-final.pdf.

McLaughlin, M. (2006). Implementation research in education. In M. Honig (Ed.), *New directions in education policy implementation* (pp. 209–28). Albany: State University of New York Press.

McLendon, M. K., & Hearn, J. C. (2013). The resurgent interest in performance-based funding for higher education. *Academe, 99*(6), 25–30.

Merton, R. K. (1968). *Social theory and social structure* (rev. and enlarged ed.). New York: Free Press.

Merton, R. K. (1976). *Sociological ambivalence and other essays.* New York: Free Press.

Mica, A., Peisert, A., & Winczorek, J. (Eds.). (2012). *Sociology and the unintended.* New York: Peter Lang.

Miller, G. J. (2005). The political evolution of principal-agent models. *Annual Review of Political Science, 8,* 203–25.

Miller, T. (2014). *Ensuring quality in the context of outcomes-based funding.* Washington, DC: HCM Strategists.

Missouri Department of Higher Education. (2014). *State of Missouri performance funding for higher education (vol. 3)*. Jefferson City, MO: Author. Retrieved from http://dhe.mo .gov/documents/PerformanceFundingPublicationVo.32014.pdf.

Moden, G. O., & Williford, A. M. (2002). Ohio's challenge: A clash of performance funding and base budgeting. In J. C. Burke (Ed.), *Funding public colleges and universities for performance: Popularity, problems, and prospects* (pp. 169–94). Albany, NY: Rockefeller Institute Press.

Moe, T. M. (1984). The new economics of organization. *American Journal of Political Science, 28*(4), 739–77.

Monaghan, D., & Goldrick-Rab, S. (2016). *Is community college already free?* Policy Brief 16-01. Madison: University of Wisconsin, Wisconsin HOPE Lab. Retrieved from http:// wihopelab.com/publications/Wisconsin_HOPE_Lab_Policy_Brief%2016-01_Is _Community_College_Already_Free.pdf.

Morest, V. S., & Jenkins, D. (2007). *Institutional research and the culture of evidence at community colleges*. New York: Columbia University, Teachers College, Community College Research Center.

Moynihan, D. P. (2008). *The dynamics of performance management: Constructing information and reform*. Washington, DC: Georgetown University Press.

Moynihan, D. P. (2010). The problems and paradoxes of performance-based bureaucracy. In R. F. Durant (Ed.), *The Oxford handbook of American bureaucracy* (pp. 278–302). New York: Oxford.

Moynihan, D. P., & Pandey, S. K. (2010). The big question for performance management: Why do managers use performance information? *Journal of Public Administration Research and Theory, 20*(4), 849–66.

Moynihan, D. P., Pandey, S. K., & Wright, B. E. (2012). Setting the table: How transformational leadership fosters performance information use. *Journal of Public Administration Research and Theory, 22*(1), 143–64.

National Center for Education Statistics. (2011). *Digest of education statistics, 2010*. NCES 2011-015. Washington, DC: Author.

National Center for Education Statistics. (2014). *Digest of education statistics, 2013*. NCES 2014-015. Washington, DC: Author.

National Conference of State Legislatures. (2015). Performance-based funding for higher education. Denver, CO: Author. Retrieved from http://www.ncsl.org/research /education/performance-funding.aspx.

Natow, R. S., Pheatt, L., Dougherty, K. J., Jones, S., Lahr, H., & Reddy, V. (2014). *Institutional changes to organizational policies, practices, and programs following the adoption of state-level performance funding policies*. CCRC Working Paper No. 76. New York: Columbia University, Teachers College, Community College Research Center.

Neave, G. (1998). The evaluative state reconsidered. *European Journal of Education, 33*(3), 265–84.

Ness, E. C., Deupree, M. M., & Gándara, D. (2015). *Campus responses to outcomes-based funding in Tennessee: Robust, aligned, and contested*. Nashville: Tennessee Higher Education Coordinating Board. Retrieved from http://www.tn.gov/assets/entities /thec/attachments/FordFoundationPaper.pdf.

Nodine, T., Venezia, A., & Bracco, K. (2011). *Changing course: A guide to increasing student completion in community colleges*. San Francisco: WestEd. Retrieved from http://knowledgecenter.completionbydesign.org/sites/default/files/changing_course_V1_fb_10032011.pdf.

Offenstein, J., & Shulock, N. (2010). *Taking the next step: The promise of intermediate measures for meeting postsecondary completion goals*. Boston: Jobs for the Future.

Ohio Association of Community Colleges. (2013). *SSI allocation recommendations*. Columbus, OH: Author.

Ohio Board of Regents. (1996). *Higher Education Funding Commission: Final report and recommendations*. Columbus, OH: Author.

Ohio Board of Regents. (2007, May). *Ohio has a revised articulation & transfer policy*. Columbus, OH: Author. Retrieved from http://regents.ohio.gov/transfer/pathways/policy.php.

Ohio Board of Regents. (2008). *Strategic plan for higher education 2008–2017*. Columbus, OH: Author.

Ohio Board of Regents. (2009a). *State Share of Instruction handbook: Providing the methodology for allocating State Share of Instruction funds for fiscal year 2010 and fiscal year 2011 for use by: Community and technical colleges*. Columbus, OH: Author.

Ohio Board of Regents. (2009b). *State Share of Instruction handbook: Providing the methodology for allocating State Share of Instruction funds for fiscal year 2010 and fiscal year 2011 for use by: University main campuses*. Columbus, OH: Author.

Ohio Board of Regents. (2010). *State Share of Instruction: Final FY 2010 & 2011*. Columbus, OH: Author. Retrieved from http://regents.ohio.gov/financial/selected_budget_detail/operating_budget_1011/campus-ssi-allocations.pdf.

Ohio Board of Regents. (2011a). *State Share of Instruction handbook: Providing the methodology for allocating State Share of Instruction funds for fiscal year 2012 and fiscal year 2013 for use by: Community and technical colleges*. Columbus, OH: Author. Retrieved from http://www.ohiohighered.org/files/uploads/financial/ssi/HANDBOOK%20CC.pdf.

Ohio Board of Regents. (2011b). *State Share of Instruction handbook: Providing the methodology for allocating State Share of Instruction funds for fiscal year 2012 and fiscal year 2013 for use by: University main campuses*. Columbus, OH: Author. Retrieved from http://www.ohiohighered.org/files/uploads/financial/ssi/HANDBOOK%20UM.pdf.

Ohio Board of Regents. (2011c). *State Share of Instruction handbook: Providing the methodology for allocating State Share of Instruction funds for fiscal year 2012 and fiscal year 2013 for use by: University regional campuses*. Columbus, OH: Author. Retrieved from http://www.ohiohighered.org/files/uploads/financial/ssi/HANDBOOK%20UB.pdf.

Ohio Board of Regents. (2012a). *Recommendations of the Ohio Higher Education Funding Commission*. Columbus, OH: Author.

Ohio Board of Regents. (2012b). *Working together for student success: Lessons from Ohio's College-ABLE Partnership Project*. Columbus, OH: Author.

Ohio Board of Regents. (2012c). *FY12_13_SSI_10_22_actuals_V2*. Columbus, OH: Author. Retrieved from https://www.ohiohighered.org/files/uploads/financial/ssi/FY12_13_SSI_Actual_FY11_Oct_31.pdf.

Ohio Board of Regents. (2012d). *Complete College Ohio: Task force report and recommendations.* Columbus, OH: Author. Retrieved from https://www.ohiohighered.org/sites/ohiohighered.org/files/uploads/completion/CCO-task-force-report_FINAL.pdf.

Ohio Board of Regents. (2013a). *State Share of Instruction handbook: Providing the methodology for allocating State Share of Instruction funds for fiscal year 2012 and fiscal year 2014 for use by: Community and technical colleges.* Columbus, OH: Author. Retrieved from https://www.ohiohighered.org/node/2519.

Ohio Board of Regents. (2013b). *State Share of Instruction handbook: Providing the methodology for allocating State Share of Instruction funds for fiscal year 2012 and fiscal year 2014 for use by: University regional and main campuses.* Columbus, OH: Author. Retrieved from https://www.ohiohighered.org/node/2519.

Ohio Board of Regents. (2013c). *FY2014 SSI distributions 11-15-2013.* Columbus, OH: Author. Retrieved from https://www.ohiohighered.org/node/2519.

Ohio Board of Regents. (2013d). *Draft State Share of Instruction FY2014 with FY2013 actuals.* Columbus, OH: Author.

Ohio Board of Regents. (2013e). *Total headcount enrollment by institution and by campus: Fall term 2003 to 2012: University System of Ohio institutions.* Columbus, OH: Author. Retrieved from https://www.ohiohighered.org/sites/ohiohighered.org/files/uploads/data/statistical-profiles/enrollment/headcount_institution_campus_03-12.pdf.

Ohio Board of Regents. (2013f). *Degrees and certificates awarded by Ohio public institutions: Fiscal Years 2003 to 2012: University System of Ohio institution.* Columbus, OH: Author. Retrieved from https://www.ohiohighered.org/sites/ohiohighered.org/files/completions_public_03-12.pdf.

Ohio Board of Regents. (2014). *State Share of Instruction report.* Columbus, OH: Author. Retrieved from https://www.ohiohighered.org/sites/ohiohighered.org/files/uploads/financial/ssi/SSI_Performance-Based-Funding-Evaluation-Report_Dec2014.pdf.

Ohio Board of Regents. (2015a). *State Share of Instruction handbook: Providing the methodology for allocating State Share of Instruction funds for fiscal year 2014 and fiscal year 2015 for use by: Community and technical colleges.* Columbus, OH: Author. Retrieved from https://www.ohiohighered.org/content/fy_2015_operating_budget_details.

Ohio Board of Regents. (2015b). *State Share of Instruction handbook: Providing the methodology for allocating State Share of Instruction funds for fiscal year 2014 and fiscal year 2015 for use by: University regional and main campuses.* Columbus, OH: Author. Retrieved from https://www.ohiohighered.org/content/fy_2015_operating_budget_details.

Ohio Board of Regents. (2015c). *FY2015 second half SSI distributions for community colleges.* Columbus, OH: Author. Retrieved from https://www.ohiohighered.org/content/fy_2015_operating_budget_details.

Olivas, M., & Baez, B. (2011). The legal environment: The implementation of legal change on campus. In P. A. Altbach, P. J. Gumport, & R. O. Berdahl (Eds.), *American higher education in the twenty-first century* (3rd ed., pp. 170–94). Baltimore: Johns Hopkins University Press.

O'Neal, L. M. (2007). *Performance funding in Ohio's four-year institutions of higher education: A case study* (doctoral dissertation). Available from ProQuest Dissertations and Theses database (UMI No. AAT 3272928).

Organisation for Economic Co-operation and Development. (2012). *Assessment of higher education learning outcomes feasibility study report.* (2 vols.) Paris: Author. Retrieved from http://www.oecd.org/site/ahelo/backgrounddocumentsfortheahelofeasibilitys tudyconference.htm.

Petrick, R. (2010, Feb. 9). *Funding based on course completions: The Ohio model (v. 1.0).* Presentation to the Texas Higher Education Coordinating Board, Austin, TX.

Petrick, R. (2012). The Ohio experience with outcomes-based funding. In A. P. Kelly & M. Schneider (Eds.), *Getting to graduation* (pp. 269–92). Baltimore: Johns Hopkins University Press.

Pfeffer, J., & Salancik, G. (1978). *The external control of organizations.* New York: Harper & Row.

Pheatt, L., Lahr, H., Dougherty, K. J., Jones, S. M., Natow, R. S., & Reddy, V. (2014). *Obstacles to the effective implementation of performance funding: A multi-state cross-case analysis.* CCRC Working Paper No. 77. New York: Columbia University, Teachers College, Community College Research Center.

Postsecondary Analytics. (2013). *What's working? Outcomes-based funding in Tennessee.* Washington, DC: HCM Associates.

Power, M. (1994). The audit society. In A. G. Hopwood & P. Miller (Eds.), *Accounting as social and institutional practice* (pp. 299–316). London: Cambridge University Press.

Pressman, J., & Wildavsky, A. (1973). *Implementation.* Berkeley: University of California Press.

Quint, J. C., Jaggars, S. S., Byndloss, D. C., & Magazinnik, A. (2013). *Bringing developmental education to scale: Lessons from the Developmental Education Initiative.* New York: MDRC. Retrieved from http://www.mdrc.org/sites/default/files/Bringing%20 Developmental%20Education%20to%20Scale%20FR.pdf.

Rabovsky, T. (2012). Accountability in higher education: Exploring impacts on state budgets and institutional spending patterns. *Journal of Public Administration Research and Theory, 22*(4), 675–700.

Rabovsky, T. (2014a). Support for performance-based funding: The role of political ideology, performance, and dysfunctional information environments. *Public Administration Review, 74*(6), 761–74.

Rabovsky, T. (2014b). Using data to manage for performance at public universities. *Public Administration Review, 74*(2), 260–72.

Radford, A. W., Berkner, L., Wheeless, S. C., & Shepherd, B. (2010). *Persistence and attainment of 2003–04 Beginning Postsecondary Students: After 6 years.* NCES 2011-151. Washington, DC: National Center for Education Statistics.

Radin, B. A. (2006). *Challenging the performance movement: Accountability, complexity, and democratic values.* Washington, DC: Georgetown University Press.

Reddy, V., Lahr, H., Dougherty, K. J., Jones, S. M., Natow, R. S., & Pheatt, L. (2014). *Policy instruments in service of performance funding: A study of performance funding in three states.* CCRC Working Paper No. 75. New York: Columbia University, Teachers College, Community College Research Center.

Reindl, T., & Jones, D. P. (2012). *Raising the bar: Strategies for increasing postsecondary educational attainment with limited resources.* Washington, DC: National Governors

Association. Retrieved from http://www.nga.org/files/live/sites/NGA/files/pdf/1206 RedesignJonesReindl.pdf.

Reindl, T., & Reyna, R. (2011). *From information to action: Revamping higher education accountability systems.* Washington, DC: National Governors Association. Retrieved from http://www.nga.org/files/live/sites/NGA/files/pdf/1107C2CACTIONGUIDE.PDF.

Rhoades, G. (1998). *Managed professionals: Unionized faculty and restructuring academic labor.* Albany: State University of New York Press.

Richardson, R. C., Bracco, K. R., Callan, P. M., & Finney, J. E. (1999). *Designing state higher education systems for a new century.* Phoenix: Oryx Press.

Rothstein, R. (2008a). *Grading education: Getting accountability right.* New York: Teachers College Press.

Rothstein, R. (2008b). *Holding accountability to account: How scholarship and experience in other fields inform exploration of performance incentives in education.* Working Paper No. 2008-04. Washington, DC: Economic Policy Institute. Retrieved from http://www.epi.org/publication/wp_accountability/.

Rouse, C., Hannaway, J., Goldhaber, D., & Figlio, D. (2007). *Feeling the Florida heat? How low-performing schools respond to voucher and accountability pressure.* Washington, DC: Urban Institute.

Rutherford, A., & Rabovsky, T. (2014). Evaluating impacts of performance funding policies on student outcomes in higher education. *The ANNALS of the American Academy of Political and Social Science, 655*(1), 185–206.

Rutschow, E. Z., Richburg-Hayes, L., Brock, T., Orr, G., Cerna, O., Cullinan, D., & Martin, K. (2011). *Turning the tide: Five years of Achieving the Dream in community colleges.* New York: MDRC.

Ryan, W. (1976). *Blaming the victim* (2nd ed.). New York: Vintage.

Salamon, L. (2002). The new governance and the tools of public action: An introduction. In L. Salamon (Ed.), *The tools of government: A guide to the new governance* (pp. 1–47). New York: Oxford.

Sanford, T., & Hunter, J. M. (2011). Impact of performance funding on retention and graduation rates. *Educational Policy Analysis Archives, 19*(33), 1–30. Retrieved from http://epaa.asu.edu/ojs.

Santiago. P., Tremblay, K., Basri, E., & Arnale, E. (2008). *Tertiary education for the knowledge society (vol. 1).* Paris: Organization for Economic Cooperation and Development.

Sauder, M., & Espeland, W. N. (2009). The discipline of rankings. *American Sociological Review, 74*(1), 63–82.

Schick, A. (2002). Opportunity, strategy, and tactics in reforming public management. *OECD Journal on Budgeting, 2*(3), 7–34.

Schick, A. (2003). The performing state: Reflection on an idea whose time has come but whose implementation has not. *OECD Journal on Budgeting, 3*(2), 71–103.

Schmidtlein, F. A., & Berdahl, R. O. (2011). Autonomy and accountability: Who controls academe? In P. A. Altbach, P. J. Gumport, & R. O. Berdahl (Eds.), *American higher education in the twenty-first century* (3rd ed., pp. 69–87). Baltimore: Johns Hopkins University Press.

Schneider, A. L., & Ingram, H. (1997). *Policy design for democracy.* Lawrence: University of Kansas Press.

Scott-Clayton, J. (2012). *Information constraints and student aid policy.* NBER Working Paper No. 17811. Cambridge, MA: National Bureau of Economic Research. Retrieved from http://www.nber.org/papers/w17811.

Scrivener, S., Weiss, M. J., Ratledge, A., Rudd, T., Sommo, C., & Fresques, H. (2015). *Doubling graduation rates: Three-year effects of CUNY's accelerated study in associate programs (ASAP) for developmental education student.* New York: MDRC.

Shaw, K. (2015). *Conducting research on outcomes-based funding policy: Identifying and addressing the substantive and methodological challenges.* Paper presented to the annual meeting of the Association for the Study of Higher Education, Denver, CO. Philadelphia: Research for Action.

Shin, J. C. (2010). Impacts of performance-based accountability on institutional performance in the U.S. *Higher Education, 60*(1), 47–68.

Shin, J. C., & Milton, M. (2004). The effects of performance budgeting and funding programs on graduation rate in public four-year colleges and universities. *Education Policy Analysis Archives, 12*(22), 1–26. Retrieved from http://epaa.asu.edu/ojs.

Shulock, N. (2011). *Concerns about performance-based funding and ways that states are addressing the concerns.* Sacramento: California State University, Institute for Higher Education Leadership and Policy.

Shulock, N., & Jenkins, D. (2011). *Performance incentives to improve community college completion: Learning from Washington State's Student Achievement Initiative.* State Policy Brief. New York: Columbia University, Teachers College, Community College Research Center. Retrieved from http://ccrc.tc.columbia.edu/publications/performance-incentives-college-completion.html.

Smith. A. L. (2015, Sept. 25). Faculty members see promise in unified way to measure student learning. *Chronicle of Higher Education.*

Smith, K. B., & Larimer, C. W. (2009). *The public policy theory primer.* Boulder, CO: Westview.

Snyder, M. J. (2011, Oct.). *Role of performance funding in higher education's reform agenda: A glance at some state trends.* Presentation given at the Annual Legislative Institute on Higher Education, National Conference of State Legislatures, Denver, CO. Washington, DC: HCM Strategists.

Snyder, M. J. (2015). *Driving better outcomes: Typology and principles to inform outcomes-based funding models.* Washington, DC: HCM Strategists. Retrieved from http://hcmstrategists.com/drivingoutcomes/wp-content/themes/hcm/pdf/Driving%20Outcomes.pdf.

SPEC Associates. (2012a). *National evaluation of Lumina Foundation's productivity work: Interim report for Tennessee.* Detroit: Author.

SPEC Associates. (2012b). *National evaluation of Lumina Foundation's productivity work: Interim report for Indiana.* Detroit: Author.

Spillane, J. P., Reiser, B., & Gomez, L. M. (2006). Policy implementation and cognition. In M. Honig (Ed.), *New directions in education policy implementation* (pp. 47–63). Albany: State University of New York Press.

State Higher Education Executive Officers. (2013). *State higher education finance fiscal year 2012.* Boulder, CO: Author.

Stecher, B., & Kirby, S. N. (2004). *Organizational improvement and accountability: Lessons for education from other sectors.* Santa Monica, CA: RAND Corp.

Stensaker, B. (2003). Trance, transparency and transformation: The impact of external quality monitoring on higher education. *Quality in Higher Education, 9*(2), 151–59.

Stinson, C. S. (2003). *A historical review and financial analysis of higher education funding in Tennessee* (doctoral dissertation, East Tennessee University). Retrieved from http://dc .etsu.edu/etd/826.

Stokes, K. (2011, Dec. 1). Indiana to base larger portion of college funding on performance. *StateImpact—Indiana.* Retrieved from http://indianapublicmedia.org/stateimpact/2011 /12/01/indiana-to-base-larger-portion-of-college-funding-on-performance.

Stone, D. (2012). *Policy paradox: The art of political decision making* (3rd ed.). New York: Norton.

Sunderman. G. L., & Kim, J. S. (2007). The expansion of federal power and the politics of implementing the No Child Left Behind Act. *Teachers College Record, 109*(5), 1057–85.

Tandberg, D. A, & Hillman, N. W. (2014). State higher education performance funding: Data, outcomes, and causal relationships. *Journal of Education Finance, 39*(3), 222–43.

Tandberg, D. A., Hillman, N. W., & Barakat, M. (2014). State higher education performance funding for community colleges: Diverse effects and policy implications. *Teachers College Record, 116*(12), 1–31.

Tennessee Higher Education Commission. (2008). *Making opportunity affordable: Planning grant proposal.* Nashville: Author.

Tennessee Higher Education Commission. (2010). *2010–2015 performance funding quality assurance.* Nashville: Author.

Tennessee Higher Education Commission. (2011a). *Outcomes formula technical details.* Nashville: Author.

Tennessee Higher Education Commission. (2011b). *Outcomes based formula explanation.* Nashville: Author.

Tennessee Higher Education Commission. (2011c). *Tennessee higher education fact book, 2010–2011.* Nashville: Author. Retrieved from http://www.state.tn.us/thec/Legislative /Reports/2011/2010-11%20Fact%20Book.PDF.

Tennessee Higher Education Commission. (2012a). *2012–13 outcomes formula model.* Nashville: Author.

Tennessee Higher Education Commission. (2012b). *Outcomes based formula model data definitions* (Rev. 6-27-2012). Nashville: Author.

Tennessee Higher Education Commission. (2014a). *2014–2015 Outcomes formula spreadsheet.* Nashville: Author. Retrieved from http://www.state.tn.us/thec/Divisions/Fiscal /funding_formula/dynamic_model/2014-15%20Outcomes%20Formula%20-%20 EMAIL.xlsx.

Tennessee Higher Education Commission. (2014b). *Tennessee higher education fact book, 2013–2014.* Nashville: Author.

Tennessee Higher Education Commission. (2015a). *2015–20 Outcomes funding formula.* Nashville: Author.

Tennessee Higher Education Commission. (2015b). *Members of the Statutory Formula Review Committee.* Nashville: Author. Retrieved from http://www.tn.gov/thec/article /2015-20-funding-formula.

Tennessee Higher Education Commission. (2015c). *2015–16 outcomes-based formula.* Nashville: Author. Retrieved from http://www.tn.gov/thec/article/2010-2015-funding -formula.

Tennessee Higher Education Commission. (2015d). *Outcomes-based formula model data definitions.* Nashville: Author. Retrieved from http://www.tn.gov/thec/article/2010-2015 -funding-formula.

Tennessee Higher Education Commission. (2015e). *2015–2020 outcomes-based funding formula overview.* Nashville: Author. Retrieved from http://www.tn.gov/thec/article /2015-20-funding-formula.

Timmermans, S., & Epstein, S. (2010). A world of standards but not a standard world: Toward a sociology of standards and standardization. *Annual Review of Sociology, 36*(1), 69–89.

Tinto, V. (2012). *Completing college: Rethinking institutional action.* Chicago: University of Chicago Press.

Titus, M. (2004). An examination of the influence of institutional context on student persistence at 4-year colleges and universities: A multi-level approach. *Research in Higher Education, 45*(7), 673–99.

Townley, B., Cooper, D. J., & Oakes, L. (2003). Performance measures and the rationalization of organizations. *Organization Studies, 24*(7), 1045–71.

Townsley, S. (2014). Personal communication from Associate Commissioner for Information and Research, Indiana Commission for Higher Education, Indianapolis.

Tyack, D. (1974). *The one best system: A history of American urban education.* Cambridge, MA: Harvard University Press.

Umbricht, M. R., Fernandez, F., & Ortagus, J. C. (2015). An examination of the (un)intended consequences of performance funding in higher education. *Educational Policy,* 1–31. DOI: 10.1177/0895904815614398.

University of Tennessee. (2011, Aug. 22). *UT, TBR announce 50 guaranteed transfer pathways between community colleges and universities.* Knoxville, TN: Author. Retrieved from http://www.tennessee.edu/media/releases/082211_transfer.html.

US Bureau of the Census. (2012). *Statistical abstract of the United States, 2012.* Washington, DC: Government Printing Office.

US Department of Education. (2011). *College completion tool kit.* Washington, DC: Author. Retrieved from http://www.whitehouse.gov/sites/default/files/college_completion_tool _kit.pdf.

US Office of the President. (2013). *FACT SHEET on the President's plan to make college more affordable: A better bargain for the middle class.* Washington, DC: Author. http://www .whitehouse.gov/the-press-office/2013/08/22/fact-sheet-president-s-plan-make-college -more-affordable-better-bargain-.

Van Thiel, S., & Leeuw, F. L. (2002). The performance paradox in the public sector. *Public Performance & Management Review, 25*(3), 267–81.

Van Vught, F. A. (1994). Policy models and policy instruments in higher education. In J. Smart (Ed.), *Higher education: Handbook of theory and research* (vol. 10). Dordrecht, Netherlands: Springer.

Wells, S. J., & Johnson, M. A. (2001). Selecting outcome measures for child welfare settings: Lessons for use in performance management. *Children and Youth Services Review, 23*(2), 169–99.

Witham, K. A., & Bensimon, E. M. (2012). Creating a culture of inquiry around equity and student success. In S. D. Museus & U. M. Jayakumar (Eds.), *Creating campus cultures: Fostering success among racially diverse student populations* (pp. 46–67). New York: Routledge.

Wright, D. L. (2015). *Structuring state policy for student success: Applying incentives in the Volunteer State*. Washington, DC: HCM Strategists.

Yorks, L. (2005). Adult learning and the generation of new knowledge and meaning: Creating liberating spaces for fostering adult learning through practitioner-based collaborative action inquiry. *Teachers College Record, 107*(6), 1217–44.

Yorks, L., & Marsick, V. (2000). Organizational learning and transformation. In J. Mezirow & Associates (Eds.), *Learning as transformation: Critical perspectives in a theory in process* (pp. 253–81). San Francisco: Jossey-Bass.

Yorks, L., Neuman, J. H., Kowalski, D. R., Kowalski, R. (2007). Lessons learned from a 5-year project within the Department of Veterans Affairs. *Journal of Applied Behavioral Science, 43*(3), 252–372.

Ziskin, M. B., Hossler, D., Rabourn, K., Cekic, O., & Hwang, Y. (2014). *Outcomes-based funding: Current status, promising practices and emerging trends*. Toronto: Higher Education Quality Council of Ontario.

Zumeta, W., & Kinne, A. (2011). Accountability policies: Directions old and new. In D. E. Heller (Ed.), *The states and public higher education policy: Affordability, access, and accountability* (2nd ed., pp. 173–99). Baltimore: Johns Hopkins University Press.

Index

Page numbers in *italics* signify tables.